RECONSTRUCTION

INTERPRETATIONS OF AMERICAN HISTORY

★ ★ ★ JOHN HIGHAM AND BRADFORD PERKINS, EDITORS

RECONSTRUCTION

EDITED BY

STAUGHTON LYND
Yale University

HARPER & ROW, PUBLISHERS
NEW YORK, EVANSTON, AND LONDON

CONTENTS

v

EDITORS' INTRODUCTION

This volume—and companions in the series, "Interpretations of American History"—makes a special effort to cope with one of the basic dilemmas confronting every student of history. On the one hand, historical knowledge shares a characteristic common to all appraisals of human affairs. It is partial and selective. It picks out some features and facts of a situation while ignoring others that may be equally pertinent. The more selective an interpretation is, the more memorable and widely applicable it can be. On the other hand, history has to provide what nothing else does: a total estimate, a multifaceted synthesis, of man's experience in particular times and places. To study history, therefore, is to strive simultaneously for a clear, selective focus and for an integrated, over-all view.

In that spirit, each volume of the series aims to resolve the varied literature on a major topic or event into a meaningful whole. One interpretation, we believe, does not deserve as much of a student's attention as another simply because they are in conflict. Instead of contriving a balance between opposing views, or choosing polemical material simply to create an appearance of controversy, Professor Lynd has exercised his own judgment on the relative importance of different aspects or interpretations of a problem. We have asked him to select some of what he considers the best, most persuasive writings bearing on Reconstruction, indicating in the introductory essay and headnotes his reasons for considering these accounts convincing or significant. When appropriate, he has also brought out the relation between older and more recent approaches to the subject. The editor's own competence and experience in the field enable him to provide a sense of order and to indicate the evolution and complexity of interpretations. He is, then, like other editors in this series, an informed participant rather than a mere observer, a student sharing with other students the results of his own investigations of the literature on a crucial phase of American development.

JOHN HIGHAM
BRADFORD PERKINS

RECONSTRUCTION

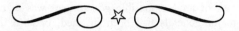

INTRODUCTION

A generation ago Charles Beard suggested that the American Civil War was a "second American Revolution." In many ways, as Beard pointed out, the war of 1861–1865 was more revolutionary than the war of 1776–1783. Property was confiscated on a much more extensive scale, notably $2 billion worth of slaves. When in his Second Inaugural President Abraham Lincoln said that if necessary the war should continue until every drop of blood drawn by the lash had been paid for by a drop drawn by the sword, he spoke more wisely than he knew: for the number of men on both sides who died in the Civil War (more than 500,000) was approximately equal to the number of slaves in the United States in 1776.

Radical Republicans, such as Congressman Thaddeus Stevens of Pennsylvania, were well aware that they were living through a revolution. They did not need the young French reporter Georges Clemenceau to tell them that this was an upheaval comparable to 1640 in England or 1789 in France. In 1867 Senator Howard of Michigan defended the policy of military reconstruction against the charge that it would recreate Cromwell's "oppressive and tyrannical" major generals. The history of

Parts of this introduction appeared in the editor's "Rethinking Slavery and Reconstruction," *Journal of Negro History,* L (1965), pp. 198–209.

Cromwell's rule, Howard insisted, had been written by men hostile to the revolution. In fact England was then bubbling with counter-revolution and the task of any responsible government was to crush such conspiracy. The major generals had been justified, because the 1650's, like the 1860's, were a "time of war, of civil war, of conspiracy, of public danger."

Far more common, as the popular tags "Jacobin" and "Bourbon" attest, was an analogy to revolutionary France. The most radical Congressional debate in American history took place in the spring of 1862 on the question of confiscating land owned by rebels. In defending Robespierre's confiscations against the charge that they were "not precedents to be followed, but warnings to be heeded," Howard and other Radicals invoked Old Testament exemplars. Representative Cutler reminded the House that when 250 princes of Israel rebelled against Moses and Aaron, they put the problem in the hands of the Lord. "Did he argue the right of coercion with them? . . . No, sir; he sent them quickly down to hell, and passed a general confiscation act." Senator Charles Sumner, later to use the story of Naboth's vineyard in protesting President U. S. Grant's plan to annex Santo Domingo, used it in 1862 to justify confiscation of Confederate lands. Sumner conceded that French confiscation "aroused at the time the eloquent indignation of Burke, and still causes a sigh among all who think less of principles than of privileges." But:

Cruel as were many of the consequences, this confiscation must be judged as a part of that mighty revolution whose temper it shared; nor will it be easy to condemn anything but its excesses, unless you are ready to say that the safety of France, torn by domestic foes and invaded abroad, was not worth securing, or that equality before the law, which is now the most assured possession of that great nation, was not worth obtaining.

Reconstruction, therefore, must be viewed as the consolidation of a revolution, not merely as the peace settlement following a war. Something went wrong, and the upshot was oppression for the Southern Negro, bitter resentment among Southern whites, and puzzled frustration on the part of Northern men of goodwill.

The story of Reconstruction can be divided into: (1.) A preparatory period (1861–1865) in which rehearsals for Reconstruction were enacted in Tennessee, Louisiana, Arkansas, and the sea islands off South Carolina, as these fell to the Union army; (2.) The period of Presidential Reconstruction (April–December 1865) in which Andrew Johnson attempted to bring the Confederate states rapidly back into the Union, without Negro suffrage; (3.) Congressional Reconstruction (1866–1877), highlighted by the Fourteenth Amendment of 1866, and the Reconstruction Acts of 1867, which imposed military rule on the defeated states until they remade their governments on a basis of universal manhood suffrage.

Until recently historians' discussion tended to focus on Congressional Reconstruction, and on the questions: Just how bad were the Reconstruction state governments, and whose fault was it? Howard K. Beale, in a 1940 article called "On Rewriting Reconstruction History," noted that before the turn of the century histories of Reconstruction were simple projections of embittered sectionalism. "Thus Hilary Herbert and his corroborators presented a Southern indictment of Northern policies, and Henry Wilson's history was a brief for the North." As Beale observed, the first scholarly works on Reconstruction, by William A. Dunning, James F. Rhodes, and Dunning's graduate students at Columbia University, on the whole reflected the Southern stereotype of Reconstruction history.

The emphasis of the Dunning school was upon the harm done to the South by Radical Reconstruction and upon the sordid political and economic motives behind Radicalism. Rhodes and the Dunning group drew a picture of a South that—but for outside interference—might have made a happy and practical readjustment suited to the new social, economic, and political order. Rhodes, however, while crediting the President's faults to weakness rather than to wickedness, yet accepted the older picture of Andrew Johnson and blamed his mistakes for much of the disaster that overtook the South. Then still another group rehabilitated Johnson. . . .

In fact Beale himself was a principal proponent of this rehabilitation. He wrote in the preface to his *The Critical Year*: "I have not been convinced by Rhodes's simple explanation that the unreasoning obstinacy of Johnson and the South in the face of an overwhelming popular verdict for the Fourteenth Amendment was responsible for the subsequent extremes of reconstruction." Transferring Beard's emphasis on economic motives for the genesis of Civil War to the analysis of Reconstruction, Beale sought to demolish the last remnant of historical justification for postwar Northern policy. As Don Fehrenbacher comments: "By disparaging the outcome of the war and the motives of Radical Republicanism, the Beard thesis tended to merge with the Dunning interpretation of Reconstruction."

Well into the New Deal, the historian's view of Reconstruction largely accepted the long-standing Southern contention that the Negro himself was the essential reason that Reconstruction failed. Alan Harper has observed that Dunning's approach to Reconstruction, like that of Ulrich Phillips to slavery, laid central emphasis on the white man's alleged necessity to keep the Negro under social control. Thus Harper quotes Dunning as deploring the North's failure to recognize that

. . . the root of the trouble in the South had been, not the institution of slavery, but the coexistence in one society of two races so distinct in characteristics as to render coalescence impossible; that slavery had been a *modus vivendi* through which social life was possible; and that, after its disappearance, its place must be taken by some set of conditions which, if more humane and beneficent in accidents, must in essence express the same fact of racial inequality.

It is hardly an exaggeration to say that until the publication of W. E. B. Du Bois' *Black Reconstruction* in 1935 no other prominent historian had questioned the conclusion that the great mistake of Reconstruction was to give the vote to the unprepared Southern Negro.

Since *Black Reconstruction,* liberal historians have occupied themselves with redeeming the reputation of the Reconstruction government in the Southern states. In contrast, the selections in this book have been chosen to illuminate the North's attempt to find a blueprint for deliberate social change which would accomplish its revolutionary goals in the South. The question of the character of the Southern state governments created by the Reconstruction Acts is given much less than the conventional emphasis. I have three reasons for weighting the presentation in this way. First, the spectrum of historians' views on corruption, the behavior of Negro officeholders, the influence of railroad speculators and kindred topics is well exhibited in *Reconstruction in the South,* edited by Edwin Rozwenc. Second, in my opinion liberal historians of the last generation who have sought to correct the traditional image of cigar-smoking Negro legislators voting themselves gold spittoons have added very little to Du Bois' 1910 article on "Reconstruction and its Benefits," included in the present volume. Finally, in our time analysis of the failure of Reconstruction has properly been influenced by the new civil rights struggle (what C. Vann Woodward terms "the Second Reconstruction") and the transformation of underdeveloped societies overseas. Accordingly, we are now less disposed to blame the tragedy of Reconstruction on any of the stock characters of earlier historiography—whether freedman, scalawag, carpetbagger, Bourbon, or redneck—and to ask instead, What strategy of planned social change might have succeeded?

This is a difficult question, to which there have been two fundamental answers. One is that the failure of Reconstruction shows the futility of trying to coerce deep-seated attitudes by legal or military force. In sending troops back into the South in 1867, the North destroyed the possibility of unforced evolutionary change in the relation of whites and

Negroes. Education and economic betterment offered the only hope for lasting melioration of the Negro's position; improvement might have come about if Congress had not sought to shortcut the process artificially by giving the Negro the ballot at bayonet-point.

A sophisticated version of this view is exemplified in *Andrew Johnson and Reconstruction,* by Eric McKitrick. Ostensibly a critical revision of the overgenerous portrait of Andrew Johnson created by such scholars as Beard and Howard Beale, McKitrick's book also represents a return to the attitude of Rhodes: Johnson's lenient policy was better than Stevens-Sumner harshness, but Johnson erred in his manner of carrying it out. It is, writes McKitrick, "rather hard to avoid the conclusion that of the two policies it was Johnson's which contained the greatest long-range wisdom and which best seemed to serve the interests of the country at large." McKitrick follows Rhodes in believing that the most enlightened Northern statesman was Massachusetts governor and capitalist John A. Andrew, and that could Andrew have settled matters with his Southern counterparts, men of power and "natural leaders" like Confederate general Wade Hampton, a better way forward could have been found.

The other answer goes something like this: The only thing wrong with Congressional Reconstruction was that it stopped too soon. The North was right in assuming that if Southerners were compelled to behave equitably, in time their attitudes would also change. But the North should have realized that this process could not happen overnight. Unfortunately, influenced from the beginning by motives more economic than idealistic, deprived of leadership by the deaths of Stevens and Sumner, and distracted by the Panic of 1873, the North abandoned Radical Republican policies before they had been fairly tried.

McKitrick's book was published in 1960, the year of the sit-ins; subsequent treatments, reflecting the Southern student movement and its demand for federal intervention, have tended to argue that the Radical Republicans were right. Whereas McKitrick accepted John A. Andrew's conviction that the men who led the Confederacy would inevitably dominate the postwar South, John Hope Franklin ended his *Reconstruction After The Civil War* (1961) with the lament that the South returned to the Union "with a leadership strikingly like that of the South which had seceded in 1860." Britisher W. R. Brock's *An American Crisis* (1963), an intensive study of the formation of Congressional policy for the South from 1865 to 1867, leaned toward the conclusion that Sumner and Stevens were realistic in suggesting that the Southern states be governed as territories during a prolonged period of social transformation. Their policy failed, Brock implied, because it was not applied long enough: "though one may blame them for their determination to have a revolution it is a little unfair to blame them for being forced to stop half-way." When in 1965 Kenneth Stampp too ventured on the dark and bloody ground of Reconstruction, the circle of slavery-and-Reconstruction historiography was closed; for Stampp, whose book on *The Peculiar Institution* championed the thesis that the slave was a white man with a black skin who consciously resented and resisted his oppression, now presented a version of Reconstruction comparable to his interpretation of slavery. Stampp concluded:

> The Fourteenth and Fifteenth Amendments, which could have been adopted only under the conditions of radical reconstruction, make the blunders of that era, tragic though they were, dwindle into insignificance. For if it was worth four years of civil war to save the Union, it was worth a few years of radical reconstruction to give the American Negro the ultimate promise of equal civil and political rights.

Neither of these views compels conviction. Their common weakness is that each reveals itself under scrutiny as a sophisticated paraphrase of the sectional stereotypes three quarters of a century old. The South wishes it had been left alone; the North regrets it did not intervene more vigorously.

Each position presupposes a set of assumptions about the strategy of social change. One of the virtues of Howard Zinn's *The Southern Mystique* is that, in attempting to articulate the rationale for a coercive approach to the new reconstruction of the South, he makes it possible for historians of the old reconstruction to rephrase their disagreement with more clarity. In asking the federal government to manipulate the white Southerner's environment so as to induce him to act decently toward the Negro, Zinn argues as Radical Republicans argued in 1867. Similarly, Southerners Claude Sitton and C. Vann Woodward, in charging Zinn with quasi-totalitarianism and insensitivity to the need for change to be organic and spontaneous if it is to be lasting, express much the same apprehension voiced in the 1870s by Liberal Republicans and Southern moderates against (as it seemed to them) bayonet rule *ad infinitum*.

The persistence of this cleavage, separating Northern radical from Southern liberal by a line thin but hard, must dampen optimism. Each body of assumptions is internally consistent. Yet the two arguments and their respective exponents are somehow opaque to one another; and so after a century of tragedy the nation blunders on, trying first one nostrum, then the other, invoking now this rationale and now that, but never confident and certain of its course.

All of which is to say that in the controversy over Reconstruction, as in the controversy over the nature of the first American Revolution, it hardly suffices to lay old stereotypes low. They will creep and seep back in unless merely negative analysis is supplemented by an alternative explanation, a more convincing way of telling the story. In 1959, Bernard Weisberger summarized the achievements of the anti-Dunning revisionists:

They show, first of all, that the so-called "scalawags" were not all the ragged underlings of Southern society, but included—at least early in the period—many erstwhile Southern Whigs, high in status and thoroughly baptized in the church of the Lost Cause. The nucleus of a Southern Republican party, they were displaced by extremist pressure from overardent Radicals, both Negro and white, on the one hand, and die-hard "white line" supporters on the other. Often, however, the issues on which they were challenged had as much to do with patronage and with profit as with race. Secondly, the Republican state governments chosen under the operation of the Reconstruction Acts of 1867 were not composed exclusively of corruptionists, white or Negro, and achieved a number of praiseworthy social and educational reforms. Thirdly, such corruption as did exist was shared in by many white and respectable Southerners, later to become "Bourbons," who did not scruple to profit by the lavish gifts of the sinful "carpetbag" governments to Southern development companies. Moreover, when restored to control, these "Conservatives" continued to keep the doors of the state treasuries hospitably open to businessmen who had formerly supported the Radicals. Fourthly, the restored "Conservatives" were willing to live with Negro suffrage, provided they could control its outcome. The "sin" of enfranchising the illiterate freedman was apparently washed whiter than snow, once he switched to the Democratic ticket. Fifthly, life somehow went on under "bayonet rule." Crops, capital, and order *were* restored, after all, and there were cakes and ale as well as heartbreak and ugliness. Violence there was; but the legend of Negro militiamen's "atrocities," perpetuated in Thomas Dixon's *The Klansman,* is as baseless as the implication in Albion Tourgee's *A Fool's Errand* that every square Southern mile contained a secretly buried victim of the Klan. Lastly, neither in Congress nor in the South were the Radicals the purposeful and unified group of conspirators that they have been made out to be by friendly biographers of Andrew Johnson. Johnson himself, pilloried though he was by his enemies, added to his own woes by personal hardheadedness, political stumbling, and a blind belief that the incantation of constitutional formulas could change the brute facts of power distribution.

Yet, Weisberger remarked,

. . . twenty years after these premonitory signs, the indicated tide of revision has not fully set in. Certainly the work still needs to be done. The New Deal, the Second World War, and the Cold War have all set in motion what some have called a "New Reconstruction" of the South—with fresh patterns in industry, urban life, population movement, agrarian practice, social and political leadership, and capitalization forming almost faster than the census takers can reveal them. The school desegregation crisis has, since 1954, moved the race question into disturbing but unescapable prominence. It is more important than ever that progress be made towards understanding the issues raised in the "old" Reconstruction of 1865 to 1877. Yet something seems to have blunted the purpose of the historical guild, and the discovery of what this something is deserves professional attention.

This judgment still holds at the present writing.

In my opinion a third point of view is in the process of crystalizing. It seeks to escape the debate as to whether Northern policy was too soft or too hard by contending that it was hard in the wrong way, or more precisely, in the wrong area of social life. This third view holds that the fundamental error in Reconstruction policy was that it did not give the freedman land of his own. Whether by confiscation of the property of leading rebels, by a vigorous Southern homestead policy, or by some combination of the two, Congress should have given the ex-slaves the economic independence to resist political intimidation. Lacking such an economic substratum, manhood suffrage was inevitably artificial; supported by the presence of Union soldiers, it collapsed when they were withdrawn. (Negroes continued to vote in large numbers in some Southern states after the end of Reconstruction, but rarely did they vote independently.)

This is not a new view. Such a "third course" was advocated at the time by Thaddeus Stevens, who was reluctant to enact Negro suffrage until the plantations of leading rebels were divided. Among historians W. E. B. Du Bois has concurred most clearly. Writing in 1901, at a time when historians and the public at large were convinced that the error in Reconstruction was (as *The Atlantic Monthly* put it) "giving the negro the ballot before he was qualified to use it," Du Bois argued subtly that, to begin with, the freedman required the ballot to defend his new liberty, but also that to give him only the ballot and not the land was to end "a civil war by beginning a race feud." "A far better policy" would have included "a permanent Freedman's Bureau, with a national system of Negro schools; a carefully supervised employment and labor office; a system of impartial protection before the regular courts; and such institutions for social betterment as savings-banks, land and building associations, and social settlements." Unwilling to contemplate so vast a plan of social engineering, the nation came to regard "Negro suffrage as a final answer to all present perplexities": "the Freedman's Bureau died, and its child was the Fifteenth Amendment."

The much-patronized abolitionists were far more aware of the need for such undergirding economic change than is often supposed. Stevens was not alone. Willie Lee Rose shows how stubbornly the ex-slaves and their abolitionist allies fought for land ownership in the sea island "rehearsal for reconstruction"; while James McPherson, in his splendid study of abolitionist agitation during and after the war, demonstrates that the vision of forty acres and a mule as a keystone of reconstruction was widespread, even commonplace, in the abolitionist press. Nothing that actually happened induced a Wendell Phillips or a Frederick Douglass to change their minds. Reviewing the failure of Reconstruction in the *North American Review,* Phillips stated: "Planted on his own land, sure of bread—instead of being merely a wage-slave—the negro's suffrage would have been a very different experiment." And Douglass declared in 1880 that had Stevens' strategy been followed, "the negro would not today be on his knees, as he is, supplicating the old master class to give him leave to toil."

In a pocket history of the United States distributed to American servicemen overseas during World War II, two deans of the historical profession (Allan Nevins and Henry Steele Commager) said that the Reconstruction state legislatures "were probably the worst that have ever been known in any English-speaking land." That was yesterday's history. Tomorrow's history will be along the lines laid down by McPherson, when he writes: "The South was not 'reconstructed' economically, and consequently the other measures of reconstruction rested upon an unstable foundation."

A NOTE TO STUDENTS AND TEACHERS

If desired, this pamphlet can be read from beginning to end so as to sense the development of Reconstruction historiography. But it is also possible to read the essays in an order which corresponds, not to the time they were written, but to the period of Reconstruction with which they deal.

Thus McKitrick's essay (No. 12) deals with the summer and fall of 1865, the period of Presidential Reconstruction. The diary of Clemenceau (No. 1) begins in the fall of 1865 and continues to the passage of the Fifteenth Amendment in 1869, the period of most active Congressional policy-making. Du Bois' chapter on the Freedmen's Bureau (No. 3) covers roughly the same period, but viewed from the standpoint of the South.

The selections by Rhodes and Beale (Nos. 4, 7) deal with the motivation of the men who fashioned Congressional Reconstruction in 1866–1867. Later views of the same subject are represented by the essays of Hesseltine, Sharkey, and Brock (Nos. 8, 10, 11 and 14).

Several selections survey the end and aftermath of Reconstruction in the South, among them Tourgée's (no. 2), Du Bois' (No. 5), Dunning's (No. 6), and Shugg's (No. 9).

PROSPECT
AND RETROSPECT:
TWO CONTEMPORARY VIEWS

The Power of Avenging Justice

GEORGES CLEMENCEAU

At the close of the Civil War the hopes of democratic idealists all over
the world turned to America, where representative institutions had shown
their capacity to survive massive armed insurrection. Georges Clemenceau,
then a young medical student and freelance writer, later the head of the
French government in World War I, came to the United States in September
1865 to view the new birth of freedom firsthand. His journal gives a sympathetic picture of the hopes and discouragements of Radical Republican
decision-makers during the years when Reconstruction policy was shaped.
Beginning just before Congress assembled to question the fruits of "Presi-

Reprinted from *American Reconstruction 1865–1870 and the Impeachment of
President Johnson* by Georges Clemenceau. Fernand Baldensperger, Editor. Trans-
lated by Margaret MacVeagh. Used by permission of the publisher, The Dial Press,
Inc. (New York, 1928, pp. 25–41, 97–98, 292–297).

dential Reconstruction" in December 1865, the journal extends through the final creative act of "Congresional Reconstruction," the adoption and ratification of the Fifteenth Amendment in 1869–1870.

Although a partisan of Charles Sumner and Thaddeus Stevens, Clemenceau saw clearly many of the defects in Radical Republicanism which subsequent historians have stressed. He noted that it would be "difficult to require the Southern states to give the negro freedmen all the rights of citizenship if the blacks do not yet enjoy these in the North." Like Wendell Phillips and Frederick Douglass, Clemenceau understood the need for the freedmen to have land of their own. And while he lauded the Radicals for their leadership of the revolution (as he called it), Clemenceau recognized that the Republicans were also the party of "industrial aristocracy," "political centralization," and "Puritan intolerance."

SEPTEMBER 28, 1865. THE POLITICAL PARTIES OF THE COUNTRY ARE just now passing through an interesting phase. Republicans and Democrats vie with each other in expressing their friendship for Mr. Johnson, the Democrats seeking to win him over, and the Republicans to keep their claim on him. Both parties have held their conventions, in Albany, New York, and the copperheads praised Johnson to the skies, the same Johnson whom three short months ago they were calling "Dionysius the Tyrant," accusing of the murder of Mrs. Surratt, Booth's accomplice,[1] and threatening with dire vengeance unless he made haste to drop from his cabinet Stanton, his Secretary of War.

Indeed a surprising change! At the bottom of it is the hope of the Democrats that they may harvest for their party's advantage the fruits of the policies which Johnson appears to be adopting. The vital question just now in American politics is that of negro suffrage. Johnson declares that he will allow each state to settle it independently, whereas the radical Republicans would like to have him assert his authority and settle it once for all. The moderate Republicans are undecided and disturbed about it. They do not wish to join issue openly with the President, and they are consoling themselves for his action in passing the problem of negro suffrage over to the former slave owners and rebels for solution, with the thought that, as Congress must ratify the new constitutions of the Southern states, the question of negro suffrage is simply deferred and will reappear sooner or later before the Federal legislative authority.

When this happens, however, it will be difficult to require the South-

---

[1] EDITOR'S NOTE: The reference, of course, is to the leader of the assassination plot against Lincoln and members of his cabinet, John Wilkes Booth.

ern states to give the negro freedmen all the rights of citizenship if the blacks do not yet enjoy these in the North. . . .

In all the discussions, I note that the question of universal suffrage does not arise. Each state is to be left free to define its voting qualifications for itself. The point is that, whatever regulation is made, no distinction shall exist between blacks and whites. Even Horace Greeley, the editor of the *Tribune,* does not claim universal suffrage for the negroes. A recent statement by him says: "We would readily consent to admitting to the suffrage only those who can read and write, or those who pay taxes, or are engaged in some trade. Any standard which would limit the voting privilege to the competent and deserving, would be acceptable to us." But the rules and restrictions relating to the suffrage should be applied to all on the same basis, in his opinion. The Southern states contain many poor whites, who are not better qualified to vote than the most ignorant and degraded negroes.

The question of negro suffrage took a most important place also in the convention of Massachusetts Republicans, recently held in Worcester. Charles Sumner,[2] chairman of the convention, made a very long speech which was garbled to some extent in the telegraphic report. He emphasized the necessity of giving the negroes the suffrage in order to create in the Southern states a voting faction of unquestionable loyalty, to prevent any reestablishment of slavery in any form, and to avoid putting a helpless race at the mercy of a dominant race, with no political redress. He protested vigorously against Mr. Johnson's policies, and would like to withhold full exercise of their former rights from the Southerners until they have given positive guarantees to the Union. When once the Federal garrisons have been entirely withdrawn from the South, and the freedmen's bureau abolished, the blacks will have no protection whatever from their former masters. Mr. Sumner believes time to be an essential factor in the adjustment of political affairs, and Mr. Johnson's solutions appear to him over hasty. His own advice would be to go slow in every respect. He would prefer to continue the military occupation of the Southern states until all spirit of revolt has entirely died out, and to keep the freedmen's bureaux in operation. This would mean that the Southern states would not be self-governing, as in the past, until their new constitutions were formed and approved by Congress. He would prefer not to have the country leave the solution of all unsettled problems to the executive power, and believes that the legislative power should be entrusted with far more responsibility in these matters. This hasty summary of his speech is all I can give. It has

[2] EDITOR'S NOTE: Charles Sumner, Senator from Massachusetts, was the foremost Radical Republican in the Senate.

influenced public opinion profoundly, as does every utterance of this distinguished, upright, and justly popular statesman.

I cannot deny that many progressive men have not been able to decide among the contradictory views concerning Southern Reconstruction, and are still without any convictions. Many who do not want to oppose Mr. Johnson openly, believing him sincerely devoted to the liberal and popular cause, still are afraid that his moderation and generosity, perhaps too expansive, will allow the Southern states to resume the share of power which they held so long, and that the spirit of compromise, which plunged the United States step by step into the Civil War will once again obscure the issues, veiling the appearance of the danger spots until they grow deep and ineradicable. There is a feeling that the South is now at the mercy of the North, and that for the first time the opportunity is at hand to quell definitely, once for all, the temper of oligarchical pride which worked such disaster to the Republic. There is a widespread feeling of pity for the blacks, who behaved so admirably during the war, committed no excesses nor cruelties, and shed their blood for the Union in the hope of becoming its citizens. Now they are being forced to bargain for, perhaps in the end to lose entirely, the rights which they have already purchased so dearly.

The real misfortune of the negro race is in owning no land of his own. There cannot be real emancipation for men who do not possess at least a small portion of the soil. We have had an example in Russia. In spite of the war, and the confiscation bills, which remain dead letters, every inch of land in the Southern states belongs to the former rebels. The population of free negroes has become a nomad population, congregated in the towns and suffering wretchedly there, destined to be driven back eventually by poverty into the country, where they will be forced to submit to the harshest terms imposed by their former masters. It would be too much to expect those masters of their own accord to conciliate the negroes by conceding them a little land in order to secure their cooperation. They are still too blinded by passion to see their own best interests.

Thus on every hand political and social difficulties arise. But the people of the United States have a peculiar faculty for adjusting themselves to circumstances and learning by experience, suddenly changing their course and thus nearly always disappointing prophets of disaster. The Americans will make mistakes but they will quickly find out how to remedy them. They will lose their way temporarily among the problems which beset them, trying out and abandoning unsatisfactory solutions, but in the end, when truth and justice have taken some kind of shape and revealed themselves to the eyes of the world, the people will seize upon them. So we must reserve our judgment for a time. For the present I will do no more than indicate the fluctuations of public opinion. The events of the last four years have taught me never to give up hope for this country.

· · ·

August 10, 1867. It must be admitted that the radicals, who will forever have the glorious distinction of having led to a successful conclusion the far-reaching revolution through which the country has just passed, are not above criticism. They represent the party of the industrial aristocracy, and for this reason are the rabid enemies of free trade. They are the authors of the incredible tariff, which would be unendurable except for the immense resources of this country and the abundance of paper money. Their idea of protection is prohibition, and the rich factory owners of New England will listen to no reason on this score. And yet, there has already been a deep division within the Republican party on this subject. It is sufficient to say that Mr. William Cullen Bryant, poet and newspaper man, well known for his radical opinions, is the president of the League for Free Trade in New York. The symptom takes on an added significance from the fact that when the South has finally been reconstructed, and the revolution finished, economic questions will be the first to come up for discussion, and it is on this foundation the two new parties will establish their respective platforms. The Republican party stands for political centralization (but it must be understood at once that this does not take a dangerous form here) and Puritan intolerance. The Republicans are the men who insist on keeping Sunday, as they understand the word, and it is they who made the laws forbidding the retail sale of strong liquors on Sunday, as in New York, or even forbidding their sale altogether, as in Massachusetts.

On these two points it is certain that the real mass of people, the body of the Republican party, is not in accord with its leaders, and this is enough to explain the reason why the Republicans lost nearly ten thousand votes in Maine in the last election. Of course, one must count in the losses all who do not wish to give the right of suffrage to the negroes, but the number of these is less than one would suppose, in view of the fact that the greater number of them were already ranged among the Democrats. . . .

· · ·

April 21, 1869. Like the Sibyl who continued to double the price of her books, in which the destinies of Rome were prophesied, as long as Tarquin refused to buy them, the North has become more and more exacting with every refusal of the concessions which it demanded. It is because they would not consent at the beginning to give civil rights to the negroes that the Southern states are now being forced to give them political rights.[3] Years might have elapsed before the North decided to do complete justice to the black race, but the obstinacy of the slave holders forced it upon them, and the negroes now owe almost as much to the hatred of the one class as to the friendship of the other.

• • •

June 8, 1869. Although General Grant[4] is openly trying to pacify the South, it must be admitted in justice to him that, far from deserting the cause of the blacks, as Mr. Johnson did so promptly, he has surprised even the radicals by his insistence on not only preaching, but also practising the doctrine of the equality of the races. He is, in fact, the first President who has dared to give to a black man a post in the administration. It is hard to say what Mr. Lincoln would have done had he lived, but it seems entirely probable that he would have hesitated to do any such thing. Perhaps he would never have thought of it, for, though circumstances made of him a revolutionary, he was at heart essentially a conservative, and so moderate that the leaders of the Republican party several times accused him of holding back. If he had thought of it, I feel quite sure he would not have acted upon the idea, and all who know how strong and deep rooted were the prejudices of the Northern Republicans against the African race, even after the war, will understand that Mr. Lincoln might have been afraid to stir up against his own party a reaction dangerous by its violence, if not by its duration.

Since then, many blacks have been appointed to civil posts and, although the Democratic newspapers have thought it incumbent upon them to shout loud protests, public opinion has approved of this act of justice and of reparation, in which the President bravely led the way. I say bravely, because Mr. Lincoln and General Grant, though they played important rôles in one of the most radical revolutions known in history, were the instruments and not the promoters of it.

Neither of these men was a reformer cherishing a more or less definitely formulated cause, nor did he owe his achievement of power to either a sudden wave or a slowly rising tide of popular enthusiasm. Both of them were purely and simply representatives of popular opinion,

---

[3] EDITOR'S NOTE: Clemenceau refers to the rejection of the Fourteenth Amendment by Southern state legislatures in 1866–1867.

[4] EDITOR'S NOTE: U. S. Grant was elected President in 1868, succeeding Andrew Johnson.

without which they would have no power at all and opposed to which they would be completely ruined. Consequently, there is nothing surprising in the spectacle of their changing and adapting themselves to opinion, for the truth is that all their efforts and their ambition have been concentrated on this. But, as a matter of course, this adaptation does not take place by chance; it is rather a development in a predetermined direction, a natural evolution, operating in them at the same time as in the whole people. . . .

• • •

August 6, 1869. The Fifteenth Amendment has been accepted.[5]

There is only one method of ending all difficulties, and that is justice, not force. It is true that in this case, by a rare chance, force was ranged on the side of justice and a happy combination of circumstances brought it about that the victors were those who deserved to win. But they could not have changed the course of the world in four years. Never could they have pacified men's minds and won them over to the new ideals, unless even the conquered had felt that all humanity had spoken the verdict and lifted its hand to bear down upon them; if they had not realized, in short, that it was useless now to defend with the pen what they had as a last resort tried to defend with the sword, and that the hour had come to abandon their cause. It is perfectly possible to fight, making more or less plausible pretexts, for an idea which one would not dare to support in words, but once defeated, there is nothing more to do in such a case but cry for mercy.

It is this most formidable opposition which has died down in four years, together with all those other opposing forces which have considerably less strength in action, but which are gathering headway every day in other countries of the world. The power which crushed the one is the same power that nourishes and eventually will assure the triumph of the others—avenging justice.

• • •

November 3, 1869. The blacks must henceforth work to better themselves. They have the right to education, they must learn; they have the right to work, they must work; lastly, they have civil and political rights which are effective and powerful weapons, they must use them in their

---

[5] EDITOR'S NOTE: The Fifteenth Amendment, passed by Congress in 1869 and ratified by the states in 1870, provided that the right to vote should not be denied or abridged on grounds of race, color, or previous servitude.

own defense. They must gird. up their loins, and struggle for their existence, in Darwin's phrase, for their physical as well as their moral existence. In a word, they must become men. . . .

This Short-Sighted Plan

ALBION W. TOURGÉE

Like Clemenceau, Tourgée was sympathetic to the aims of Congressional Reconstruction, but fourteen years of experience in attempting to administer that plan in the South led him to be bitterly critical of it as a means. Born in a hotbed of abolitionism, the Western Reserve of Ohio, Tourgée enlisted in the 27th New York Volunteers in the first week of the Civil War. In October 1865 he settled in Greensboro, North Carolina to practice law. Here he became an advocate of Negro suffrage, organizer of a Union League, editor of the short-lived *Union Register*, and a member of the constitutional convention elected under the Reconstruction Acts of 1867. Thereafter he served for six years on the state Superior Court, denouncing the Ku Klux Klan and in turn being denounced and threatened himself. In 1879 Tourgée returned to the North and published anonymously a novel describing his experience, *A Fool's Errand*.

Tourgée is often regarded merely as a chronicler of KKK violence. This was one of his central concerns, and as Harriet Beecher Stowe insisted that her work was based on fact, so the author of "the *Uncle Tom's Cabin* of Reconstruction" included in a later edition of his novel an appendix on the Klan intended to refute his critics. But Tourgée was far from being a fanatical Radical. He expressed a subtle awareness of the reciprocal misunderstandings between North and South, and criticized Congressional Reconstruction for its unrealistic assumption that the Southern aristocracy could be deprived of power simply by excluding it from the vote and political office. Perhaps Tourgée's strongest feeling was that Congress, having for better or worse embarked on a program of basic social change, then failed to give protection or support to those in the South who sought to make that program succeed.

Albion W. Tourgée, *A Fool's Errand* (New York: Fords, Howard & Hulbert, 1880), pp. 119–125.

HOW THE WISE MEN BUILDED

IT MUST HAVE BEEN WELL UNDERSTOOD BY THE WISE MEN WHO devised this short-sighted plan of electing a President beyond a peradventure of defeat,[1] that they were giving the power of the re-organized, subordinate republics, into the hands of a race unskilled in public affairs, poor to a degree hardly to be matched in the civilized world, and so ignorant that not five out of a hundred of its voters could read their own ballots, joined with such Adullamites among the native whites as might be willing to face a proscription which would shut the house of God in the face of their families, together with the few men of Northern birth, resident in that section since the close of the war,—either knaves or fools, or partaking of the nature of both,—who might elect to become permanent citizens, and join in the movement.

Against them was to be pitted the wealth, the intelligence, the organizing skill, the pride, and the hate of a people whom it had taken four years to conquer in open fight when their enemies outnumbered them three to one, who were animated chiefly by the apprehension of what seemed now about to be forced upon them by this miscalled measure of "Reconstruction"; to wit, the equality of the negro race.

It was done, too, in the face of the fact that within the preceding twelvemonth the white people of the South, by their representatives in the various Legislatures of the Johnsonian period, had absolutely refused to recognize this equality, even in the slightest matters, by *refusing to allow the colored people to testify in courts of justice* against white men, or to protect their rights of person and property in any manner from the avarice, lust, or brutality of their white neighbors. It was done in the very face of the "Black Codes," which were the first enactments of Provisional Legislatures, and which would have established a serfdom more complete than that of the Russian steppes before the *ukase* of Alexander.[2]

And the men who devised this plan called themselves honest and wise statesmen. More than one of them has since then hugged himself in gratulation under the belief, that, by his co-operation therein, he had cheaply achieved an immortality of praise from the liberty-lovers of the

[1] EDITOR'S NOTE: Tourgée refers to the Reconstruction Acts of 1867 which required each Southern state to hold an election for a state constitutional convention, with the further provision that adult male Negroes be permitted to vote for delegates to each convention and that they be enfranchised in each constitution. Tourgee regarded this as a device to ensure the election of a Republican President in 1868, by creating "rotten boroughs" of Negro Republican voters.

[2] EDITOR'S NOTE: The so-called Black Codes were laws passed by Southern state legislatures during the period of Presidential Reconstruction restricting the freedom of Negroes to own land, bear arms, move from place to place, etc.

earth! After having forced a proud people to yield what they had for more than two centuries considered a right,—the right to hold the African race in bondage,—they proceeded to outrage a feeling as deep and fervent as the zeal of Islam or the exclusiveness of Hindoo caste, by giving to the ignorant, unskilled, and dependent race—a race who could not have lived a week without the support or charity of the dominant one—equality of political right! Not content with this, they went farther, and, by erecting the rebellious territory into self-regulating and sovereign States, they abandoned these parties like cocks in a pit, to fight out the question of predominance without the possibility of national interference. They said to the colored man, in the language of one of the pseudo-philosophers of that day, "Root, hog, or die!"

It was cheap patriotism, cheap philanthropy, cheap success!

Yet it had its excuse, which we are bound to set forth. The North and the South had been two households in one house—two nations under one name. The intellectual, moral, and social life of each had been utterly distinct and separate from that of the other. They no more understood or appreciated each other's feelings or development than John Chinaman comprehends the civilization of John Bull. It is true they spoke the same language, used the same governmental forms, and, most unfortunately, thought they comprehended each other's ideas. Each thought they knew the thought and purpose of the other better than the thinker knew his own. The Northern man despised his Southern fellow-citizen in bulk, as a good-natured *braggadocio*, mindful of his own ease, fond of power and display, and with no animating principle which could in any manner interfere with his interest. The Southern man despised his Northern compeer as cold-blooded, selfish, hypocritical, cowardly, and envious.

This is how they played at cross-purposes, each thinking that he knew the other's heart far better than he sought to know his own.

ANTE BELLUM

NORTHERN IDEA OF SLAVERY	SOUTHERN IDEA OF SLAVERY
Slavery is wrong, politically, and economically. It is tolerated only for the sake of peace and quiet. The negro is a man, and has equal inherent rights with the white race.	The negro is fit only for slavery. It is sanctioned by the Bible, and it must be right; or, if not exactly right, is unavoidable, now that the race is among us. We can not live with them in any other condition.

NORTHERN IDEA OF THE SOUTHERN IDEA

Those Southern fellows know that slavery is wrong, and incompatible with the theory of our government; but it is a good thing for them. They grow fat and rich, and have a good time, on account of it; and no one can blame them for not wanting to give it up.

SOUTHERN IDEA OF THE NORTHERN IDEA

Those Yankees are jealous because we make slavery profitable, raising cotton and tobacco, and want to deprive us of our slaves from envy. They don't believe a word of what they say about its being wrong, except a few fanatics. The rest are all hypocrites.

POST BELLUM

THE NORTHERN IDEA OF THE SITUATION

The negroes are free now, and must have a fair chance to make themselves something. What is claimed about their inferiority may be true. It is not likely to approve itself, but, true or false, they have a right to equality before the law. That is what the war meant, and this must be secured to them. The rest they must get as they can, or do without, as they choose.

THE SOUTHERN IDEA OF THE SITUATION

We have lost our slaves, our bank stock, every thing, by the war. We have been beaten, and have honestly surrendered: slavery is gone, of course. The slave is now free, but he is not white. We have no ill will towards the colored man as such and in his place; but he is not our equal, can not be made our equal, and we will not be ruled by him, or admit him as a co-ordinate with the white race in power. We have no objection to his voting, so long as he votes as his old master, or the man for whom he labors, advises him; but, when he chooses to vote differently, he must take the consequences.

THE NORTHERN IDEA OF THE SOUTHERN IDEA

Now that the negro is a voter, the Southern people will have to treat him well, because they will need his vote. The negro will remain

THE SOUTHERN IDEA OF THE NORTHERN IDEA

The negro is made a voter simply to degrade and disgrace the white people of the South. The North cares nothing about the negro as true to the government and party which gave him liberty, and in order to secure its preservation. Enough of the Southern whites will go with them, for the sake of office and power, to enable them to retain permanent control of those States for an indefinite period. The negroes will go to work, and things will gradually adjust themselves. The South has no right to complain. They would have the negroes as slaves, kept the country in constant turmoil for the sake of them, brought on the war because we would not catch their runaways, killed a million of men; and now they can not complain if the very weapon by which they held power is turned against them, and is made the means of righting the wrongs which they have themselves created. It may be hard; but they will learn to do better hereafter.

a man, but only enfranchises him in order to humiliate and enfeeble us. Of course, it makes no difference to the people of the North whether he is a voter or not. There are so few colored men there, that there is no fear of one of them being elected to office, going to the Legislature, or sitting on the bench. The whole purpose of the measure is to insult and degrade. But only wait until the States are restored and the "Blue Coats" are out of the way, and we will show them their mistake.

There was just enough of truth in each of these estimates of the other's characteristics to mislead. The South, as a mass, was honest in its belief of the righteousness of slavery, both morally and politically. The North, in like manner, was equally honest in its conviction with regard to the wickedness of slavery, and its inconsistency with republican institutions; yet neither credited the other with honesty. The South was right in believing that the North cared little or nothing for the negro *as a man,* but wrong in the idea that the theory of political equality and manhood suffrage was invented or imposed from any thought of malice, revenge, or envy toward the South. The wish to degrade did not enter into the Northern mind in this connection. The idea that "of one blood are all the nations of the earth," and that "race, color, or previous condition of servitude," can not be allowed to affect the legal or political rights of any, *was* a living principle in the Northern mind, as little capable of suppression as the sentiment of race-antagonism by which it was met, and whose intensity it persistently discredited.

There was another thing which the wise men who were rebuilding the citadel of Liberty in such hot haste quite forgot. In judging of the South, and predicting its future course, they pictured it to themselves as the North would be with an infusion, so to speak, of newly-enfranchised blacks amounting to one-third of its aggregate population: in other words, they accounted the result of emancipation as the only differential feature by which the South was distinguishable from the North. They did not estimate aright the effects, upon the white people of the South, of an essentially different civilization and development. They said, "The South has heretofore differed from the North *only* in the institution of slavery. That is now removed; only the freedmen remain as a sign of its existence: therefore, the South is as the North would be with this element added to its population." It was a strange mistake. The ideas of generations do not perish in an hour. Divergent civilizations can not be made instantly identical by uprooting a single institution.

Among the peculiarities which marked the difference between Northern and Southern society was one so distinct and evident, one which had been so often illustrated in our political history, that it seems almost impossible that shrewd observers of that history should for a moment have overlooked or underestimated it. This is the influence of family position, social rank, or political prominence. Leadership, in the sense of a blind, unquestioning following of a man, without his being the peculiar exponent of an idea, is a thing almost unknown at the North: at the South it is a power. Every family there has its clientelage, its followers, who rally to its head as quickly, and with almost as unreasoning a faith, as the old Scottish clansmen, summoned by the burning cross. By means of this fact slavery had been perpetuated for fifty years. It was through this peculiarity that secession and rebellion became dominant there. This fact seems to have been dimly recognized, though not at all understood or appreciated, by those who originated what are known as the Reconstruction Acts. They seem to have supposed, that, if this class were deprived of actual political position, they would thereby be shorn of political influence: so it was provided that all who had any such prominence as to have been civil or military officers before the war, and had afterwards engaged in rebellion, should not be allowed to vote, or hold office, until relieved from such disability.

It was a fatal mistake. The dead leader has always more followers than his living peer. Every henchman of those lordlings at whom this blow was aimed felt it far more keenly than he would if it had lighted on his own cheek. The king of every village was dethroned; the magnate of every crossroads was degraded. Henceforward, each and every one of their satellites was bound to eternal hostility toward these measures and to all that might result therefrom.

So the line of demarkation was drawn. Upon the one side were found only those who constituted what was termed *respectable people*,—the bulk of those of the white race who had ruled the South in *ante bellum* days, who had fostered slavery, and been fattened by it, who had made it the dominant power in the nation, together with the mass of those whose courage and capacity had organized rebellion, and led the South in that marvelous struggle for separation. On the other side were the pariahs of the land, to designate the different classes of which, three words were used: "Niggers," the newly-enfranchised African voters; "Scalawags," the native whites who were willing to accept the reconstruction measures; and "Carpetbaggers," all men of Northern birth, resident in the South, who should elect to speak or act in favor of such reconstruction.

The ban of proscription spared neither age nor sex, and was never relaxed. In business or pleasure, in friendship or religion, in the market or the church, it was omnipotent. Men were excluded from the Lord's Communion for establishing sabbath schools for colored people. Those who did not curse the measure, its authors, and the government by which it was administered, were henceforth shunned as moral and social lepers. The spirit of the dead Confederacy was stronger than the mandate of the nation to which it had succumbed in battle. . . .

NEGRO SUFFRAGE, PRO AND CON

Of The Dawn of Freedom

W. E. B. DU BOIS

By the turn of the century novelists, politicians, and historians in all parts of the United States were in fundamental agreement in their view of Reconstruction in the South. The Negro-dominated legislatures of the States of the former Confederacy—so this version had it—initiated an era of unparalleled corruption and misgovernment. The illiterate freedman, the crafty carpetbagger who manipulated the freedman's vote, the shiftless scalawag, and the decent Southern white man fearful for his life, his property, and his daughter, all became familiar stereotypes.

Among scholars the sole prominent dissenter was the young Negro historian, W. E. B. Du Bois. Born in Massachusetts, educated at Fisk, at Harvard, and in Germany, Du Bois contributed an article to *The Atlantic Monthly* in 1901 which appeared two years later, slightly revised, in *The*

W. E. B. Du Bois, *The Souls of Black Folk* (New York: Paperback edition, Fawcett World Library, 1961), pp. 23–41.

Souls of Black Folk under the title "Of The Dawn Of Freedom." The essay was and remains significant, both for its famous opening phrase ("The problem of the twentieth century is the problem of the color-line") and for its challenge to the then-prevailing view of Southern Reconstruction.

Du Bois believed that the heart of the Reconstruction effort was the Freedmen's Bureau, an agency which (as he saw it) should have been made permanent and endowed with extensive powers over employment, education, and the administration of justice. Unprepared to take so large a step in social engineering, Congress, according to Du Bois, fell back on enfranchisement as a cure for all ills. Despite the fact that "every sensible man, black and white, would easily have chosen" restricted rather than full and immediate suffrage, "the Freedmen's Bureau died, and its child was the Fifteenth Amendment."

> Careless seems the great Avenger;
>   History's lessons but record
> One death-grapple in the darkness
>   'Twixt old systems and the Word;
> Truth forever on the scaffold,
>   Wrong forever on the throne;
> Yet that scaffold sways the future,
>   And behind the dim unknown
> Standeth God within the shadow
>   Keeping watch above His own.
>
>   LOWELL

THE PROBLEM OF THE TWENTIETH CENTURY IS THE PROBLEM OF the color-line,—the relation of the darker to the lighter races of men in Asia and Africa, in America and the islands of the sea. It was a phase of this problem that caused the Civil War, and however much they who marched South and North in 1861 may have fixed on the technical points of union and local autonomy as a shibboleth, all nevertheless knew, as we know, that the question of Negro slavery was the real cause of the conflict. Curious it was, too, how this deeper question ever forced itself to the surface despite effort and disclaimer. No sooner had Northern armies touched Southern soil than this old question, newly guised, sprang from the earth,—What shall be done with Negroes? Peremptory military commands, this way and that, could not answer the query; the Emancipation Proclamation seemed but to broaden and intensify the difficulties; and the War Amendments made the Negro problems of to-day.

It is the aim of this essay to study the period of history from 1861 to 1872 so far as it relates to the American Negro. In effect, this tale of the dawn of Freedom is an account of that government of men called the Freedmen's Bureau,—one of the most singular and interesting of the attempts made by a great nation to grapple with vast problems of race and social condition.

The war has naught to do with slaves, cried Congress, the President, and the Nation; and yet no sooner had the armies, East and West, penetrated Virginia and Tennessee than fugitive slaves appeared within their lines. They came at night, when the flickering camp-fires shone like vast unsteady stars along the black horizon: old men and thin, with gray and tufted hair; women, with frightened eyes, dragging whimpering hungry children; men and girls, stalwart and gaunt,—a horde of starving vagabonds, homeless, helpless, and pitiable, in their dark distress. Two methods of treating these newcomers seemed equally logical to opposite sorts of minds. Ben Butler, in Virginia, quickly declared slave property contraband of war, and put the fugitives to work; while Fremont, in Missouri, declared the slaves free under martial law. Butler's action was approved, but Fremont's was hastily countermanded, and his successor, Halleck, saw things differently. "Hereafter," he commanded, "no slaves should be allowed to come into your lines at all; if any come without your knowledge, when owners call for them deliver them." Such a policy was difficult to enforce; some of the black refugees declared themselves freemen, others showed that their masters had deserted them, and still others were captured with forts and plantations. Evidently, too, slaves were a source of strength to the Confederacy, and were being used as laborers and producers. "They constitute a military resource," wrote Secretary Cameron, late in 1861; "and being such, that they should not be turned over to the enemy is too plain to discuss." So gradually the tone of the army chiefs changed; Congress forbade the rendition of fugitives, and Butler's "contrabands" were welcomed as military laborers. This complicated rather than solved the problem, for now the scattering fugitives became a steady stream, which flowed faster as the armies marched.

Then the long-headed man with care-chiselled face who sat in the White House saw the inevitable, and emancipated the slaves of rebels on New Year's, 1863. A month later Congress called earnestly for the Negro soldiers whom the act of July, 1862, had half grudgingly allowed to enlist. Thus the barriers were levelled and the deed was done. The stream of fugitives swelled to a flood, and anxious army officers kept inquiring: "What must be done with slaves, arriving almost daily? Are we to find food and shelter for women and children?"

It was a Pierce of Boston who pointed out the way, and thus became in a sense the founder of the Freedmen's Bureau. He was a firm friend of Secretary Chase; and when, in 1861, the care of slaves and abandoned lands developed upon the Treasury officials, Pierce was specially detailed from the ranks to study the conditions. First, he cared for the refugees at Fortress Monroe; and then, after Sherman had captured Hilton Head, Pierce was sent there to found his Port Royal experiment of making free workingmen out of slaves.[1] Before his experiment was barely started, however, the problem of the fugitives had assumed such proportions that it was taken from the hands of the over-burdened Treasury Department and given to the army officials. Already centres of massed freedmen were forming at Fortress Monroe, Washington, New Orleans, Vicksburg and Corinth, Columbus, Ky., and Cairo, Ill., as well as at Port Royal. Army chaplains found here new and fruitful fields; "superintendents of contrabands" multiplied, and some attempt at systematic work was made by enlisting the able-bodied men and giving work to the others.

Then came the Freedmen's Aid societies, born of the touching appeals from Pierce and from these other centres of distress. There was the American Missionary Association, sprung from the *Amistad,* and now full-grown for work; the various church organizations, the National Freedmen's Relief Association, the American Freedmen's Union, the Western Freedmen's Aid Commission,—in all fifty or more active organizations, which sent clothes, money, school-books, and teachers southward. All they did was needed, for the destitution of the freedmen was often reported as "too appalling for belief," and the situation was daily growing worse rather than better.

And daily, too, it seemed more plain that this was no ordinary matter of temporary relief, but a national crisis; for here loomed a labor problem of vast dimensions. Masses of Negroes stood idle, or, if they worked spasmodically, were never sure of pay; and if perchance they received pay, squandered the new thing thoughtlessly. In these and other ways were camp-life and the new liberty demoralizing the freedmen. The broader economic organization thus clearly demanded sprang up here and there as accident and local conditions determined. Here it was that Pierce's Port Royal plan of leased plantations and guided workmen pointed out the rough way. In Washington the military governor, at the urgent appeal of the superintendent, opened confiscated estates to the cultivation of the fugitives, and there in the shadow of the dome gathered black farm villages. General Dix gave over estates to the freedmen of Fortress Monroe, and so on, South and West. The government and benevolent

---

[1] EDITOR'S NOTE: Hilton Head and Port Royal were locations in the "sea islands" near the coast of South Carolina and Georgia, which were captured by Union forces in the fall of 1861 and became the scene of the first experiments in Reconstruction.

societies furnished the means of cultivation, and the Negro turned again slowly to work. The systems of control, thus started, rapidly grew, here and there, into strange little governments, like that of General Banks in Louisiana, with its ninety thousand black subjects, its fifty thousand guided laborers, and its annual budget of one hundred thousand dollars and more. It made out four thousand pay-rolls a year, registered all freedmen, inquired into grievances and redressed them, laid and collected taxes, and established a system of public schools. So, too, Colonel Eaton, the superintendent of Tennessee and Arkansas, ruled over one hundred thousand freedmen, leased and cultivated seven thousand acres of cotton land, and fed ten thousand paupers a year. In South Carolina was General Saxton, with his deep interest in black folk. He succeeded Pierce and the Treasury officials, and sold forfeited estates, leased abandoned plantations, encouraged schools, and received from Sherman, after that terribly picturesque march to the sea, thousands of the wretched camp followers.

Three characteristic things one might have seen in Sherman's raid through Georgia, which threw the new situation in shadowy relief: the Conqueror, the Conquered, and the Negro. Some see all significance in the grim front of the destroyer, and some in the bitter sufferers of the Lost Cause. But to me neither soldier nor fugitive speaks with so deep a meaning as that dark human cloud that clung like remorse on the rear of those swift columns, swelling at times to half their size, almost engulfing and choking them. In vain were they ordered back, in vain were bridges hewn from beneath their feet; on they trudged and writhed and surged, until they rolled into Savannah, a starved and naked horde of tens of thousands. There too came the characteristic military remedy: "The islands from Charleston south, the abandoned rice-fields along the rivers for thirty miles back from the sea, and the country bordering the St. John's River, Florida, are reserved and set apart for the settlement of Negroes now made free by act of war." So read the celebrated "Field-order Number Fifteen."

All these experiments, orders, and systems were bound to attract and perplex the government and the nation. Directly after the Emancipation Proclamation, Representative Eliot had introduced a bill creating a Bureau of Emancipation; but it was never reported. The following June a committee of inquiry, appointed by the Secretary of War, reported in favor of a temporary bureau for the "improvement, protection, and employment of refugee freedmen," on much the same lines as were afterwards followed. Petitions came into President Lincoln from distinguished citizens and organizations, strongly urging a comprehensive and unified plan of dealing with the freedmen, under a bureau which should be "charged with the study of plans and execution of measures for easily guiding, and in every way judiciously and humanely aiding, the passage of our emancipated and yet to be emancipated blacks from the old condition of forced labor to their new state of voluntary industry."

Some half-hearted steps were taken to accomplish this, in part, by putting the whole matter again in charge of the special Treasury agents. Laws of 1863 and 1864 directed them to take charge of and lease abandoned lands for periods not exceeding twelve months, and to "provide in such leases, or otherwise, for the employment and general welfare" of the freedmen. Most of the army officers greeted this as a welcome relief from perplexing "Negro affairs," and Secretary Fessenden, July 29, 1864, issued an excellent system of regulations, which were afterward closely followed by General Howard.[2] Under Treasury agents, large quantities of land were leased in the Mississippi Valley, and many Negroes were employed; but in August, 1864, the new regulations were suspended for reasons of "public policy," and the army was again in control.

Meanwhile Congress had turned its attention to the subject; and in March the House passed a bill by a majority of two establishing a Bureau for Freedmen in the War Department. Charles Sumner, who had charge of the bill in the Senate, argued that freedmen and abandoned lands ought to be under the same department, and reported a substitute for the House Bill attaching the Bureau to the Treasury Department. This bill passed, but too late for action by the House. The debates wandered over the whole policy of the administration and the general question of slavery, without touching very closely the specific merits of the measure in hand. Then the national election took place; and the administration, with a vote of renewed confidence from the country, addressed itself to the matter more seriously. A conference between the two branches of Congress agreed upon a carefully drawn measure which contained the chief provisions of Sumner's bill, but made the proposed organization a department independent of both the War and the Treasury officials. The bill was conservative, giving the new department "general superintendence of all freedmen." Its purpose was to "establish regulations" for them, protect them, lease them lands, adjust their wages, and appear in civil and military courts as their "next friend." There were many limitations attached to the powers thus granted, and the organization was made permanent. Nevertheless, the Senate defeated the bill, and a new conference committee was appointed. This committee reported a new bill, February 28, which was whirled through

---

[2] EDITOR'S NOTE: Oliver O. Howard was head of the Freedmen's Bureau throughout its short and controversial career.

just as the session closed, and became the act of 1865 establishing in the War Department a "Bureau of Refugees, Freedmen, and Abandoned Lands."

This last compromise was a hasty bit of legislation, vague and uncertain in outline. A Bureau was created, "to continue during the present War of Rebellion, and for one year thereafter," to which was given "the supervision and management of all abandoned lands and the control of all subjects relating to refugees and freedmen," under "such rules and regulations as may be presented by the head of the Bureau and approved by the President." A Commissioner, appointed by the President and Senate, was to control the Bureau, with an office force not exceeding ten clerks. The President might also appoint assistant commissioners in the seceded States, and to all these offices military officials might be detailed at regular pay. The Secretary of War could issue rations, clothing, and fuel to the destitute, and all abandoned property was placed in the hands of the Bureau for eventual lease and sale to ex-slaves in forty-acre parcels.

Thus did the United States government definitely assume charge of the emancipated Negro as the ward of the nation. It was a tremendous undertaking. Here at a stroke of the pen was erected a government of millions of men,—and not ordinary men either, but black men emasculated by a peculiarly complete system of slavery, centuries old; and now, suddenly, violently, they come into a new birthright, at a time of war and passion, in the midst of the stricken and embittered population of their former masters. Any man might well have hesitated to assume charge of such a work, with vast responsibilities, indefinite powers, and limited resources. Probably no one but a soldier would have answered such a call promptly; and, indeed, no one but a soldier could be called, for Congress had appropriated no money for salaries and expenses.

Less than a month after the weary Emancipator passed to his rest, his successor assigned Major-Gen. Oliver O. Howard to duty as Commissioner of the new Bureau. He was a Maine man, then only thirty-five years of age. He had marched with Sherman to the sea, had fought well at Gettysburg, and but the year before had been assigned to the command of the Department of Tennessee. An honest man, with too much faith in human nature, little aptitude for business and intricate detail, he had had large opportunity of becoming acquainted at first hand with much of the work before him. And of that work it has been truly said that "no approximately correct history of civilization can ever be written which does not throw out in bold relief, as one of the great landmarks of political and social progress, the organization and administration of the Freedmen's Bureau."

On May 12, 1865, Howard was appointed; and he assumed the duties of his office promptly on the 15th, and began examining the field of work. A curious mess he looked upon: little despotisms, communistic experiments, slavery, peonage, business speculations, organized charity, unorganized almsgiving,—all reeling on under the guise of helping the freedmen, and all enshrined in the smoke and blood of war and the cursing and silence of angry men. On May 19 the new government—for a government it really was—issued its constitution; commissioners were to be appointed in each of the seceded states, who were to take charge of "all subjects relating to refugees and freedmen," and all relief and rations were to be given by their consent alone. The Bureau invited continued cooperation with benevolent societies, and declared: "It will be the object of all commissioners to introduce practicable systems of compensated labor," and to establish schools. Forthwith nine assistant commissioners were appointed. They were to hasten to their fields of work; seek gradually to close relief establishments, and make the destitute self-supporting; act as courts of law where there were no courts, or where Negroes were not recognized in them as free; establish the institution of marriage among ex-slaves, and keep records; see that freedmen were free to choose thir employers, and help in making fair contracts for them; and finally, the circular said: "Simple good faith, for which we hope on all hands for those concerned in the passing away of slavery, will especially relieve the assistant commissioners in the discharge of their duties toward the freedmen, as well as promote the general welfare."

No sooner was the work thus started, and the general system and local organization in some measure begun, than two grave difficulties appeared which changed largely the theory and outcome of Bureau work. First, there were the abandoned lands of the South. It had long been the more or less definitely expressed theory of the North that all the chief problems of Emancipation might be settled by establishing the slaves on the forfeited lands of their masters,—a sort of poetic justice, said some. But this poetry done into solemn prose meant either wholesale confiscation of private property in the South, or vast appropriations. Now Congress had not appropriated a cent, and no sooner did the proclamations of general amnesty appear than the eight hundred thousand acres of abandoned lands in the hands of the Freedmen's Bureau melted quickly away. The second difficulty lay in perfecting the local organization of the Bureau throughout the wide field of work. Making a new machine and sending out officials of duly ascertained fitness for a great work of social reform is no child's task; but this task was even harder, for a new central organization had to be fitted on a heterogeneous and confused but already existing system of relief and control of ex-slaves; and the agents available for this work must be sought for in an army still busy with war operations,—men in the very nature of the case ill fitted for delicate social work,—or among the questionable camp followers of an invading host. Thus, after a year's work, vigorously as it was pushed, the problem looked even more difficult to grasp and solve than at the beginning. Nevertheless, three things that year's work did, well worth the doing: it relieved a vast amount of physical suffering; it transported seven thousand fugitives from congested centres back to the farm; and, best of all, it inaugurated the crusade of the New England schoolma'am.

The annals of this Ninth Crusade are yet to be written,—the tale of a mission that seemed to our age far more quixotic than the quest of St. Louis seemed to his. Behind the mists of ruin and rapine waved the calico dresses of women who dared, and after the hoarse mouthings of the field guns rang the rhythm of the alphabet. Rich and poor they were, serious and curious. Bereaved now of a father, now of a brother, now of more than these, they came seeking a life work in planting New England schoolhouses among the white and black of the South. They did their work well. In that first year they taught one hundred thousand souls, and more.

Evidently, Congress must soon legislate again on the hastily organized Bureau, which had so quickly grown into wide significance and vast possibilities. An institution such as that was well-nigh as difficult to end as to begin. Early in 1866 Congress took up the matter, when Senator Trumbull, of Illinois, introduced a bill to extend the Bureau and enlarge its powers. This measure received, at the hands of Congress, far more thorough discussion and attention than its predecessor. The war cloud had thinned enough to allow a clearer conception of the work of Emancipation. The champions of the bill argued that the strengthening of the Freedmen's Bureau was still a military necessity; that it was needed for the proper carrying out of the Thirteenth Amendment, and was a work of sheer justice to the ex-slave, at a trifling cost to the government. The opponents of the measure declared that the war was over, and the necessity for war measures past; that the Bureau, by reason of its extraordinary powers, was clearly unconstitutional in time of peace, and was destined to irritate the South and pauperize the freedmen, at a final cost of possibly hundreds of millions. These two arguments were unanswered, and indeed unanswerable: the one that the extraordinary powers of the Bureau threatened the civil rights of all citizens; and the other that the government must have power to do what manifestly must be done, and that present abandonment of the freedmen meant their practical re-enslavement. The bill which finally passed enlarged and made permanent the Freedmen's Bureau. It was promptly vetoed by President Johnson as "unconstitutional," "unnecessary," and "extrajudicial," and failed of passage over the veto. Meantime, however, the breach between Congress and the President began to broaden, and a modified form of the lost bill was finally passed over the President's second veto, July 16.

The act of 1866 gave the Freedmen's Bureau its final form,—the form by which it will be known to posterity and judged of men. It extended the existence of the Bureau to July, 1868; it authorized additional assistant commissioners, the retention of army officers mustered out of regular service, the sale of certain forfeited lands to freedmen on nominal terms, the sale of Confederate public property for Negro schools, and a wider field of judicial interpretation and cognizance. The government of the unreconstructed South was thus put very largely in the hands of the Freedmen's Bureau, especially as in many cases the departmental military commander was now made also assistant commissioner. It was thus that the Freedmen's Bureau became a full-fledged government of men. It made laws, executed them and interpreted them; it laid and collected taxes, defined and punished crime, maintained and used military force, and dictated such measures as it thought necessary and proper for the accomplishment of its varied ends. Naturally, all these powers were not exercised continuously nor to their fullest extent; and yet, as General Howard has said, "scarcely any subject that has to be legislated upon in civil society failed, at one time or another, to demand the action of this singular Bureau."

To understand and criticise intelligently so vast a work, one must not forget an instant the drift of things in the later sixties. Lee had surrendered, Lincoln was dead, and Johnson and Congress were at loggerheads; the Thirteenth Amendment was adopted, the Fourteenth pending, and the Fifteenth declared in force in 1870. Guerrilla raiding, the ever-present flickering after-flame of war, was spending its forces against the Negroes, and all the Southern land was awakening as from some wild dream to poverty and social revolution. In a time of perfect calm, amid willing neighbors and streaming wealth, the social uplifting of four million slaves to an assured and self-sustaining place in the body politic and economic would have been a herculean task; but when to the inherent difficulties of so delicate and nice a social operation were added the spite and hate of conflict, the hell of war; when suspicion and cruelty were rife, and gaunt Hunger wept beside Bereavement,—in such a case, the work of any instrument of social regeneration was in large part foredoomed to failure. The very name of the Bureau stood for a thing in the South which for two centuries and better men had refused even to argue,—that life amid free Negroes was simply unthinkable, the maddest of experiments.

The agents that the Bureau could command varied all the way from unselfish philanthropists to narrow-minded busybodies and thieves; and even though it be true that the average was far better than the worst, it was the occasional fly that helped spoil the ointment.

Then amid all crouched the freed slave, bewildered between friend and foe. He had emerged from slavery,—not the worst slavery in the world, not a slavery that made all life unbearable, rather a slavery that had here and there something of kindliness, fidelity, and happiness,— but withal slavery, which, so far as human aspiration and desert were concerned, classed the black man and the ox together. And the Negro knew full well that, whatever their deeper convictions may have been, Southern men had fought with desperate energy to perpetuate this slavery under which the black masses, with half-articulate thought, had writhed and shivered. They welcomed freedom with a cry. They shrank from the master who still strove for their chains; they fled to the friends that had freed them, even though those friends stood ready to use them as a club for driving the recalcitrant South back into loyalty. So the cleft between the white and black South grew. Idle to say it never should have been; it was as inevitable as its results were pitiable. Curiously incongruous elements were left arrayed against each other,—the North, the government, the carpet-bagger, and the slave, here; and there, all the South that was white, whether gentleman or vagabond, honest man or rascal, lawless murderer or martyr to duty.

Thus it is doubly difficult to write of this period calmly, so intense was the feeling, so mighty the human passions that swayed and blinded men. Amid it all, two figures ever stand to typify that day to coming age,—the one, a gray-haired gentleman, whose fathers had quit themselves like men, whose sons lay in nameless graves; who bowed to the evil of slavery because its abolition threatened untold ill to all; who stood at last, in the evening of life, a blighted, ruined form, with hate in his eyes;—and the other, a form hovering dark and mother-like, her awful face black with the mists of centuries, had aforetime quailed at that white master's command, had bent in love over the cradles of his sons and daughters, and closed in death the sunken eyes of his wife,—aye, too, at his behest had laid low to his lust, and borne a tawny man-child to the world, only to see her dark boy's limbs scattered to the winds by midnight marauders riding after "damned Niggers." These were the saddest sights of that woful day; and no man clasped the hands of these two passing figures of the present-past; but, hating, they went to their long home, and, hating, their children's children live to-day.

Here, then, was the field of work for the Freedmen's Bureau; and since, with some hesitation, it was continued by the act of 1868 until

1869, let us look upon four years of its work as a whole. There were, in 1868, nine hundred Bureau officials scattered from Washington to Texas, ruling, directly and indirectly, many millions of men. The deeds of these rulers fall mainly under seven heads: the relief of physical suffering, the overseeing of the beginnings of free labor, the buying and selling of land, the establishment of schools, the paying of bounties, the administration of justice, and the financiering of all these activities.

Up to June, 1869, over half a million patients had been treated by Bureau physicians and surgeons, and sixty hospitals and asylums had been in operation. In fifty months twenty-one million free rations were distributed at a cost of over four million dollars. Next came the difficult question of labor. First, thirty thousand black men were transported from the refuges and relief stations back to the farms, back to the critical trial of a new way of working. Plain instructions went out from Washington: the laborers must be free to choose their employers, no fixed rate of wages was prescribed, and there was to be no peonage or forced labor. So far, so good; but where local agents differed *toto cœlo* in capacity and character, where the *personnel* was continually changing, the outcome was necessarily varied. The largest element of success lay in the fact that the majority of the freedmen were willing, even eager, to work. So labor contracts were written,—fifty thousand in a single State,—laborers advised, wages guaranteed, and employers supplied. In truth, the organization became a vast labor bureau,—not perfect, indeed, notably defective here and there, but on the whole successful beyond the dreams of thoughtful men. The two great obstacles which confronted the officials were the tyrant and the idler,—the slaveholder who was determined to perpetuate slavery under another name; and the freedman who regarded freedom as perpetual rest,—the Devil and the Deep Sea.

In the work of establishing the Negroes as peasant proprietors, the Bureau was from the first handicapped and at last absolutely checked. Something was done, and larger things were planned; abandoned lands were leased so long as they remained in the hands of the Bureau, and a total revenue of nearly half a million dollars derived from black tenants. Some other lands to which the nation had gained title were sold on easy terms, and public lands were opened for settlement to the very few freedmen who had tools and capital. But the vision of "forty acres and a mule" —the righteous and reasonable ambition to become a landholder, which the nation had all but categorically promised the freedmen—was destined in most cases to bitter disappointment. And those men of marvellous hindsight who are today seeking to preach the Negro back to the present peonage of the soil know well, or ought to know, that the opportunity of binding the Negro peasant willingly to the soil was lost on that day when the Commissioner of the Freedmen's Bureau had to go to South Carolina and tell the weeping freedmen, after their years of toil, that their land was not theirs, that there was a mistake—somewhere. If by 1874 the Georgia Negro alone owned three hundred and fifty thousand acres of land, it was by grace of his thrift rather than by bounty of the government.

The greatest success of the Freedmen's Bureau lay in the planting of the free school among Negroes, and the idea of free elementary education among all classes in the South. It not only called the school-mistresses through the benevolent agencies and built them school-houses, but it helped discover and support such apostles of human culture as Edmund Ware, Samuel Armstrong, and Erastus Cravath. The opposition to Negro education in the South was at first bitter, and showed itself in ashes, insult, and blood; for the South believed an educated Negro to be a dangerous Negro. And the South was not wholly wrong; for education among all kinds of men always has had, and always will have, an element of danger and revolution, of dissatisfaction and discontent. Nevertheless, men strive to know. Perhaps some inkling of this paradox, even in the unquiet days of the Bureau, helped the bayonets allay an opposition to human training which still to-day lies smouldering in the South, but not flaming. Fisk, Atlanta, Howard, and Hampton were founded in these days, and six million dollars were expended for educational work, seven hundred and fifty thousand dollars of which the freedmen themselves gave of their poverty.

Such contributions, together with the buying of land and various other enterprises, showed that the ex-slave was handling some free capital already. The chief initial source of this was labor in the army, and his pay and bounty as a soldier. Payments to Negro soldiers were at first complicated by the ignorance of the recipients, and the fact that the quotas of colored regiments from Northern States were largely filled by recruits from the South, unknown to their fellow soldiers. Consequently, payments were accompanied by such frauds that Congress, by joint resolution in 1867, put the whole matter in the hands of the Freedmen's Bureau. In two years six million dollars was thus distributed to five thousand claimants, and in the end the sum exceeded eight million dollars. Even in this system fraud was frequent; but still the work put needed capital in the hands of practical paupers, and some, at least, was well spent.

The most perplexing and least successful part of the Bureau's work lay in the exercise of its judicial functions. The regular Bureau court consisted of one representative of the employer, one of the Negro, and one of the Bureau. If the Bureau could have maintained a perfectly judicial attitude, this arrangement would have been ideal, and must in time have gained confidence; but the nature of its other activities and the character of its *personnel* prejudiced the Bureau in favor of the black litigants, and led without doubt to much injustice and annoyance. On the other hand, to leave the Negro in the hands of Southern courts was impossible. In a distracted land where slavery had hardly fallen, to keep the strong from wanton abuse of the weak, and the weak from bloating insolently over the half-shorn strength of the strong, was a thankless, hopeless task. The former masters of the land were peremptorily ordered about, seized, and imprisoned, and punished over and again, with scant courtesy from army officers. The former slaves were intimidated, beaten, raped, and butchered by angry and revengeful men. Bureau courts tended to become centres simply for punishing whites, while the regular civil courts tended to become solely institutions for perpetuating the slavery of blacks. Almost every law and method ingenuity could devise was employed by the legislatures to reduce the Negroes to serfdom,—to make them the slaves of the State, if not of individual owners; while the Bureau officials too often were found striving to put the "bottom rail on top," and gave the freedmen a power and independence which they could not yet use. It is all well enough for us of another generation to wax wise with advice to those who bore the burden in the heat of the day. It is full easy now to see that the man who lost home, fortune, and family at a stroke, and saw his land ruled by "mules and niggers," was really benefited by the passing of slavery. It is not difficult now to say to the young freeman, cheated and cuffed about who has seen his father's head beaten to a jelly and his own mother namelessly assaulted, that the meek shall inherit the earth. Above all, nothing is more convenient than to heap on the Freedmen's Bureau all the evils of that evil day, and damn it utterly for every mistake and blunder that was made.

All this is easy, but it is neither sensible nor just. Some one had blundered, but that was long before Oliver Howard was born; there was criminal aggression and heedless neglect, but without some system of control there would have been far more than there was. Had that control been from within, the Negro would have been reenslaved, to all intents and purposes. Coming as the control did from without, perfect men and methods would have bettered all things; and even with imperfect agents and questionable methods, the work accomplished was not undeserving of commendation.

Such was the dawn of Freedom; such was the work of the Freedmen's Bureau, which, summed up in brief, may be epitomized thus: for some fifteen million dollars, beside the sums spent before 1865, and the dole of benevolent societies, this Bureau set going a system of free labor, established a beginning of peasant proprietorship, secured the recognition of black freedmen before courts of law, and founded the free common school in the South. On the other hand, it failed to begin the establishment of good-will between ex-masters and freedmen, to guard its work wholly from paternalistic methods which discouraged self-reliance, and to carry out to any considerable extent its implied promises to furnish the freedmen with land. Its successes were the result of hard work, supplemented by the aid of philanthropists and the eager striving of black men. Its failures were the result of bad local agents, the inherent difficulties of the work, and national neglect.

Such an institution, from its wide powers, great responsibilities, large control of moneys, and generally conspicuous position, was naturally open to repeated and bitter attack. It sustained a searching Congressional investigation at the instance of Fernando Wood in 1870. Its archives and few remaining functions were with blunt discourtesy transferred from Howard's control, in his absence, to the supervision of Secretary of War Belknap in 1872, on the Secretary's recommendation. Finally, in consequence of grave intimations of wrong-doing made by the Secretary and his subordinates, General Howard was court-martialed in 1874. In both of these trials the Commissioner of the Freedmen's Bureau was officially exonerated from any wilful misdoing, and his work commended. Nevertheless, many unpleasant things were brought to light,—the methods of transacting the business of the Bureau were faulty; several cases of defalcation were proved, and other frauds strongly suspected; there were some business transactions which savored of dangerous speculation, if not dishonesty; and around it all lay the smirch of the Freedmen's Bank.

Morally and practically, the Freedmen's Bank was part of the Freedmen's Bureau, although it had no legal connection with it. With the prestige of the government back of it, and a directing board of unusual respectability and national reputation, this banking institution had made a remarkable start in the development of that thrift among black folk which slavery had kept them from knowing. Then in one sad day came the crash,—all the hard-earned dollars of the freedmen disappeared; but that was the least of the loss,—all the faith in saving went too, and much of the faith in men; and that was a loss that a Nation which to-day sneers at Negro shiftlessness has never yet made good. Not even ten additional years of slavery could have done so much to throttle the thrift of the freedmen as the mismanagement and bankruptcy of the series of savings banks chartered by the Nation for their especial aid. Where all the blame should rest, it is hard to say; whether the Bureau and the Bank died chiefly by reason of the blows of its selfish friends or the dark machinations of its foes, perhaps even time will never reveal, for here lies unwritten history.

Of the foes without the Bureau, the bitterest were those who attacked not so much its conduct or policy under the law as the necessity for any such institution at all. Such attacks came primarily from the Border States and the South; and they were summed up by Senator Davis, of Kentucky, when he moved to entitle the act of 1866 a bill "to promote strife and conflict between the white and black races . . . by a grant of unconstitutional power." The argument gathered tremendous strength South and North; but its very strength was its weakness. For, argued the plain common-sense of the nation, if it is unconstitutional, unpractical, and futile for the nation to stand guardian over its helpless wards, then there is left but one alternative,—to make those wards their own guardians by arming them with the ballot. Moreover, the path of the practical politician pointed the same way; for, argued this opportunist, if we cannot peacefully reconstruct the South with white votes, we certainly can with black votes. So justice and force joined hands.

The alternative thus offered the nation was not between full and restricted Negro suffrage; else every sensible man, black and white, would easily have chosen the latter. It was rather a choice between suffrage and slavery, after endless blood and gold had flowed to sweep human bondage away. Not a single Southern legislature stood ready to admit a Negro, under any conditions, to the polls; not a single Southern legislature believed free Negro labor was possible without a system of restrictions that took all its freedom away; there was scarcely a white man in the South who did not honestly regard Emancipation as a crime, and its practical nullification as a duty. In such a situation, the granting of the ballot to the black man was a necessity, the very least a guilty nation could grant a wronged race, and the only method of compelling the South to accept the results of the war. Thus Negro suffrage ended a civil war by beginning a race feud. And some felt gratitude toward the race thus sacrificed in its swaddling clothes on the altar of national integrity; and some felt and feel only indifference and contempt.

Had political exigencies been less pressing, the opposition to government guardianship of Negroes less bitter, and the attachment to the slave system less strong, the social seer can well imagine a far better policy,—a permanent Freedmen's Bureau, with a national system of Negro schools; a carefully supervised employment and labor office; a system of impartial protection before the regular courts; and such institutions for social betterment as savings-banks, land and building associations, and social settlements. All this vast expenditure of money and brains might have formed a great school of prospective citizenship, and solved in a way we have not yet solved the most perplexing and persistent of the Negro problems. That such an institution was unthinkable in 1870 was due in part to certain acts of the Freedmen's Bureau itself. It came to regard its work as merely temporary, and Negro suffrage as a final answer to all present perplexities. The political ambition of many of its agents and *protégés* led it far afield into questionable activities, until the South, nursing its own deep prejudices came easily to ignore all the good deeds of the Bureau and hate its very name with perfect hatred. So the Freedmen's Bureau died, and its child was the Fifteenth Amendment.

The passing of a great human institution before its work is done, like the untimely passing of a single soul, but leaves a legacy of striving for other men. The legacy of the Freedmen's Bureau is the heavy heritage of this generation. To-day, when new and vaster problems are destined to strain every fibre of the national mind and soul, would it not be well to count this legacy honestly and carefully? For this much all men know: despite compromise, war, and struggle, the Negro is not free. In the backwoods of the Gulf States, for miles and miles, he may not leave the plantation of his birth; in well-nigh the whole rural South the black farmers are peons, bound by law and custom to an economic slavery, from which the only escape is death or the penitentiary. In the most cultured sections and cities of the South the Negroes are a segregated servile caste, with restricted rights and privileges. Before the courts, both in law and custom, they stand on a different and peculiar basis. Taxation without representation is the rule of their political life. And the result of all this is, and in nature must have been, lawlessness and crime. That is the large legacy of the Freedmen's Bureau, the work it did not do because it could not.

I have seen a land right merry with the sun, where children sing, and rolling hills lie like passioned women wanton with harvest. And there in the King's Highway sat and sits a figure veiled and bowed, by which the traveller's footsteps hasten as they go. On the tainted air broods fear. Three centuries' thought has been the raising and unveiling of that bowed human heart, and now behold a century new for the duty and the deed. The problem of the Twentieth Century is the problem of the color-line.

A Policy of Injustice

JAMES F. RHODES

Corollary to the picture of Southern Reconstruction as a saturnalia of corruption and injustice was the conception of the Radical Republicans as crafty and vindictive conspirators. One among many portraits of the fanatical Radical was James Ford Rhodes' vignette of Senator Charles Sumner.

Rhodes was born in Cleveland of New England parents. He became a coal and iron magnate, numbering among his intimates his brother-in-law Mark Hanna and John D. Rockefeller, Sr. At the age of thirty-seven Rhodes retired to write a history of the United States in the years 1850–1877. Rhodes was both pro-abolitionist and prejudiced toward the Negro. Thus he condemned Sumner for failing to accept the conclusion of Sumner's close friend, the biologist Louis Agassiz, that Negroes were biologically inferior to white men. John R. Lynch, a Negro Congressman from Mississippi during Reconstruction, wrote in reviewing Rhodes' volumes that "so far as the Reconstruction period is concerned, it is not only inaccurate and unreliable but it is the most biased, partisan, and prejudiced historical work I have ever read."

In fact, Rhodes' narrative was solidly based on extensive research. While fundamentally sympathetic to President Johnson's approach to Reconstruction as opposed to the radicalism of Sumner and Stevens, Rhodes also strongly condemned Johnson for urging the Southern states to reject the Fourteenth Amendment.

"SIR," DECLARED SUMNER IN THE SENATE JANUARY 21, 1870, "I am the author of the provision" in the Reconstruction Act conferring universal negro suffrage. While this is not exactly true, yet even at this time [1870] when negro suffrage was popular and many senators were eager to show that they had a share in its accomplishment, Sumner was by no means unduly arrogant when he claimed for himself that

James Ford Rhodes, *History of the United States from the Compromise of* 1850 *to the Final Restoration of Home Rule at the South in* 1877, 7 vols. (New York: The Macmillan Company, 1904–1906), Vol. VI, pp. 35–42.

which was then regarded an honour. Edward L. Pierce, his appreciative friend and faithful biographer, has justly written, "For weal or woe, whether it was well or not for the black man and the country, it is to Sumner's credit or discredit as a statesman that suffrage, irrespective of color or race, became fixed and universal in the American system." Discussing the suffrage provision of the Reconstruction Act, Pierce referred to "Sumner who led" and "the statesmen who followed": this in my judgment is a correct statement of the case although Sumner was not a parliamentary leader like Stevens. While both often antagonized their supporters, Stevens possessed the power of compelling them to fall into line when the crucial vote was taken, but Sumner's leadership lay in a constant urging of a consistent policy. In the autumn of 1865 Andrew [1] attempted to win him over but the cavalier response showed that the senator was fixed in his idea that drastic measures were necessary to protect the negro, although otherwise he might have had sympathy with the poverty-stricken gentlemen and literateurs of the South, as he had not the slightest feeling of vindictiveness.

At Sumner's back were the ministers and school-teachers of New England and of the West, where New England ideas held sway, and his known following increased his influence in the Senate. He was the "scholar in politics"; and as such, what might have been expected of him before venturing to advocate in the Senate the immediate enfranchisement of such an ignorant mass of an alien race? It was an age of science —the era of Darwin and Spencer, of Huxley and Tyndall. The influence of heredity and the great fact of race were better understood than ever before. Sumner's study it is true was literature, not science, but these facts were permeating literature. "Science has now made visible to everybody," wrote Matthew Arnold, "the great and pregnant elements of difference which lie in race." And Sumner had an intimate friend with whom he had often sat at table, and who in his domestic trouble sent him this word, "My dear Sumner, you have my deepest and truest silent sympathy"; and this friend, Louis Agassiz, was one of the most distinguised men of science in America. Had the senator asked advice of the scientist this is the word he would have received: "We should beware," Agassiz had written to Dr. Samuel G. Howe in August 1863, "how we give to the blacks rights, by virtue of which they may endanger the progress of the whites before their temper has been tested by a prolonged experience. Social equality I deem at all times impracticable,—a natural impossibility, from the very character of the negro race. Let us consider for a moment

[1] EDITOR'S NOTE: Some historians believe that Governor John A. Andrew of Massachusetts was the man best qualified to find a middle way between President Johnson and the Radical Republicans.

the natural endowments of the negro race as they are manifested in history on their native continent as far as we can trace them back, and compare the result with what we know of our own destinies, in order to ascertain within the limits of probability, whether social equality with the negro is really an impossibility. We know of the existence of the negro race, with all its physical peculiarities, from the Egyptian monuments, several thousand years before the Christian era. Upon these monuments the negroes are so represented as to show that in natural propensities and mental abilities they were pretty much what we find them at the present day,—indolent, playful, sensual, imitative, subservient, good-natured. versatile, unsteady in their purpose, devoted and affectionate. From this picture I exclude the character of the half-breeds, who have, more or less, the character of their white parents. Originally found in Africa, the negroes seem at all times to have presented the same characteristics wherever they have been brought into contact with the white race; as in Upper Egypt along the borders of the Carthaginian and Roman settlements in Africa, in Senegel in juxtaposition with the French, in Congo in juxtaposition with the Portuguese, about the Cape and on the eastern coast of Africa in justaposition with the Dutch and the English. While Egypt and Carthage grew into powerful empires and attained a high degree of civilization; while in Babylon, Syria, and Greece were developed the highest culture of antiquity, the negro race groped in barbarism and *never originated a regular organization among themselves.* This is important to keep in mind, and to urge upon the attention of those who ascribe the condition of the modern negro wholly to the influence of slavery. . . . I am not prepared to state what political privileges they are fit to enjoy now; though I have no hesitation in saying that they should be equal to other men before the law. The right of owning property, of bearing witness, of entering into contracts, of buying and selling, of choosing their own domicile, would give them ample opportunity of showing in a comparatively short time what political rights might properly and safely be granted to them in successive instalments. No man has a right to what he is unfit to use. Our own best rights have been acquired successively. I cannot, therefore, think it just or safe to grant at once to the negro all the privileges which we ourselves have acquired by long struggles. History teaches us what terrible reactions have followed too extensive and too rapid changes. Let us beware of granting too much to the negro race in the beginning lest it become necessary hereafter to deprive them of some of the privileges which they may use to their own and our detriment."

Let me emphasize the fact that this was written in 1863. What the whole country has only learned through years of costly and bitter experience was known to this leader of scientific thought before we ventured on the policy of trying to make negroes intelligent by legislative acts: and this knowledge was to be had for the asking by the men who were shaping the policy of the nation.

Sumner showed no appreciation of the great fact of race, nor, so far as my considerable reading of the debates in Congress goes, did any of the men who took a prominent part in this legislation. Sherman indeed declaimed against negro rule. "Beware, sir," he said, "lest in guarding against rebels you destroy the foundation of republican institutions. I like rebels no better than the Senator from Massachusetts [Sumner]; but, sir, I will not supersede one form of oligarchy in which the blacks were slaves by another in which the whites are disenfranchised outcasts. Let us introduce no such horrid deformity into the American Union." Senator Howard too did not want to see governments "based exclusively upon the votes of black persons"; but the general impression which one obtains is that the Republicans believed that the negro would equal the white man could he have education and his other chances. Sumner did not embrace universal negro suffrage without some reflection. He said to John C. Ropes that to enfranchise this uneducated mass was foreign to his convictions and his whole habit of thought, but the fact of it was the suffrage was necessary to protect the negro. He moved to amend the supplemental bill so as to require the Southern States to establish a system of public schools open to both negroes and whites, but this amendment was lost by a tie vote. Sumner's disappointment was so keen at this result that on reaching his house after the adjournment of the Senate he burst into tears.

In my judgment Sumner did not show wise constructive statesmanship in forcing unqualified negro suffrage on the South. While the work of destruction was going on, his services to the anti-slavery cause were of the utmost value. We may all agree with Moorfield Storey that "Charles Sumner was a great man in his absolute fidelity to principle . . . his unflinching courage, his perfect sincerity, his persistent devotion to duty, his indifference to selfish considerations, his high scorn of anything petty or mean"; but he failed in his Reconstruction policy from regarding only one side of the problem. The point made by George S. Boutwell that Sumner was very "unpractical in the affairs of government" and left no mark upon the statutes except an insignificant amendment to a law excluding Mongolians from citizenship does not seem to me of great importance. I do not mean to imply that the knack of drawing bills is not a high quality. That power of legislative expression which secures the support of fellow lawgivers and at the same time gives a clear meaning to the enacted law is a desirable possession but Sumner made a powerful impress upon the legislation of his time without it. Nor was he a man of one idea. His large knowledge of the world and the manifold connections he had formed at home and abroad enabled him to be of great service to his country as chairman of the Committee on Foreign Relations; yet even here we shall not appreciate his service by reading his pompous speeches but must look for it in his private correspondence and in reports of private conversations.

Sumner persuaded himself that suffrage was an "essential right," not a privilege; and he said in the Senate, "Whatever you enact for human rights is constitutional. There can be no State rights against human rights." Nearly two years before the reconstruction legislation was enacted Richard H. Dana wrote: "Sumner who has high and great instincts and great moral energy never had any logic, could never see a fallacy on his own side, could never see the joke against himself. He is a good seer but a bad guide. He never did care a farthing for the Constitution, is impatient of law and considers his oath to have been not to the Constitution but to the Declaration of Independence. If the negro votes he does not care how the result is obtained or what else may follow." His lack of imagination prevented his putting himself into the place of the defeated Southerners; could he have done so he was capable of espousing their cause as did Andrew. "Sumner," wrote Dr. Holmes, "seems to me to have less imagination, less sense of humor or wit than almost any man of intellect I ever knew. P. B. said of him in the Temple Place days that if you told him the moon was made of green cheese he would say, 'No, it cannot be so' and give you solid reasons to the contrary." Could Fessenden, Sherman, Trumbull and Andrew (had he been in the Senate) have framed a scheme of reconstruction capable of being adopted, it would have been far better than the actual one of which Stevens and Sumner are the reputed fathers. Sumner lent his great influence to a policy of injustice to a prostrate foe, to a policy at variance with the political philosophy of Burke, and the teaching of modern science, contrary to the spirit of Lincoln's second inaugural and to his every pronouncement on reconstruction: he exemplified the dictum of Bishop Stubbs, "that the worst cause has often been illustrated with the most heroic virtue."

Reconstruction and Its Benefits[1]

W. E. B. DU BOIS

In this 1910 article in the *American Historical Review* Du Bois confronted directly the question: What happened in the South between 1867, when Congress required the Southern States to make new governments based on Negro suffrage, and 1877 when the last Federal troops were withdrawn? Modern revisionist scholars have added very little to the essentials of Du Bois' argument.

On the one hand, Du Bois maintained that the misdeeds of Negro legislators had been exaggerated. Contemporary comment on their work was often admiring. Whites as well as Negroes took part in corruption, particularly in the larger frauds involving "the manipulation of state and railway bonds and of bank-notes." Du Bois concluded in a famous sentence: "There was one thing that the white South feared more than negro dishonesty, ignorance, and incompetency, and that was negro honesty, knowledge, and efficiency."

On the other hand, Du Bois argued, the Reconstruction legislatures did much that was good. They democratized government, by abolishing property qualifications, equalizing apportionment, and protecting the rights of women and debtors. "There is no doubt that the thirst of the black man for knowledge . . . gave birth to the public free-school system of the South." The soundness of the Reconstruction state constitutions, said Du Bois, is suggested by the fact that the Redeemers in many states left them unchanged for decades.

The careful reader will notice that while in 1903 Du Bois viewed immediate suffrage for all freedmen as an inadequate substitute for a comprehensive program of social and economic change, in 1910 his concern was to defend Negro enfranchisement. He presented still a third, more Marxist analysis in his sprawling classic *Black Reconstruction* (1935).

THERE IS DANGER TO-DAY THAT BETWEEN THE INTENSE FEELING OF the South and the conciliatory spirit of the North grave injustice will be done the negro American in the history of Reconstruction. Those who see in negro suffrage the cause of the main evils of Reconstruction

[1] Paper read at the annual meeting of the American Historical Association in New York, December, 1909.

W. E. B. Du Bois, "Reconstruction and Its Benefits," *American Historical Review*, Vol. XV (July, 1910), pp. 781–799.

must remember that if there had not been a single freedman left in the South after the war the problems of Reconstruction would still have been grave. Property in slaves to the extent of perhaps two thousand million dollars had suddenly disappeared. One thousand five hundred more millions, representing the Confederate war debt, had largely disappeared. Large amounts of real estate and other property had been destroyed, industry had been disorganized, 250,000 men had been killed and many more maimed. With this went the moral effect of an unsuccessful war with all its letting down of social standards and quickening of hatred and discouragement—a situation which would make it difficult under any circumstances to reconstruct a new government and a new civilization. Add to all this the presence of four million freedmen and the situation is further complicated. But this complication is very largely a matter of well-known historical causes. Any human being "doomed in his own person, and his posterity, to live without knowledge, and without the capacity to make anything his own, and to toil that another may reap the fruits,"[2] is bound, on sudden emancipation, to loom like a great dread on the horizon.

How to train and treat these ex-slaves easily became a central problem of Reconstruction, although by no means the only problem. Three agencies undertook the solution of this problem at first and their influence is apt to be forgotten. Without them the problems of Reconstruction would have been far graver than they were. These agencies were: (a) the negro church, (b) the negro school, and (c) the Freedmen's Bureau. After the war the white churches of the South got rid of their negro members and the negro church organizations of the North invaded the South. The 20,000 members of the African Methodist Episcopal Church in 1856 leaped to 75,000 in 1866 and 200,000 in 1876, while their property increased sevenfold. The negro Baptists with 150,000 members in 1850 had fully a half million in 1870. There were, before the end of Reconstruction, perhaps 10,000 local bodies touching the majority of the freed population, centering almost the whole of their social life, and teaching them organization and autonomy. They were primitive, ill-governed, at times fantastic groups of human beings, and yet it is difficult to exaggerate the influence of this new responsibility—the first social institution fully controlled by black men in America, with traditions that rooted back to Africa and with possibilities which make the 35,000 negro American churches today, with their three and one-half million members, the most powerful negro institutions in the world.

With the negro church, but separate from it, arose the school as the

2 State *v.* Mann, *North Carolina Reports,* 2 Devereux 263.

first expression of the missionary activity of Northern religious bodies. Seldom in the history of the world has an almost totally illiterate population been given the means of self-education in so short a time. The movement started with the negroes themselves and they continued to form the dynamic force behind it. "This great multitude rose up simultaneously and asked for intelligence." [3] The education of this mass had to begin at the top with the training of teachers, and within a few years a dozen colleges and normal schools started; by 1877, 571,506 negro children were in school. There can be no doubt that these schools were a great conservative steadying force to which the South owes much. It must not be forgotten that among the agents of the Freedmen's Bureau were not only soldiers and politicians but school-teachers and educational leaders like Ware and Cravath.

Granted that the situation was in any case bad and that negro churches and schools stood as conservative educative forces, how far did negro suffrage hinder progress, and was it expedient? The difficulties that stared Reconstruction politicians in the face were these: (a) They must act quickly. (b) Emancipation had increased the political power of the South by one-sixth: could this increased political power be put in the hands of those who, in defense of slavery, had disrupted the Union? (c) How was the abolition of slavery to be made effective? (d) What was to be the political position of the freedmen?

Andrew Johnson said in 1864, in regard to calling a convention to restore the state of Tennessee,

Who shall restore and re-establish it? Shall the man who gave his influence and his means to destroy the Government? Is he to participate in the great work of re-organization? Shall he who brought this misery upon the State be permitted to control its destinies? If this be so, then all this precious blood of our brave soldiers and officers so freely poured out will have been wantonly spilled.[4]

To settle these and other difficulties, three ways were suggested: (1) the Freedmen's Bureau, (2) partial negro suffrage, and (3) full manhood suffrage for negroes.

The Freedmen's Bureau was an attempt to establish a government guardianship over the negroes and insure their economic and civil rights. Its establishment was a herculean task both physically and socially, and it not only met the solid opposition of the white South, but even the North looked at the new thing as socialistic and over-paternal. It accomplished

[3] First General Report of the Inspector of Schools, Freedmen's Bureau.
[4] McPherson, *Reconstruction*, p. 46.

a great task but it was repudiated. Carl Schurz in 1865 felt warranted in saying

that not half of the labor that has been done in the south this year, or will be done there next year, would have been or would be done but for the exertions of the Freedmen's Bureau. . . . No other agency, except one placed there by the national government, could have wielded that moral power whose interposition was so necessary to prevent the southern society from falling at once into the chaos of a general collision between its different elements.[5]

Notwithstanding this the Bureau was temporary, was regarded as a makeshift and soon abandoned.

Meantime, partial negro suffrage seemed not only just but almost inevitable. Lincoln in 1864 "cautiously suggested" to Louisiana's private consideration, "whether some of the colored people may not be let in, as, for instance, the very intelligent, and especially those who have fought gallantly in our ranks. They would probably help, in some trying time to come, to keep the jewel of liberty in the family of freedom." [6] Indeed, the "family of freedom" in Louisiana being somewhat small just then, who else was to be intrusted with the "jewel"? Later and for different reasons, Johnson in 1865 wrote to Mississippi:

If you could extend the elective franchise to all persons of color who can read the Constitution of the United States in English and write their names, and to all persons of color who own real estate valued at not less than two hundred and fifty dollars, and pay taxes thereon, you would completely disarm the adversary and set an example the other States will follow. This you can do with perfect safety, and you thus place the southern States, in reference to free persons of color, upon the same basis with the free States. I hope and trust your convention will do this.[7]

Meantime the negroes themselves began to ask for the suffrage—the Georgia Convention in Augusta, 1866, advocating "a proposition to give those who could write and read well, and possessed a certain property qualification, the right of suffrage." The reply of the South to these suggestions was decisive. In Tennessee alone was any action attempted that even suggested possible negro suffrage in the future, and that failed. In all other states the "Black Codes" adopted were certainly not reassuring to friends of freedom. To be sure it was not a time to look for calm, cool, thoughtful action on the part of the white South. Their economic condi-

[5] Schurz. Report to the President, 1865. *Senate Ex. Doc. No.* 2, 49 Cong., I sess., p. 40.

[6] Letter to Hahn, March 13. McPherson, p. 20.

[7] Johnson to Sharkey, August 15. *Ibid.*, p. 19.

tion was pitiable, their fear of negro freedom genuine; yet it was reasonable to expect from them something less than repression and utter reaction toward slavery. To some extent this expectation was fulfilled: the abolition of slavery was recognized and the civil rights of owning property and appearing as a witness in cases in which he was a party were generally granted the negro; yet with these went in many cases harsh and unbearable regulations which largely neutralized the concessions and certainly gave ground for the assumption that once free the South would virtually re-enslave the negro. The colored people themselves naturally feared this and protested as in Mississippi "against the reactionary policy prevailing, and expressing the fear that the Legislature will pass such proscriptive laws as will drive the freedmen from the State, or practically re-enslave them." [8]

The Codes spoke for themselves. They have often been reprinted and quoted. No open-minded student can read them without being convinced that they meant nothing more nor less than slavery in daily toil. Not only this but as Professor Burgess (whom no one accuses of being negrophile) says:

Almost every act, word or gesture of the Negro, not consonant with good taste and good manners as well as good morals, was made a crime or misdemeanor, for which he could first be fined by the magistrates and then be consigned to a condition of almost slavery for an indefinite time, if he could not pay the bill.

These laws might have been interpreted and applied liberally, but the picture painted by Carl Schurz does not lead one to anticipate this:

Some planters held back their former slaves on their plantations by brute force. Armed bands of white men patrolled the country roads to drive back the negroes wandering about. Dead bodies of murdered negroes were found on and near the highways and by-paths. Gruesome reports came from the hospitals—reports of colored men and women whose ears had been cut off, whose skulls had been broken by blows, whose bodies had been slashed by knives or lacerated with scourges. A number of such cases I had occasion to examine myself. The negro found scant justice in the local courts against the white man. He could look for protection only to the military forces of the United States still garrisoning the "States lately in rebellion" and to the Freedmen's Bureau.

All things considered, it seems probable that if the South had been permitted to have its way in 1865 the harshness of negro slavery would have been mitigated so as to make slave-trading difficult, and to make it

[8] October 7, 1865.

possible for a negro to hold property and appear in some cases in court; but that in most other respects the blacks would have remained in slavery.

What could prevent this? A Freedmen's Bureau, established for ten, twenty or forty years with a careful distribution of land and capital and a system of education for the children, might have prevented such an extension of slavery. But the country would not listen to such a comprehensive plan. A restricted grant of the suffrage voluntarily made by the states would have been a reassuring proof of a desire to treat the freedmen fairly, and would have balanced, in part at least, the increased political power of the South. There was no such disposition evident. On the other hand, there was ground for the conclusion in the Reconstruction report of June 18, 1866, that so far as slavery was concerned "the language of all the provisions and ordinances of these States on the subject amounts to nothing more than an unwilling admission of an unwelcome truth." This was of course natural, but was it unnatural that the North should feel that better guarantees were needed to abolish slavery? Carl Schurz wrote:

I deem it proper, however, to offer a few remarks on the assertion frequently put forth, that the franchise is likely to be extended to the colored man by the voluntary action of the Southern whites themselves. My observation leads me to a contrary opinion. Aside from a very few enlightened men, I found but one class of people in favor of the enfranchisement of the blacks: it was the class of Unionists who found themselves politically ostracised and looked upon the enfranchisement of the loyal negroes as the salvation of the whole loyal element. . . . The masses are strongly opposed to colored suffrage; anybody that dares to advocate it is stigmatized as a dangerous fanatic.

The only manner in which, in my opinion, the southern people can be induced to grant to the freedman some measure of self-protecting power in the form of suffrage, is to make it a condition precedent to "readmission".[9]

Even in Louisiana, under the proposed reconstruction

not one negro was allowed to vote, though at that very time the wealthy intelligent free colored people of the state paid taxes on property assessed at $15,000,000 and many of them were well known for their patriotic zeal and love for the Union. Thousands of colored men whose homes were in Louisiana, served bravely in the national army and navy, and many of the so-called negroes in New Orleans could not be distinguished by the most intelligent strangers from the best class of white gentlemen, either by color or manner, dress or language, still, as it was known by tradition and common fame that they were not of pure Caucasion descent, they could not vote.[10]

[9] Report to the President, 1865. *Senate Ex. Doc. No.* 2, 39 Cong., 1 sess., p. 44.
[10] Brewster, *Sketches of Southern Mystery, Treason, and Murder,* p. 116.

The United States government might now have taken any one of three courses:

1. Allowed the whites to reorganize the states and take no measures to enfranchise the freedmen.

2. Allowed the whites to reorganize the states but provided that after the lapse of a reasonable length of time there should be no discrimination in the right of suffrage on account of "race, color or previous condition of servitude".

3. Admitted all men, black and white, to take part in reorganizing the states and then provided that future restrictions on the suffrage should be made on any basis except "race, color and previous condition of servitude."

The first course was clearly inadmissible since it meant virtually giving up the great principle on which the war was largely fought and won, *i. e.,* human freedom; a giving of freedom which contented itself with an edict, and then turned the "freed" slaves over to the tender mercies of their impoverished and angry ex-masters was no gift at all. The second course was theoretically attractive but practically impossible. It meant at least a prolongation of slavery and instead of attempts to raise the freedmen, it gave the white community strong incentives for keeping the blacks down so that as few as possible would ever qualify for the suffrage. Negro schools would have been discouraged and economic fetters would have held the black man as a serf for an indefinite time. On the other hand, the arguments for universal negro suffrage from the start were strong and are still strong, and no one would question their strength were it not for the assumption that the experiment failed. Frederick Douglass said to President Johnson: "Your noble and humane predecessor placed in our hands the sword to assist in saving the nation, and we do hope that you, his able successor, will favorably regard the placing in our hands the ballot with which to save ourselves." [11] And when Johnson demurred on account of the hostility between blacks and poor whites, a committee of prominent colored men replied:

Even if it were true, as you allege, that the hostility of the blacks toward the poor whites must necessarily project itself into a state of freedom, and that this enmity between the two races is even more intense in a state of freedom than in a state of slavery, in the name of Heaven, we reverently ask, how can you, in view of your professed desire to promote the welfare of the black man, deprive him of all means of defence, and clothe him whom you regard as his enemy in the panoply of political power? [12]

Carl Schurz expressed this argument most emphatically:

[11] Frederick Douglass to Johnson, February 7, 1866. McPherson, p. 52.
[12] McPherson, p. 56.

The emancipation of the slaves is submitted to only in so far as chattel slavery in the old form could not be kept up. But although the freedman is no longer considered the property of the individual master, he is considered the slave of society, and all independent State legislation will share the tendency to make him such.

The solution of the problem would be very much facilitated by enabling all the loyal and free-labor elements in the south to exercise a healthy influence upon legislation. It will hardly be possible to secure the freedman against oppressive class legislation and private persecution, unless he be endowed with a certain measure of political power.[13]

To the argument of ignorance Schurz replied:

The effect of the extension of the franchise to the colored people upon the development of free labor and upon the security of human rights in the south being the principal object in view, the objections raised on the ground of the ignorance of the freedman become unimportant. Practical liberty is a good school. . . . It is idle to say that it will be time to speak of negro suffrage when the whole colored race will be educated, for the ballot may be necessary to him to secure his education.[14]

The granting of full negro suffrage meant one of two alternatives to the South: (a) the uplift of the negro for sheer self-preservation; this is what Schurz and the saner North expected; as one Southern superintendent said: "the elevation of this class is a matter of prime importance since a ballot in the hands of a black citizen is quite as potent as in the hands of a white one." Or (b) a determined concentration of Southern effort by actual force to deprive the negro of the ballot or nullify its use. This is what happened, but even in this case so much energy was taken in keeping the negro from voting that the plan for keeping him in virtual slavery and denying him education failed. It took ten years to nullify negro suffrage in part and twenty years to escape the fear of federal intervention. In these twenty years a vast number of negroes had risen so far as to escape slavery forever. Debt peonage could be fastened on part of the rural South, and was, but even here the new negro landholder appeared. Thus despite everything the Fifteenth Amendment and that alone struck the death knell of slavery.

The steps that ended in the Fifteenth Amendment were not, however, taken suddenly. The negroes were given the right by universal suffrage to join in reconstructing the state governments and the reasons for it were cogently set forth in the report of the Joint Committee on Reconstruction in 1866, which began as follows:

---

[13] Report to the President, 1865. *Senate Ex. Doc. No.* 2, 39 Cong., 1 sess., p. 45.
[14] *Ibid.,* p. 43.

A large proportion of the population had become, instead of mere chattels, free men and citizens. Through all the past struggle these had remained true and loyal, and had, in large numbers, fought on the side of the Union. It was impossible to abandon them without securing them their rights as free men and citizens. The whole civilized world would have cried out against such base ingratitude, and the bare idea is offensive to all right-thinking men. Hence it became important to inquire what could be done to secure their rights, civil and political.[15]

The report then proceeded to emphasize the increased political power of the South and recommended the Fourteenth Amendment since

it appeared to your committee that the rights of these persons by whom the basis of representation had been thus increased should be recognized by the General Government. While slaves, they were not considered as having any rights, civil or political. It did not seem just or proper that all the political advantages derived from their becoming free should be confined to their former masters, who had fought against the Union, and withheld from themselves, who had always been loyal.[16]

It was soon seen that this expedient of the Fourteenth Amendment was going to prove abortive and that determined and organized effort would be used to deprive the freedmen of the ballot. Thereupon the United States said the final word of simple justice, namely: the states may still regulate the suffrage as they please but they may not deprive a man of the right to vote simply because he is a negro.

For such reasons the negro was enfranchised. What was the result? No language has been spared to describe these results as the worst imaginable. Nor is it necessary to dispute for a moment that there were bad results, and bad results arising from negro suffrage; but it may be questioned if the results were as bad as painted or if negro suffrage was the prime cause.

Let us not forget that the white South believed it to be of vital interest to its welfare that the experiment of negro suffrage should fail ignominiously, and that almost to a man the whites were willing to insure this failure either by active force or passive acquiescence; that beside this there were, as might be expected, men, black, and white, Northern and Southern, only too eager to take advantage of such a situation for feathering their own nests. The results in such case had to be evil but to charge the evil to negro suffrage is unfair. It may be charged to anger, poverty, venality, and ignorance; but the anger and poverty were the almost inevitable aftermath of war; the venality was much greater among whites than negroes,

[15] *House Reports No. 30, 39 Cong., I sess., p. xiii.*
[16] *Ibid.*

and while ignorance was the curse of the negroes, the fault was not theirs, and they took the initiative to correct it.

The chief charges against the negro governments are extravagance, theft, and incompetency of officials. There is no serious charge that these governments threatened civilization or the foundations of social order. The charge is that they threatened property, and that they were inefficient. These charges are in part undoubtedly true, but they are often exaggerated. When a man has, in his opinion, been robbed and maltreated he is sensitive about money matters. The South had been terribly impoverished and saddled with new social burdens. In other words, a state with smaller resources was asked not only to do a work of restoration but a larger social work. The property-holders were aghast. They not only demurred, but, predicting ruin and revolution, they appealed to secret societies, to intimidation, force, and murder. They refused to believe that these novices in government and their friends were aught but scamps and fools. Under the circumstances occurring directly after the war, the wisest statesman would have been compelled to resort to increased taxation and would in turn have been execrated as extravagant and even dishonest. When now, in addition to this, the new legislators, white and black, were undoubtedly in a large number of cases extravagant, dishonest, and incompetent, it is easy to see what flaming and incredible stories of Reconstruction governments could gain wide currency and belief. In fact, the extravagance, although great, was not universal, and much of it was due to the extravagant spirit pervading the whole country in a day of inflated currency and speculation. The ignorance was deplorable but a deliberate legacy from the past, and some of the extravagance and much of the effort was to remedy this ignorance. The incompetency was in part real and in part emphasized by the attitude of the whites of the better class.

When incompetency gains political power in an extravagant age the result is widespread dishonesty. The dishonesty in the reconstruction of the South was helped on by three circumstances:

1. The former dishonesty in the political South.

2. The presence of many dishonest Northern politicians.

3. The temptation to Southern politicians at once to profit by dishonesty and to discredit negro government.

4. The poverty of the negro.

(1) Dishonesty in public life has no monopoly of time or place in America. To take one state: In 1839 it was reported in Mississippi that ninety per cent of fines collected by sheriffs and clerks were unaccounted for. In 1841 the state treasurer acknowledges himself "at a loss to determine the precise liabilities of the state and her means of paying the same." And in 1839 the auditor's books had not been posted for eighteen months,

no entries made for a year, and no vouchers examined for three years. Congress gave Jefferson College, Natchez, more than 46,000 acres of land; before the war this whole property had "disappeared" and the college was closed. Congress gave to Mississippi among other states the "16th section" of the public lands for schools. In thirty years the proceeds of this land in Mississippi were embezzled to the amount of at least one and a half millions of dollars. In Columbus, Mississippi, a receiver of public moneys stole $100,000 and resigned. His successor stole $55,000, and a treasury agent wrote: "Another receiver would probably follow in the footsteps of the two. You will not be surprised if I recommend his being retained in preference to another appointment." From 1830 to 1860 Southern men in federal offices alone embezzled more than a million dollars—a far larger sum then than now. There might have been less stealing in the South during Reconstruction without negro suffrage but it is certainly highly instructive to remember that the mark of the thief which dragged its slime across nearly every great Northern state and almost up to the presidential chair could not certainly in those cases be charged against the vote of black men. This was the day when a national secretary of war was caught stealing, a vice-president presumably took bribes, a private secretary of the president, a chief clerk of the Treasury, and eighty-six government officials stole millions in the whiskey frauds, while the Credit Mobilier filched fifty millions and bribed the government to an extent never fully revealed; not to mention less distinguished thieves like Tweed.

Is it surprising that in such an atmosphere a new race learning the a-b-c of government should have become the tools of thieves? And when they did was the stealing their fault or was it justly chargeable to their enfranchisement?

Undoubtedly there were many ridiculous things connected with Reconstruction governments: the placing of ignorant field-hands who could neither read nor write in the legislature, the gold spittoons of South Carolina, the enormous public printing bill of Mississippi—all these were extravagant and funny, and yet somehow, to one who sees beneath all that is bizarre, the real human tragedy of the upward striving of downtrodden men, the groping for light among people born in darkness, there is less tendency to laugh and gibe than among shallower minds and easier consciences. All that is funny is not bad.

Then too a careful examination of the alleged stealing in the South reveals much. First, there is repeated exaggeration. For instance it is said that the taxation in Mississippi was fourteen times as great in 1874 as in 1869. This sounds staggering until we learn that the state taxation in 1869 was only ten cents on one hundred dollars, and that the expenses of government in 1874 were only twice as great as in 1860, and that too with a depreciated currency. It could certainly be argued that the state government in Mississippi was doing enough additional work in 1874 to warrant greatly increased cost. A Southern white historian acknowledges that

the work of restoration which the government was obliged to undertake, made increased expenses necessary. During the period of the war, and for several years thereafter, public buildings and state institutions were permitted to fall into decay. The state house and grounds, the executive mansion, the penitentiary, the insane asylum, and the buildings for the blind, deaf, and dumb were in a dilapidated condition, and had to be extended and repaired. A new building for the blind was purchased and fitted up. The reconstructionists established a public school system and spent money to maintain and support it, perhaps too freely, in view of the impoverishment of the people. When they took hold, warrants were worth but sixty or seventy cents on the dollar, a fact which made the price of building materials used in the work of construction correspondingly higher. So far as the conduct of state officials who were intrusted with the custody of public funds is concerned, it may be said that there were no great embezzlements or other cases of misappropriation during the period of Republican rule.[17]

The state debt of Mississippi was said to have been increased from a half million to twenty million when in fact it had not been increased at all.

The character of the real thieving shows that white men must have been the chief beneficiaries and that as a former South Carolina slaveholder said:

The legislature, ignorant as it is, could not have been bribed without money, that must have been furnished from some source that it is our duty to discover. A legislature composed chiefly of our former slaves has been bribed. One prominent feature of this transaction is the part which native Carolinians have played in it, some of our own household men whom the state, in the past, has delighted to honor, appealing to their cupidity and avarice make them the instruments to effect the robbery of their impoverished white brethren. Our former slaves have been bribed by these men to give them the privilege by law of plundering the property-holders of the state.[18]

The character of much of the stealing shows who were the thieves. The frauds through the manipulation of state and railway bonds and of bank-notes must have inured chiefly to the benefit of experienced white men, and this must have been largely the case in the furnishing and printing frauds. It was chiefly in the extravagance for "sundries and incidentals" and direct money payments for votes that the negroes received their share.

That the negroes led by astute thieves became tools and received a small

[17] Garner, *Reconstruction in Mississippi,* p. 322.
[18] Hon. F. F. Warley in Brewster's *Sketches,* p. 150.

share of the spoils is true. But two considerations must be added: much of the legislation which resulted in fraud was represented to the negroes as good legislation, and thus their votes were secured by deliberate misrepresentation. Take for instance the land frauds of South Carolina. A wise negro leader of that state, advocating the state purchase of lands, said:

One of the greatest of slavery bulwarks was the infernal plantation system, one man owning his thousand, another his twenty, another fifty thousand acres of land. This is the only way by which we will break up that system, and I maintain that our freedom will be of no effect if we allow it to continue. What is the main cause of the prosperity of the North? It is because every man has his own farm and is free and independent. Let the lands of the South be similarly divided.

From such arguments the negroes were induced to aid a scheme to buy land and distribute it; yet a large part of $800,000 appropriated was wasted and went to the white landholder's pockets. The railroad schemes were in most cases feasible and eventually carried out; it was not the object but the method that was wrong.

Granted then that the negroes were to some extent venal but to a much larger extent ignorant and deceived, the question is: did they show any signs of a disposition to learn better things? The theory of democratic government is not that the will of the people is always right, but rather that normal human beings of average intelligence will, if given a chance, learn the right and best course by bitter experience. This is precisely what the negro voters showed indubitable signs of doing. First, they strove for schools to abolish ignorance, and, second, a large and growing number of them revolted against the carnival of extravagance and stealing that marred the beginning of Reconstruction, and joined with the best elements to institute reform; and the greatest stigma on the white South is not that it opposed negro suffrage and resented theft and incompetence, but that when it saw the reform movement growing and even in some cases triumphing, and a larger and larger number of black voters learning to vote for honesty and ability, it still preferred a Reign of Terror to a campaign of education, and disfranchised negroes instead of punishing rascals.

No one has expressed this more convincingly than a negro who was himself a member of the Reconstruction legislature of South Carolina and who spoke at the convention which disfranchised him, against one of the onslaughts of Tillman:*

The gentleman from Edgefield [Mr. Tillman] speaks of the piling up of the State debt; of jobbery and peculation during the period between 1869

---

* EDITOR'S NOTE: "Pitchfork Ben" Tillman led the successful effort to disfranchise Negro voters in South Carolina, and later defended lynching in the United States Senate.

and 1873 in South Carolina, but he has not found voice eloquent enough, nor pen exact enough to mention those imperishable gifts bestowed upon South Carolina between 1873 and 1876 by Negro legislators—the laws relative to finance, the building of penal and charitable institutions, and, greatest of all, the establishment of the public school system. Starting as infants in legislation in 1869, many wise measures were not thought of, many injudicious acts were passed. But in the administration of affairs for the next four years, having learned by experience the result of bad acts, we immediately passed reformatory laws touching every department of state, county, municipal and town governments. These enactments are today upon the statute books of South Carolina. They stand as living witnesses of the Negro's fitness to vote and legislate upon the rights of mankind.

When we came into power town governments could lend the credit of their respective towns to secure funds at any rate of interest that the council saw fit to pay. Some of the towns paid as high as twenty per cent. We passed an act prohibiting town governments from pledging the credit of their hamlets for money bearing a greater rate of interest than five per cent.

Up to 1874, inclusive, the State Treasurer had the power to pay out State funds as he pleased. He could elect whether he would pay out the funds on appropriations that would place the money in the hands of the speculators, or would apply them to appropriations that were honest and necessary. We saw the evil of this and passed an act making specific levies and collections of taxes for specific appropriations.

Another source of profligacy in the expenditure of funds was the law that provided for and empowered the levying and collecting of special taxes by school districts, in the name of the schools. We saw its evil and by a constitutional amendment provided that there should only be levied and collected annually a tax of two mills for school purposes, and took away from the school districts the power to levy and to collect taxes of any kind. By this act we cured the evils that had been inflicted upon us in the name of the schools, setled the public school question for all time to come, and established the system upon an honest, financial basis.

Next, we learned during the period from 1869 to 1874, inclusive, that what was denominated the floating indebtedness, covering the printing schemes and other indefinite expenditures, amounted to nearly $2,000,000. A conference was called of the leading Negro representatives in the two houses together with the State Treasurer, also a Negro. After this conference we passed an act for the purpose of ascertaining the bona fide floating debt and found that it did not amount to more than $250,000 for the four years; we created a commission to sift that indebtedness and to scale it. Hence when the Democratic party came into power they found the floating debt covering the legislative and all other expenditures, fixed at the certain sum of $250,000. This same class of Negro legislators led by the State Treasurer, Mr. F. L. Cardoza, knowing that there were millions of fraudulent bonds charged against the credit of the State, passed another act to ascertain the true bonded indebtedness, and to provide for its settlement. Under his law, at one sweep, those entrusted with the power to do so, through Negro legislators, stamped six millions of bonds, denominated as conversion bonds, "fraudulent". The commission did not finish its work before 1876. In that year, when the Hampton government came into power, there were still to be examined into and settled under the terms of the act passed by us providing for the legitimate bonded indebtedness of the state, a little over two and a half million dollars worth of bonds and coupons which had not been passed upon.

Governor Hampton, General Hagood, Judge Simonton, Judge Wallace and in fact, all of the conservative thinking Democrats aligned themselves under the provision enacted by us for the certain and final settlement of the bonded indebtedness and appealed to their Democratic legislators to stand by the Republican legislation on the subject and to confirm it. A faction in the Democratic party obtained a majority of the Democratis in the legislature against settling the question and they endeavored to open up anew the whole subject of the state debt. We had a little over thirty members in the house and enough Republican senators to sustain the Hampton conservative faction and to stand up for honest finance, or by our votes place the debt question of the old state into the hands of the plunderers and peculators. We were appealed to by General Hagood, through me, and my answer to him was in these words: "General, our people have learned the difference between profligate and honest legislation. We have passed acts of financial reform, and with the assistance of God when the vote shall have been taken, you will be able to record for the thirty odd Negroes, slandered though they have been through the press, that they voted solidly with you all for honest legislation and the preservation of the credit of the State." The thirty odd Negroes in the legislature and their senators, by their votes did settle the debt question and saved the state $13,000,000. We were eight years in power. We had built school houses, established charitable institutions, built and maintained the penitentiary system, provided for the education of the deaf and dumb, rebuilt the jails and court houses, rebuilt the bridges and re-established the ferries. In short, we had reconstructed the State and placed it upon the road to prosperity and, at the same time, by our acts of financial reform transmitted to the Hampton Government an indebtedness not greater by more than $2,500,000 than was the bonded debt of the State in 1868, before the Republican Negroes and their white allies came into power.[19]

So, too, in Louisiana in 1872 and in Mississippi later the better element of the Republicans triumphed at the polls and joining with the Democrats instituted reforms, repudiated the worst extravagance, and started toward better things. But unfortunately there was one thing that the white South feared more than negro dishonesty, ignorance, and incompetency, and that was negro honesty, knowledge, and efficiency.

In the midst of all these difficulties the negro governments in the

[19] Speech of Thomas E. Miller, one of the six negro members of the South Carolina Constitutional Convention of 1895. The speech was not published in the *Journal* but may be found in the *Occasional Papers* of the American Negro Academy, no. 6, pp. 11–13.

South accomplished much of positive good. We may recognize three things which negro rule gave to the South:

1. Democratic government.
2. Free public schools.
3. New social legislation.

Two states will illustrate conditions of government in the South before and after negro rule. In South Carolina there was before the war a property qualification for office-holders, and, in part, for voters. The Constitution of 1868, on the other hand, was a modern democratic document starting (in marked contrast to the old constitutions) with a declaration that "We, the People", framed it, and preceded by a broad Declaration of Rights which did away with property qualifications and based representation directly on population instead of property. It especially took up new subjects of social legislation, declaring navigable rivers free public highways, instituting homestead exemptions, establishing boards of county commissioners, providing for a new penal code of laws, establishing universal manhood suffrage "without distinction of race or color," devoting six sections to charitable and penal institutions and six to corporations, providing separate property for married women, etc. Above all, eleven sections of the Tenth Article were devoted to the establishment of a complete public-school system.

So satisfactory was the constitution thus adopted by negro suffrage and by a convention composed of a majority of blacks that the state lived twenty-seven years under it without essential change and when the constitution was revised in 1895, the revision was practically nothing more than an amplification of the Constitution of 1868. No essential advance step of the former document was changed except the suffrage article.

In Mississippi the Constitution of 1868 was, as compared with that before the war, more democratic. It not only forbade distinctions on account of color but abolished all property qualifications for jury service, and property and educational qualifications for suffrage; it required less rigorous qualifications for office; it prohibited the lending of the credit of the state for private corporations—an abuse dating back as far as 1830. It increased the powers of the governor, raised the low state salaries, and increased the number of state officials. New ideas like the public-school system and the immigration bureau were introduced and in general the activity of the state greatly and necessarily enlarged. Finally, that was the only constitution ever submitted to popular approval at the polls. This constitution remained in force twenty-two years.

In general the words of Judge Albion W. Tourgée, a "carpetbagger," are true when he says of the negro governments:

They obeyed the Constitution of the United States, and annulled the bonds of states, counties, and cities which had been issued to carry on the war of rebellion and maintain armies in the field against the Union. They instituted a public school system in a realm where public schools had been unknown. They opened the ballot box and jury box to thousands of white men who had been debarred from them by a lack of earthly possessions. They introduced home rule into the South. They abolished the whipping post, the branding iron, the stocks and other barbarous forms of punishment which had up to that time prevailed. They reduced capital felonies from about twenty to two or three. In an age of extravagance they were extravagant in the sums appropriated for public works. In all of that time no man's rights of person were invaded under the forms of law. Every Democrat's life, home, fireside and business were safe. No man obstructed any white man's way to the ballot box, interfered with his freedom of speech, or boycotted him on account of his political faith.[20]

A thorough study of the legislation accompanying these constitutions and its changes since would of course be necessary before a full picture of the situation could be given. This has not been done, but so far as my studies have gone I have been surprised at the comparatively small amount of change in law and government which the overthrow of negro rule brought about. There were sharp and often hurtful economies introduced marking the return of property to power, there was a sweeping change of officials, but the main body of Reconstruction legislation stood.

This democracy brought forward new leaders and men and definitely overthrew the old Southern aristocracy. Among these new men were negroes of worth and ability. John R. Lynch when speaker of the Mississippi house of representatives was given a public testimonial by Republicans and Democrats and the leading Democratic paper said:

His bearing in office had been so proper, and his rulings in such marked contrast to the partisan conduct of the ignoble whites of his party who have aspired to be leaders of the blacks, that the conservatives cheerfully joined in the testimonial.[21]

Of the colored treasurer of South Carolina, Governor Chamberlain said:

I have never heard one word or seen one act of Mr. Cardozo's which did not confirm my confidence in his personal integrity and his political honor and zeal for the honest administration of the State Government. On every occasion, and under all circumstances, he has been against fraud and jobbery, and in favor of good measures and good men.[22]

[20] *Occasional Papers* of the American Negro Academy, no. 6, p. 10; Chicago *Weekly Inter Ocean,* December 26, 1890.
[21] Jackson (Mississippi) *Clarion,* April 24, 1873.
[22] Allen, *Governor Chamberlain's Administration in South Carolina,* p. 82.

Jonathan C. Gibbs, a colored man and the first state superintendent of instruction in Florida, was a graduate of Dartmouth. He established the system and brought it to success, dying in harness in 1874. Such men —and there were others—ought not to be forgotten or confounded with other types of colored and white Reconstruction leaders.

There is no doubt but that the thirst of the black man for knowledge —a thirst which has been too persistent and durable to be mere curiosity or whim—gave birth to the public free-school system of the South. It was the question upon which black voters and legislators insisted more than anything else and while it is possible to find some vestiges of free schools in some of the Southern States before the war yet a universal, well-established system dates from the day that the black man got political power. Common-school instruction in the South, in the modern sense of the term, was begun for negroes by the Freedmen's Bureau and missionary societies, and the state public-school systems for all children were formed mainly by negro Reconstruction governments. The earlier state constitutions of Mississippi "from 1817 to 1865 contained a declaration that 'Religion, morality and knowledge being necessary to good government, the preservation of liberty and the happiness of mankind, schools and the means of education shall forever be encouraged.' It was not, however, until 1868 that encouragement was given to any general system of public schools meant to embrace the whole youthful population." The Constitution of 1868 makes it the duty of the legislature to establish "a uniform system of free public schools, by taxation or otherwise, for all children between the ages of five and twenty-one years." In Alabama the Reconstruction Constitution of 1868 provided that "It shall be the duty of the Board of Education to establish throughout the State, in each township or other school district which it may have created, one or more schools at which the children of the State between the ages of five and twenty-one years may attend free of charge." Arkansas in 1868, Florida in 1869, Louisiana in 1868, North Carolina in 1869, South Carolina in 1868, and Virginia in 1870, established school systems. The Constitution of 1868 in Louisiana required the general assembly to establish "at least one free public school in every parish," and that these schools should make no "distinction of race, color or previous condition." Georgia's system was not fully established until 1873.

We are apt to forget that in all human probability the granting of negro manhood suffrage and the passage of the Fifteenth Amendment were decisive in rendering permanent the foundation of the negro common school. Even after the overthrow of the negro governments, if the negroes had been left a servile caste, personally free, but politically powerless, it is not reasonable to think that a system of common schools would have been provided for them by the Southern States. Serfdom and education have ever proven contradictory terms. But when Congress, backed by the nation, determined to make the negroes full-fledged voting citizens, the South had a hard dilemma before her: either to keep the negroes under as an ignorant proletariat and stand the chance of being ruled eventually from the slums and jails, or to join in helping to raise these wards of the nation to a position of intelligence and thrift by means of a public-school system. The "carpet-bag" governments hastened the decision of the South, and although there was a period of hesitation and retrogression after the overthrow of negro rule in the early seventies, yet the South saw that to abolish negro schools in addition to nullifying the negro vote would invite Northern interference; and thus eventually every Southern state confirmed the work of the negro legislators and maintained the negro public schools along with the white.

Finally, in legislation covering property, the wider functions of the state, the punishment of crime and the like, it is sufficient to say that the laws on these points established by Reconstruction legislatures were not only different from and even revolutionary to the laws in the older South, but they were so wise and so well suited to the needs of the new South that in spite of a retrogressive movement following the overthrow of the negro governments the mass of this legislation, with elaboration and development, still stands on the statute books of the South.

Reconstruction constitutions, practically unaltered, were kept in

Florida, 1868–1885 .... 17 years.
Virginia, 1870–1902 .... 32 years.
South Carolina, 1868–1895 .... 27 years.
Mississippi, 1868–1890 .... 22 years.

Even in the case of states like Alabama, Georgia, North Carolina, and Louisiana, which adopted new constitutions to signify the overthrow of negro rule, the new constitutions are nearer the model of the Reconstruction document than they are to the previous constitutions. They differ from the negro constitutions in minor details but very little in general conception.

Besides this there stands on the statute books of the South to-day law after law passed between 1868 and 1876, and which has been found wise, effective, and worthy of preservation.

Paint the "carpet-bag" governments and negro rule as black as may be, the fact remains that the essence of the revolution which the overturning of the negro governments made was to put these black men and their friends out of power. Outside the curtailing of expenses and stopping of extravagance, not only did their successors make few changes in the work which these legislatures and conventions had done, but they largely carried out their plans, followed their suggestions, and strengthened their institutions. Practically the whole new growth of the South has been accomplished under laws which black men helped to frame thirty years ago. I know of no greater compliment to negro suffrage.

The Undoing of Reconstruction

WILLIAM A. DUNNING

The most scholarly expression of the turn-of-the-century consensus regarding Reconstruction was by William Dunning of Columbia University. Born in New York, an admirer of Rhodes, pupil of John W. Burgess, and teacher of Ulrich Phillips, Dunning wrote from a standpoint which seems to us now characteristically Southern. For Dunning as for Rhodes, Charles Sumner exhibited "that narrow fanaticism which erudition and egotism combined to produce."

The following esay, a brilliant narrative of the retreat from Reconstruction by the South and the nation, reveals its bias in its conclusions. Like Ulrich Phillips, Dunning believed that "the ultimate root of the trouble in the South had been, not the institution of slavery, but the coexistence in one society of two races so distinct in characteristics as to render coalescence impossible." Reflecting the newly burgeoning imperialism of the day, Dunning observed that "in view of the questions which have been raised by our lately established relations with other races, it seems most improbable that the historian will soon, or ever, have to record a reversal of the conditions" of racial inequality then established in the South.

Yet Dunning's students began the careful state-by-state chronicling of Reconstruction. And Dunning himself, in *Reconstruction, Political And Economic* (1907), anticipated his critics by noting that the heavy spending of Reconstruction legislatures in part reflected their increased concern with

William A. Dunning, "The Undoing of Reconstruction," *The Atlantic Monthly* (1901), pp. 437–449.

social welfare; that after the Civil War corruption existed in Congress and in the North as well as in the South; and that complaints against Reconstruction often came from rural property-owners unused to being taxed.

IN JULY OF 1870, WHEN THE LAW DECLARING GEORGIA ENTITLED TO representation in Congress was finally enacted, the process of reconstruction was, from the technical point of view, complete. Each of the states which had seceded from the Union had been "made over" by the creation of a new political people, in which the freedmen constituted an important element, and the organization of a new government, in the working of which the participation of the blacks on equal terms with the whites was put under substantial guarantees. The leading motive of the reconstruction had been, at the inception of the process, to insure to the freedmen an effective protection of their civil rights,— of life, liberty, and property. In the course of the process, the chief stress came to be laid on the endowment of the blacks with full political rights,—with the electoral franchise and eligibility to office. And by the time the process was complete, a very important, if not the most important part had been played by the desire and the purpose to secure to the Republican party the permanent control of several Southern states in which hitherto such a political organization had been unknown. This last motive had a plausible and widely accepted justification in the view that the rights of the negro and the "results of the war" in general would be secure only if the national government should remain indefinitely in Republican hands, and that therefore the strengthening of the party was a primary dictate of patriotism.

Through the operation of these various motives successive and simultaneous, the completion of the reconstruction showed the following situation: (1) the negroes were in the enjoyment of the equal political rights with the whites; (2) the Republican party was in vigorous life in all the Southern states, and in firm control of many of them; and (3) the negroes exercised an influence in political affairs out of all relation to their intelligence or property, and, since so many of the whites were disfranchised, excessive even in proportion to their numbers. At the present day, in the same states, the negroes enjoy practically no political rights; the Republican party is but the shadow of a name; and the influence of the negroes in political affairs is nil. This contrast suggests what has been involved in the undoing of reconstruction.

Before the last state was restored to the Union the process was well under way through which the resumption of control by the whites was to be effected. The tendency in this direction was greatly promoted by conditions within the Republican party itself. Two years of supremacy in those states which had been restored in 1868 had revealed unmistakable evidences of moral and political weakness in the governments. The personnel of the party was declining in character through the return to the North of the more substantial of the carpet-baggers, who found Southern conditions, both social and industrial, far from what they had anticipated, and through the very frequent instances in which the "scalawags" ran to open disgrace. Along with this deterioration in the white element of the party, the negroes who rose to prominence and leadership were very frequently of a type which acquired and practiced the tricks and knavery rather than the useful arts of politics, and the vicious courses of these negroes strongly confirmed the prejudices of the whites. But at the same time that the incapacity of the party in power to administer any government was becoming demonstrable the problems with which it was required to cope were made by its adversaries such as would have taxed the capacity of the most efficient statesmen the world could produce. Between 1868 and 1870, when the cessation of the national military authority left the new state governments to stand by their own strength, there developed that widespread series of disorders with which the name of the Ku Klux is associated. While these were at their height the Republican party was ousted from control in five of the old rebel states,—Tennessee, North Carolina, Texas, Georgia, and Virginia. The inference was at once drawn that the whites of the South were pursuing a deliberate policy of overthrowing the negro party by violence. No attention was paid to the claim that the manifest inefficiency and viciousness of the Republican governments afforded a partial, if not a wholly adequate explanation of their overthrow. Not even the relative quiet and order that followed the triumph of the whites in these states were recognized as justifying the new regime. The North was deeply moved by what it considered evidence of a new attack on its cherished ideals of liberty and equality, and when the Fifteenth Amendment had become part of the Constitution, Congress passed the Enforcement Acts and the laws for the federal control of elections. To the forces making for the resumption of white government in the South was thus opposed that same apparently irresistible power which had originally overthrown it.

That the Ku Klux movement was to some extent the expression of a purpose not to submit to the political domination of the blacks is doubtless true. But many other motives were at work in the disorders, and the purely political antithesis of the races was not so clear in the origin and development of the movement as in connection with the efforts of the state governments to suppress it. Thousands of respectable whites, who viewed the Ku Klux outrages with horror, turned with equal horror from the projects of the governments to quell the disturbances by a negro militia. Here was the crux of the race issue. Respectable whites would not serve with the blacks in the militia; the Republican state governments would not—and indeed from the very nature of the case, could not—exclude the blacks from the military service; the mere suggestion of employing the blacks alone in such service turned every white into practically a sympathizer with the Ku Klux: and thus the government was paralyzed at the foundation of its authority. It was demonstrated again and again that the appearance of a body of negroes under arms, whether authorized by law or not, had for its most certain result an affray, if not a pitched battle, with armed whites, in which the negroes almost invariably got the worst of it.

On the assumption, then, that the white state governments in the South were unwilling, and the black governments were unable, to protect the negro in his rights, Congress inaugurated the policy of the "Force Acts." The primary aim was to protect the right to vote, but ultimately the purely civil rights and even the so-called "social rights," were included in the legislation. By the act of 1870, a long series of minutely specified offenses, involving violence, intimidation, and fraud, with the effect or even the intention of denying equal rights to any citizens of the United States, were made crimes and misdemeanors, and were thus brought under the jurisdiction of the federal courts. Great activity was at once displayed by the United States district attorneys throughout the South, and hundreds of indictments were brought in; but convictions were few. The whites opposed to the process of the federal courts, supported by federal troops, no such undisguised resistance as had often been employed against state officers backed by a posse comitatus or a militia company of negroes. But every advantage was taken of legal technicalities; in the regions where the Ku Klux were strong, juries and witnesses were almost invariably influenced by sympathy or terror to favor the accused; and the huge disproportion between the number of arrests and the number of convictions was skillfully employed to sustain the claim that the federal officers were using the law as the cover for a systematic intimidation and oppression of the whites. As the effect of this first act seemed to be rather an increase than a decrease in the disorders of the South, Congress passed in the following year a more drastic law. This known commonly as the Ku Klux Act, healed many technical defects in the earlier law; reformulated in most precise and far-reaching terms the conspiracy clause, which was especially designed to cover Ku Klux methods; and, finally, authorized the President, for a limited time, to suspend the writ of habeas corpus, and employ military force in the suppression of violence and crime in any given district. In addition to the punitive system thus established, Congress at the same time instituted a rigorous preventive system through the Federal Elections Laws. By acts of 1871 and 1872, every polling place, in any election for Congressmen, might be manned by officials appointed by the federal courts, with extensive powers for the detection of fraud and with authority to employ the federal troops in the repression of violence.

Through the vigorous policy thus instituted by the national government the movement toward the resumption of control by the whites in the South met with a marked though temporary check. The number of convictions obtained under the Ku Klux Act was not large, and President Grant resorted in but a single instance—that of certain counties in South Carolina, in the autumn of 1871—to the extraordinary powers conferred upon him. But the moral effect of what was done was very great, and the evidence that the whole power of the national government could and would be exerted on the side of the blacks produced a salutary change in method among the whites. The extreme and violent element was reduced to quiescence, and haste was made more slowly. No additional state was redeemed by the whites until 1874. Meanwhile, the wholesale removal of political disabilities by Congress in 1872 brought many of the old and respected Southern politicians again into public life, with a corresponding improvement in the quality of Democratic leadership. More deference began to be paid to the Northern sentiment hostile to the Grant administration which had been revealed in the presidential campaign of 1872, and the policy of the Southern whites was directed especially so as to bring odium upon the use of the military forces in the states yet to be wrested from black control.

It was upon the support of the federal troops that the whole existence of the remaining black governments in the South came gradually to depend. Between 1872 and 1876 the Republican party split in each of the states in which it still retained control, and the fusion of one faction with the Democrats gave rise to disputed elections, general disorder, and appeals by the radical Republicans to the President for aid in suppressing domestic violence. Alabama and Arkansas emerged from the turmoil in 1874 with the whites triumphant; and the federal troops, after performing useful service in keeping the factions from serious bloodshed, ceased to figure in politics. But in Louisiana and South Carolina the radical factions retained power exclusively through the presence of the troops who were employed in the former state to reconstitute both the legislature and the executive at the bidding of one of the claimants of the gubernatorial office. The very extraordinary proceedings in New Orleans greatly emphasized the unfavorable feeling at the North toward "governments resting on bayonets"; and when, upon the approach of the state election of 1875 in Mississippi, the radical governor applied for troops to preserve order, President Grant rather tartly refused to furnish them. The result was the overthrow of black government in that state. Though strenuously denied at the time, it was no deep secret that the great negro majority in the state was overcome in this campaign by a quiet but general exertion of every possible form of pressure to keep the blacks from the polls. The extravagance and corruption of the state administration had become so intolerable to the whites that questionable means of terminating it were admitted by even the most honorable without question. There was relatively little "Ku Kluxing" or open violence, but in countless ways the negroes were impressed with the idea that there would be peril for them in voting. "Intimidation" was the word that had vogue at the time, in describing such methods, and intimidation was illegal. But if a party of white men, with ropes conspicuous on their saddlebows, rode up to a polling place and announced that hanging would begin in fifteen minutes, though without any more definite reference to anybody, and a group of blacks who had assembled to vote heard the remark and promptly disappeared, votes were lost but a conviction on a charge of intimidation was difficult. Or if an untraceable rumor that trouble was impeding over the blacks was followed by the mysterious appearance of bodies of horsemen on the roads at midnight, firing guns and yelling at nobody in particular, votes again were lost, but no crime or misdemeanor could be brought home to any one. Devices like these were familiar in the South, but on this occasion they were accompanied by many other evidences of a purpose on the part of the whites to carry their point at all hazards. The negroes, though numerically much in excess of the whites, were very definitely demoralized by the aggressiveness and unanimity of the latter, and in the ultimate test of race strength the weaker gave way.

The "Mississippi plan" was enthusiastically applied in the remaining three states, Louisiana, South Carolina, and Florida, in the elections of 1876. Here, however, the presence of the federal troops and of all the paraphernalia of the Federal Elections Laws materially stiffened the courage of the negroes and the result of the state election became closely involved in the controversy over the presidential count. The Southern Democratic leaders fully appreciated the opportunity of their position in this controversy, and, through one of those bargains without words which are common in great crises, the inauguration of President Hayes was followed by the withdrawal of the troops from the support of the last radical governments, and the peaceful lapse of the whole South into the control of the whites.

With these events of 1877 the first period in the undoing of reconstruction came to an end. The second period, lasting till 1890, presented conditions so different from the first as entirely to transform the methods by which the process was continued. Two, indeed, of the three elements which have been mentioned as summing up reconstruction still characterized the situation: the negroes were precisely equal in rights with the other race, and the Republican party was a powerful organization in the South. As to the third element, the disproportionate political influence of the blacks, a change had been effected, and their power had been so reduced as to correspond much more closely to their general social significance. In the movement against the still enduring features of reconstruction the control of the state governments by the whites was of course a new condition of the utmost importance, but not less vital was the party complexion of the national government. From 1875 to 1889 neither of the great parties was at any one time in effective control of both the presidency and the two houses of Congress. As a consequence no partisan legislation could be enacted. Though the state of affairs in the South was for years a party issue of the first magnitude, the legislative deadlock had for its general result a policy of non-interference by the national government, and the whites were left to work out in their own way the ends they had in view. Some time was necessary, however, to overcome the influence of the two bodies of legislation already on the national statute book,—the Force Acts and the Federal Elections Laws.

During the Hayes[1] administration the latter laws were the subject of a prolonged and violent contest between the Democratic houses and the Republican President. The Democrats put great stress on the terror and intimidation of the whites and the violation of freemen's rights due to the presence of federal officials at the polls, and of federal troops near them. The Republicans insisted that these officials and troops were essential to enable the negroes to vote and to have their votes counted. As a matter of fact, neither of these contentions was of the highest significance so far as the South was concerned. The whites, once in control of the state electoral machinery, readily devised means of evading or neutralizing the influence of the federal officers. But the patronage in the hands of the administration party under these laws was enormous. The power to appoint supervisors and deputy marshals at election time was a tower of strength, from the point of view of

[1] EDITOR'S NOTE: Rutherford Hayes was elected President on the Republican ticket in the disputed election of 1876.

direct votes and of indirect influence. Accordingly, the attack of the Democrats upon the laws was actuated mainly by the purpose of breaking down the Republican party organization in the South. The attack was successful in Mr. Hayes's time only to the extent that no appropriation was made for the payment of the supervisors and deputy marshals for their services in the elections of 1880. The system of federal supervision remained, but gradually lost all significance save as a biennial sign that the Republican party still survived and when Mr. Cleveland became President even this relation to its original character disappeared.

The Force Acts experienced a similar decline during the period we are considering. In 1875, just before the Republicans lost control of Congress, they passed, as a sort of memorial to Charles Sumner, who had long urged its adoption, a Supplementary Civil Rights Bill, which made criminal, and put under the jurisdiction of the federal courts, any denial of equality to negroes in respect to accommodations in theatres, railway cars, hotels, and other such places. This was not regarded by the most thoughtful Republicans as a very judicious piece of legislation; but it was perceived that, with the Democrats about to control the House of Representatives there was not likely to be a further opportunity for action in aid of the blacks, and so the act was permitted to go through and take its chances of good. Already, however, the courts had manifested a disposition to question the constitutionality of the most drastic provisions of the earlier Enforcement Acts. It has been said above that indictments under these acts had been many, but convictions few. Punishments were fewer still; for skillful counsel were ready to test the profound legal questions involved in the legislation, and numbers of cases crept slowly up on appeal to the Supreme Court. In 1875, this tribunal threw out an indictment under which a band of whites who had broken up a negro meeting in Louisiana had been convicted of conspiring to prevent negroes from assembling for lawful purposes and from carrying arms; for the right to assemble and the right to bear arms, the court declared, pertained to citizenship of a state, not of the United States, and therefore redress for interference with these rights must be sought in the courts of the state. In the same year, in the case of United States v. Reese, two sections of the Enforcement Act of 1870 were declared unconstitutional, as involving the exercise by the United States of powers in excess of those granted by the Fifteenth Amendment. It was not, however, till 1882 that the bottom was taken wholly out of the Ku Klux Act. In the case of United States v. Harris the conspiracy clause in its entirety was declared unconstitutional. This was a case from Tennessee, in which a band of whites had taken a negro away from the officers of the law and mal-treated him. The court held that, under the last three amendments to the Constitution, Congress was authorized to guarantee equality in civil rights against violation by a state through its officers or agents, but not against violation by private individuals. Where assault or murder or other crime was committed by a private individual, even if the pur-pose was to deprive citizens of rights on the ground of race, the juris-diction, and the exclusive jurisdiction, was in the state courts. And because the conspiracy clause brought such offenses into the jurisdiction of the United States it was unconstitutional and void. This decision finally disposed of the theory that the failure of a state to protect the negroes in their equal rights could be regarded as a positive denial of such rights, and hence could justify the United States in interfering. It left the blacks practically at the mercy of white public sentiment in the South. A year later, in 1883, the court summarily disposed of the act of 1875 by declaring that the rights which it endeavored to guarantee were not strictly civil rights at all, but rather social rights, and that in either case the federal government had nothing to do with them. The act was therefore held unconstitutional.

Thus passed the most characteristic features of the great system through which the Republicans had sought to prevent by normal action of the courts, independently of changes in public opinion and political major-ities, the undoing of reconstruction. Side by side with the removal of the preventives, the Southern whites had made enormous positive advances in the suppression of the other race. In a very general way, the process in this period, as contrasted with the earlier, may be said to have rested, in last resort, on legislation and fraud rather than on intimidation and force. The statute books of the states, especially of those in which negro rule had lasted the longest, abounded in provisions for partisan—that is, race—advantage. These were at once devoted as remorselessly to the extinction of black preponderance as they had been before to the repression of the whites. Moreover, by revision of the constitutions and by sweeping modifications of the laws, many strongholds of the old regime were destroyed. Yet with all that could be done in this way, the fact remained that in many local-ities the negroes so greatly outnumbered the whites as to render the political ascendency of the latter impossible, except through some radi-cal changes in the laws touching the suffrage and the elections; and in respect to these two points the sensitiveness of Northern feeling rendered open and decided action highly inexpedient. Before 1880 the anticipation, and after that year the realization, of a "solid South" played a prom-inent part in national politics. The permanence of white dominion in the South seemed, in view of the past, to depend as much on the exclusion of the Republicans from power at Washington as on the maintenance of white power at the state capitals. Under all the circumstances, therefore, extralegal devices had still to be used in the "black belt."

The state legislation which contributed to confirm white control included many ingenious and exaggerated applications of the gerrymander and the prescription of various electoral regulations that were designedly too intricate for the average negro intelligence. In Mississippi appeared the "shoestring district," three hundred miles long and about twenty wide, including within its boundaries nearly all the densest black communities of the state. In South Carolina, the requirement that, with eight or more ballot boxes before him, the voter must select the proper one for each ballot in order to insure its being counted, furnished an effective means of neutralizing the ignorant black vote; for though the negroes, unable to read the lettering on the boxes, might acquire, by proper coaching, the power to discriminate among them by their relative positions, a moment's work by the whites in transposing the boxes would render useless an hour's laborious instruction. For the efficient working of this method of suppression, it was indispensable, however, that the officers of election should be whites. This suggests at once the enormous advantage gained by securing control of the state government. In the hot days of negro supremacy the electoral machinery had been ruthlessly used for partisan purposes, and when conditions were reversed the practice was by no means abandoned. It was, indeed, through their exclusive and carefully maintained control of the voting and the count that the whites found the best opportunities for illegal methods.

Because of these opportunities the resort to bulldozing and other violence steadily decreased. It penetrated gradually to the consciousness of the most brutal white politicians that the whipping or murder of a negro, no matter for what cause, was likely to become at once the occasion of a great outcry at the North while by an unobtrusive manipulation of the balloting or the count very encouraging results could be obtained with little or no commotion. Hence that long series of practices, in the regions where the blacks were numerous, that give so grotesque a character to the testimony in the contested-election cases in Congress, and to the reminiscences of candid Southerners. Polling places were established at points so remote from the densest black communities that a journey of from twenty to forty miles was necessary in order to vote; and where the roads were interrupted by ferries, the resolute negroes who attempted to make the journey were very likely to find the boats laid up for repairs. The number of polling places was kept so small as to make rapid voting indispensable to a full vote; and then the whites, by challenges and carefully premeditated quarrels among themselves, would amuse the blacks and consume time, till only enough remained for their own votes to be cast. The situation of the polls was changed without notice to the negroes, or, conversely, the report of a change was industriously circulated when none had been made. Open bribery on a large scale was too common to excite comment. One rather ingenious scheme is recorded which presents a variation on the old theme. In several of the states a poll-tax receipt was required as a qualification for voting. In an important local election, one faction had assured itself of the negro vote by a generous outlay in the payment of the tax for a large number of the blacks. The other faction, alarmed at the prospect of almost certain defeat, availed itself of the opportunity presented by the providential advent of a circus in the neighborhood and the posters announced that poll-tax receipts would be accepted for admission. As a result, the audience at the circus was notable in respect to numbers, but the negro vote at the election was insignificant.

But exploitation of the poverty, ignorance, credulity, and general childishness of the blacks was supplemented, on occasion, by deliberate and high-handed fraud. Stuffing of the boxes with illegal ballots, and manipulation of the figures in making the count, were developed into serious arts. At the acme of the development undoubtedly stood the tissue ballot. There was in those days no prescription of uniformity in size and general character of the ballots. Hence miniature ballots of tissue paper were secretly prepared and distributed to trusted voters, who, folding as many, sometimes, as fifteen of the small tickets within one of the ordinary large tickets passed the whole, without detection, into the box. Not till the box was opened were the tissue tickets discovered. Then, because the number of ballots exceeded the number of voters as indicated by the polling list, it became necessary, under the law, for the excess to be drawn out by a blindfolded man before the count began. So some one's eyes were solemnly bandaged, and he was set to drawing out ballots, on the theory that he could not distinguish those of one party from those of the other. The result is not hard to guess. In one case given by the Senate investigating committee, through whose action on the elections of 1878, in South Carolina, the theory and practice of the tissue ballot were revealed to an astonished world, the figures were as follows:—

Number of ballots in box	1163
Names on polling list	620
Excess drawn out	543
Tissue ballots left to be counted	464

Not the least interesting feature of this episode was the explanation given by the white committee, of the existence of the great mass of tissue ballots. They were prepared, it was said in order to enable the blacks who wished to vote the Democratic ticket to do so secretly, and thus to escape the ostracism and other social penalties which would be meted out to them by the majority of their race.

Under the pressure applied by all these various methods upon the negroes, the black vote slowly disappeared. And with it the Republican party faded into insignificance. In the presidential election of 1884 the total vote in South Carolina was, in round numbers, 91,000, as compared with 182,000 in 1876. In Mississippi the corresponding decrease was from 164,000 to 120,000; in Louisiana, from 160,000 to 108,000. The Republican party organization was maintained almost exclusively through the holders of federal offices in the postal and revenue service. When in 1885, a Democratic administration assumed power, this basis for continued existence was very seriously weakened, and the decline of the party was much accelerated. Save for a few judicial positions held over from early appointments, the national offices, like those of the states, were hopelessly removed from the reach of any Republican's ambition. A comparison of the congressional delegation from the states of the defunct Confederacy in the Forty-First Congress (1869–71) with that in the Fifty-First (1889–91) is eloquent of the transformation that the two decades had wrought: in the former, twenty out of the twenty-two Senators were Republican, and forty-four out of fifty-eight Representatives; in the latter, there were no Republican Senators, and but three Representatives.

Summarily, then, it may be said that the second period in the undoing of reconstruction ends with the political equality of the negroes still recognized in law, though not in fact, and with the Republican party, for all practical purposes, extinct in the South. The third period has had for its task the termination of equal rights in law as well as in fact.

The decline of negro suffrage and of the Republican party in the South was the topic of much discussion in national politics and figured in the party platforms throughout the period from 1876 to 1888; but owing to the deadlock in the party control of the national legislature the discussion remained academic in character, and the issue was supplanted in public interest by the questions of tariff, currency, and monopoly. By the elections of 1888, however, the Republicans secured not only the presidency, but also a majority in each house of Congress. The deadlock of thirteen years was broken, and at once an effort was made to resume the policy of the Enforcement Acts. A bill was brought in that was designed to make real the federal control of elections. The old acts for this purpose were, indeed, still on the statute books, but their operation was farcical; the new project, while maintaining the general lines of the old, would have imposed serious restraints on the influences that repressed the negro vote, and would have infused some vitality into the moribund Republican party in the South. It was quickly demonstrated however, that the time for this procedure had gone by. The bill received perfunctory support in the House of Representatives, where it passed by the regular party majority, but in the Senate it was rather contemptuously set aside by Republican votes. Public sentiment in the North, outside of Congress, manifested considerable hostility to the project, and its adoption as a party measure probably played a rôle in the tremendous reaction which swept the Republicans out of power in the House in 1890, and gave to the Democrats in 1892 the control of both houses of Congress and the presidency as well. The response of the Democrats to the futile project of their adversaries was prompt and decisive. In February, 1894, an act became law which repealed all existing statutes that provided for federal supervision of elections. Thus the last vestige disappeared of the system through which the political equality of the blacks had received direct support from the national government.

In the meantime, a process had been instituted in the Southern states that has given the most distinctive character to the last period in the undoing of reconstruction. The generation-long discussions of the political conditions in the South have evoked a variety of explanations by the whites of the disappearance of the black vote. These different explanations have of course all been current at all times since reconstruction was completed, and have embodied different degrees of plausibility and truth in different places. But it may fairly be said that in each of the three periods into which the undoing of reconstruction falls one particular view has been dominant and characteristic. In the first period, that of the Ku Klux and the Mississippi plan, it was generally maintained by the whites that the black vote was not suppressed, and that there was no political motive behind the disturbances that occurred. The victims of murder, bulldozing, and other violence were represented as of bad character and socially dangerous, and their treatment as merely incident to their own illegal and violent acts, and expressive of the tendency to self-help instead of judicial procedure, which had always been manifest in Southern life, and had been aggravated by the demoralization of war time. After 1877, when the falling off in the Republican vote became so conspicuous, the phenomenon was explained by the assertion that the negroes had seen the light, and had become Democrats. Mr. Lamar gravely maintained, in a famous controversy with Mr. Blaine, that the original Republican theory as to the educative influence of the ballot had been proved correct by the fact that the enfranchised race had come to recognize that their true interests lay with the Democratic party; the Republicans were estopped, he contended, by their own doctrine from finding fault with the result. A corollary of this idea that the negroes were Democrats was generally adopted later in the period, to the effect that, since there was practically no opposition to the democracy the negroes had lost interest in politics. They had got on the road to economic prosperity, and were too busy with their farms and their growing bank accounts to care for other things.

Whatever of soundness there may have been in any of these explanations, all have been superseded, during the last decade, by another, which, starting with the candid avowal that the whites are determined to rule, concedes that the elimination of the blacks from politics has been effected by intimidation, fraud, and any other means, legal or illegal, that would promote the desired end. This admission has been accompanied by expressions of sincere regret that illegal means were necessary, and by a general movement toward clothing with the forms of law the disfranchisement which has been made a fact without them. In 1890, just when the Republicans in Congress were pushing their project for renewing the federal control of elections Mississippi made the first step in the new direction. Her constitution was so revised as to provide that, to be a qualified elector, a citizen must produce evidence of having paid his taxes (including a poll tax) for the past two years, and must, in addition, "be able to read any section in the constitution of this state, or . . . be able to understand the same when read to him, or give a reasonable interpretation thereof." Much might be said in favor of such an alternative intelligence qualification in the abstract: the mere ability to read is far from conclusive of intellectual capacity. But the peculiar form of this particular provision was confessedly adopted, not from any consideration of its abstract excellence, but in order to vest in the election officers the power to disfranchise illiterate blacks without disfranchising illiterate whites. In practice, the white must be stupid indeed who cannot satisfy the official demand for a "reasonable interpretation," while the negro who can satisfy it must be a miracle of brilliancy.

Mississippi's bold and undisguised attack on negro suffrage excited much attention. In the South it met with practically unanimous approval among thoughtful and conscientious men, who had been distressed by the false position in which they had long been placed. And at the North, public opinion, accepting with a certain satirical complacency the confession of the Southerners that their earlier explanations of conditions had been false, acknowledged in turn that its views as to the political capacity of the blacks had been irrational, and manifested no disposition for a new crusade in favor of negro equality. The action of Mississippi raised certain questions of constitutional law which had to be tested before her solution of the race problem could be regarded as final. Like all the other seceded states, save Tennessee, she had been readmitted to representation in Congress, after reconstruction, on the express condition that her constitution should never be so amended as to disfranchise any who were entitled to vote under the existing provisions. The new amendment was a most explicit violation of this condition. Further, so far as the new clause could be shown to be directed against the negroes as a race, it was in contravention of the Fifteenth Amendment. These legal points had been elaborately discussed in the state convention, and the opinion had been adopted that, since neither race, color, nor previous condition of servitude was made the basis of discrimination in the suffrage, the Fifteenth Amendment had no application, and that the prohibition to modify the constitution was entirely beyond the powers of Congress, and was therefore void. When the Supreme Court of the United States was required to consider the new clause of Mississippi's constitution, it adopted the views of the convention on these points, and sustained the validity of the enactment. There was still one contingency that the whites had to face in carrying out the new policy. By the Fourteenth Amendment it is provided that if a state restricts the franchise her representation in Congress shall be proportionately reduced. There was a strong sentiment in Mississippi, as there is throughout the South, that a reduction of representation would not be an intolerable price to pay for the legitimate extinction of negro suffrage. But loss of Congressmen was by no means longed for, and the possibility of such a thing was very carefully considered. The phrasing of the franchise clause may not have been actually determined with reference to this matter; but it is obvious that the application of the Fourteenth Amendment is, to say the least, not facilitated by the form used.

The action of Mississippi in 1890 throws a rather interesting light on the value of political prophecy, even when ventured upon by the most experienced and able politicians. Eleven years earlier, Mr. Blaine, writing of the possibility of disfranchisement by educational and property tests, declared: "But no Southern state will do this, and for two reasons: first, they will in no event consent to a reduction of representative strength; and, second, they could not make any disfranchisement of the negro that would not at the same time disfranchise an immense number of whites." How sadly Mr. Blaine misconceived the spirit and underrated the ingenuity of the Southerners Mississippi made clear to everybody. Five years later South Carolina dealt no less unkindly with Mr. Lamar, who at the same time with Mr. Blaine had dipped a little prophecy on the other side. "Whenever," he said,—"and the time is not far distant,—political issues arise which divide the white men of the South, the negro will divide, too. . . . The white race, divided politically, will want him to divide." Incidentally to the conditions which produced the Populist party, the whites of South Carolina, in the years succeeding 1890, became divided into two intensely hostile factions. The weaker manifested a purpose to draw on the negroes for support, and began to expose some of the devices by which the blacks had been prevented from voting. The situation had arisen which Mr. Lamar had foreseen, but the result was as far as possible from fulfilling his prediction. Instead of competing with its rival for the black vote, the stronger faction, headed by Mr. Tillman, promptly took the ground that South Carolina must have a "white man's government," and put into effect the new Mississippi plan. A constitutional amendment was adopted in 1895 which applied the "understanding clause" for two years, and after that required of every elector either the ability to read and write or the ownership of property to the amount of three hundred dollars. In the convention which framed this amendment, the sentiment of the whites revealed very clearly, not only through its content, but especially through the frank and emphatic form in which it was expressed, that the aspirations of the negro to equality in political rights would never again receive the faintest recognition.

Since the action of South Carolina, two other states, Louisiana and North Carolina, have excluded the blacks from the suffrage by analogous constitutional amendments; and in two others still, Alabama and Virginia, conventions are considering the subject as this article goes to press (August, 1901). By Louisiana, however, a new method was devised for exempting the whites from the effect of the property and intelligence tests. The hereditary principle was introduced into the franchise by the provision that the right to vote should belong, regardless of education or property, to every one whose father or grandfather possessed the right on January 1, 1867. This "grandfather clause" has been adopted by North Carolina, also, and, in a modified form and for a very limited time, by the convention in Alabama. The basis for the hereditary right in this latter state has been found, not in the possession of the franchise by the ancestor, but in the fact of his having been a soldier in any war save that with Spain. As compared with the Mississippi device for evading the Fifteenth Amendment, the "grandfather clause" has the merit of incorporating the discrimination in favor of the whites in the written law rather than referring it to the discretion of the election officers. Whether the Supreme Court of the United States will regard it as equally successful in screening its real purpose from judicial cognizance remains to be seen.

With the enactment of these constitutional amendments by the various states, the political equality of the negro is becoming as extinct in law as it has long been in fact, and the undoing of reconstruction is nearing completion. The many morals that may be drawn from the three decades of the process it is not my purpose to suggest. A single reflection seems pertinent, however, in view of the problems which are uppermost in American politics at present. During the two generations of debate and bloodshed over slavery in the United States certain of our statesmen consistently held that the mere chattel relationship of man to man was not the whole of the question at issue. Jefferson, Clay, and Lincoln all saw more serious facts in the background. But in the frenzy of the war time public opinion fell into the train of the emotionalists, and accepted the teachings of Garrison and Sumner and Phillips and Chase, that abolition and negro suffrage would remove the last drag on our national progress. Slavery was abolished, and reconstruction gave the freedmen the franchise.

But with all the guarantees that the source of every evil was removed, it became obvious enough that the results were not what had been expected. Gradually there emerged again the idea of Jefferson and Clay and Lincoln, which had been hooted and hissed into obscurity during the prevalence of the abolitionist fever. This was that the ultimate root of the trouble in the South had been, not the institution of slavery, but the coexistence in one society of two races so distinct in characteristics as to render coalescence impossible; that slavery had been a *modus vivendi* through which social life was possible; and that, after its disappearance, its place must be taken by some set of conditions which, if more humane and beneficent in accidents, must in essence express the same fact of racial inequality. The progress in the acceptance of this idea in the North has measured the progress in the South of the undoing of reconstruction. In view of the questions which have been raised by our lately established relations with other races, it seems most improbable that the historian will soon, or ever, have to record a reversal of the conditions which this process has established.

ECONOMIC APPROACHES

Claptrap and Issues

HOWARD K. BEALE

As evaluation of the consequences of Negro suffrage dominated Reconstruction historiography prior to World War I, so between World Wars I and II the emphasis was economic. This interest was stimulated by the thesis presented by Charles and Mary Beard in their *Rise of American Civilization* (1927), that the Civil War was a "second American Revolution." According to the Beards the crux of the conflict between North and South was not slavery. Rather, the war was an attempted coup d'etat by an agrarian society (the South) which feared that Northern demographic preponderance would enable a Northern majority in Congress to pass legislation for higher tariffs, federal aid to railroads, and centralized banking. The Beards viewed Reconstruction as the attempt of a victorious capitalist class to protect its wartime gains.

The Beards' thesis as it applied to Reconstruction was elaborated in 1930 by Howard K. Beale. Focussing upon the critical election of 1866, which gave the Republican Party the Congressional strength required to override Presidential vetoes, Beale argued that the ostensible concern of Radical Republicans with the protection of the Negro was "claptrap" and that the real underlying issues were economic. Elsewhere in *The Critical Year* he sought to vindicate Andrew Johnson, stating: "I have not been convinced by Rhodes's simple explanation that the unreasoning obstinacy of Johnson and the South in the face of an overwhelming popular verdict for the Fourteenth Amendment was responsible for the subsequent extremes of reconstruction." Other scholars who at about the same time presented defenses of Johnson similar to Beale's were Claude Bowers, *The Tragic Era* (1929) and George Fort Milton, *The Age of Hate* (1930).

I N ANY CAMPAIGN THE ISSUES WHICH THE POLITICIANS RAISE AND questions which actually interest the public are apt to be confused. In 1866 they were inextricably entangled. Postwar excitement, dormant bitterness, and fear provided the Radicals with excellent raw material for a campaign of hysteria; hence most political speeches were largely claptrap. For the issues one must seek further. Important issues there were. But most of them were avoided because the Radicals regarded them as dangerous to their cause, and the Conservatives thought it futile to push them until the states were all back in the Union. On some questions opinion was hopelessly divided in both Radical and Conservative camps. The Radical campaign was waged to keep in power the party that had carried on the War and was still in the saddle in 1866. Conservatives sought to restore the Union in order to end the Radical monopoly of power and throw the government open to free competition of interests and sections, realizing full well that a return of the South would greatly improve their own chances of controlling the government. To these respective ends the leaders worked. Ultimate victory would depend upon the ebb and flow of a neutral popular opinion.

Popular opinion is at once the most potent and the most dependent of political forces; it can restrain or impel the most powerful of rulers; if roused, it overthrows governments; it can accomplish the seemingly impossible. But nevertheless it is dependent upon a complex multiplicity of delicate mechanisms. Theoretically, democracy is the panacea for all ills; the people, under ideal conditions, with all the facts truly before them, uninfluenced by prejudice, unmoved by passion, could perhaps be trusted in sagacity beyond any individual. The United States in 1866 was, however, not an abstract Utopia but a very real, average group of human beings; public opinion and democracy worked then as always, not in ideal abstract surroundings, but under the ordinary conditions of practical workaday human life. Public opinion in 1866 was dependent upon the usual unreliable channels of information: newspapers, preachers, politicians, selfish men with an ax to grind, sincere men with a reform to advocate, fearful men with chimerical dangers to prophesy, stubborn men with consistency to defend—prejudiced, conflicting, uninformed, opinionated sources of information. Public opinion was then as now, subject to its own inborn prejudices and sensitive to psychological influences, appeals to fear, to hate, to patriotism. It was influenced by defense of property and the status quo, and by attacks on privilege or invocation of economic dissatisfaction and unrest; it was affected by self-interest and opportunities for power or gain, and by feelings of generosity and magnanimity; it was above all subject to the rules of mob psychology, well known though yet unnamed. In 1866 all these factors played exaggerated rôles as they always do in the excitement of material and mental readjustment which follows war.

The people are never swayed by one interest alone; they are rarely confronted by but one issue. A single issue may overbalance all others, but the others remain. It is dangerous to project the present into the past by interpreting that past through what appears, in the light of later unpredictable developments, to have been the paramount interest. Under the American system of elections it is usually impossible for the voters at the time, or historians in the future, to ascertain with any precision the determining interests. Party leaders have sought not to define, but to evade and conceal issues. Under the American two-party system it is always difficult for an individual to know how to vote wisely. Many voters adhere to principles because they bear the party label, instead of supporting the party because it will advance certain principles. But where an individual does try to think independently it is almost impossible to determine which man or which party will best advance the largest number of political interests of the voter. The thoughtful voter usually comes to the conclusion that neither party and neither candidate suits him, and votes the least objectionable ticket. The next man with like interests may under like conditions make a reverse decision. Popular votes in America, then, only exceptionally decide public questions, or show popular sentiment upon definite issues. Party loyalty, successful advertising, mob psychology, skilful crea-

tion of confidence or, more potent still, distrust, popular fears and passions—in short, psychological elements, efficient campaign machinery,
and access to the public ear—play more significant rôles than do the
merits of issues or party platforms.

It is in the light of these realities that the election of 1866 must be
studied. Most historians and thoughtful public men now condemn
the Radical program of reconstruction. Yet it was adopted. These men
differ in analyzing the causes underlying the failure of the Johnson
policy, but they generally agree in assigning as chief among them the
unreasonable conduct of the South and the stubbornness and stupidity
of Johnson. While they condemn the man, many have come to regard
Johnson's policy as the most statesmanlike of any. Some of his bitterest
enemies lived to acknowledge this. Yet it failed. To understand its
failure and Radical success, comparative wisdom of policies and constitutional theories must be thrown aside as inconsequential; other
factors popularly thought to be determining issues must be reduced
to their true 1866 proportions, and the methods and spirit of the campaign must be studied. Reconstruction was decided not through a consideration of the wisdom of various plans, but by a skilful use of the
tools of political campaigning.

The Radicals for one reason or another feared the return of Southerners to participation in government. After a great war, bitterness
was natural. Men who had lost loved ones in battle, did not look with
pleasure upon the return to power of the men who had slain them.
Allowed to cool and tempered by a return of friendly commercial and
political intercourse, this sentiment would soon have subsided, for
magnanimity to a vanquished foe is not difficult. In the West and in
the border communities, numerous relationships had bound North and
South before the War; between these sections passions had fired more
quickly, and conflict had raged more violently than between the South
and more distant New England. But after all, reconciliation was easier
between two interrelated sections which knew each other's good qual-
ities, than between the South and a remote Northeast which condemned
each other as inherently wicked, and hated each other with the hate
of long years of abolition controversy.

While resentment against Copperheads was most violent in the West
and border East, bitterness toward the South was cooling rapidly in
non-abolitionist circles and, let alone, would gradually have died out.
Abolitionists, however, had embraced as part of their creed belief in
Southern wickedness, expressed in their definition of the Constitution
as "a covenant with death and an agreement with hell." Many New
England teachers and preachers throughout the North continued with

all sincerity to paint Southerners as disciples of the devil. Those who held this view of the South, opposed its return to participation in government.

To many, abolitionism had become a religion which made it a God-given duty, now that the slaves were free, to elevate them to civil and political equality with the white man. Many such "Niggerheads" knew nothing of the Southern negro, but they devoutly believed in their own theories; others of them actually worked with the negroes as missionaries and teachers, but like many reformers were blinded to practical difficulties by their own enthusiasm. Typical of these sincere "friends of the negro" was Charles Sumner.

Men did actually believe that if the "rebels" were allowed to regain political power, they would yet overturn the government. Many feared the return of "traitors" to offices from which loyal men would be displaced. But often such expressions of fear merely signified that a man dreaded to see good Republicans replaced by Democrats.

Many Northerners honestly saw in the Black Codes a Southern attempt to reenslave the black; others were interested in the negro chiefly because his vote would be a Republican one, and would counteract that of his white neighbor.

But a considerable group dreaded the return of Southerners to power not because they feared disaster to the nation, but because they foresaw in it injury to themselves, their section, or their class. For many years Southern statesmen had controlled the destinies of the country. Since the days when her own young-bloods had urged secession for New England, the industrial Northeast had been a "minority section." It was not powerless on questions where South and West divided, or where factors which bisected every community were concerned, but on such issues as the tariff or an agricultural or industrial dispute New England and the increasingly industrial Northeast were still a minority section. For thirty years Southerners or Northern "Doughfaces" had been supreme in the federal government. Now after a long and bloody war, a purely Northern party had conquered the South and won for itself and its section long-sought power which was not lightly to be surrendered. Sheer love of power made many men hesitate before voluntarily relinquishing it by allowing Southerners to return to Congress. To politicians, whose chief function is to elect themselves and members of their party to office, retention of control seemed a sufficient cause for Radicalism, but this motive could not be publicly avowed.

For years before the War, the Northeast had been unable to get protection for industry. Then during the Civil War high taxes on industry had made necessary a high tariff, and, with the South out of the way and the North rather evenly divided, protectionists had managed to make the tariffs more than cover the taxes they supposedly offset. If the South were readmitted before this high tariff was permanently established, the protectionists would be overwhelmed.

Bondholders throughout the country feared, and were encouraged to fear, a repudiation of the debt through a return of Southern representatives. The South was traditionally opposed to national banks; hence, Eastern bankers and supporters of the new national banking system dreaded to see the South return. Hard money men, deflationists, business men who wished federal protection in the extension of their business into what they feared would be an inhospitable South, land speculators who sought confiscated lands, and new corporations that feared government regulation or sought government aid, shared this dread. The growing capital-owning group of the Northeast,[1] then, sought to keep the South out until through negro suffrage it could be brought under Northern control. The agricultural and debtor classes, on the other hand, would have welcomed Southern aid in Washington. Here was really in a new phase the familiar American struggle of East against West, old settled region against frontier, business against agriculture, city against country, "haves" against "have-nots," that made a civil war of the American Revolution, that turned Jeffersonians against Hamiltonians, Jacksonian Democrats against Whigs, and more recently farm bloc against Wall Street. This old antagonism and not a difference of opinion on the condition of Southerners, was what divided Conservatives and Radicals in 1866.

Radical leaders faced a perplexing problem. They were only a minority group. The two major issues motivating their campaign were their stand on various economic questions and their desire to secure the Republican Party in power. But the Radical leaders could not ask the people to support them merely because of their desire for power. Still less did they dare raise the economic questions. Indeed, they had to fight desperately against their being raised by the Conservatives, for on economic issues they would have lost half their party.

On the reconstruction issue unconfused, the major portion of the people originally supported Johnson; hence, the Radicals had to raise mere shibboleths. Had other Radicals been as fair-minded, as public-spirited, and as tolerant as Governor Andrew, Johnson's reputation would not have been destroyed, and there would have been no split between Congress and the President. Andrew, though a negro suffragist,

[1] Except the merchants.

deprecated the Radical tactics. "I am opposed to public meetings," he said, "called in support of . . . any man, leader or party. . . . Now, if one set of men get up meetings for Paul, another set will get up meetings for Apollos. The result will be antagonism, not patriotism; and intensifying, and exaggerating the importance and value, of the relatively unimportant, chance-utterances of individuals in controversial moods; which ought if possible, to be forgotten. . . . I, for one, desire not to encourage popular excitement, most of all, not to aid in making any." But in the creation of this very situation which Andrew deplored, lay the Radicals' best hope of success.

The repudiation shibboleth was safe throughout the country. In the East economic issues could be insinuated into the campaign, for Eastern supporters knew well the stand Radical leaders would take on them; in the West, when the Conservatives raised them, they were shouted down as nonpolitical and irrelevant. Talk of the return of rebels to power conveyed a plain second meaning to the protectionist and to the creditor, whereas it was taken at face value in the West. If the South could be excluded, or admitted only with negro suffrage, the new industrial order which the Northeast was developing, would be safe. Intentionally, then, the issues were befogged. Definite economic questions of importance confronted the country, issues on which a majority, even without the South, would have supported Johnson against the Radicals, issues which ten years later arose to plague the country. In 1866 these questions were pushed into the background, the South was kept out, and the Northeast succeeded in establishing minority government until the new industrial forces were strongly enough entrenched to withstand attacks.

Throughout the campaign constitutional arguments bulked large. It was a day when constitutional theories were required for all practice. But in our Anglo-Saxon world constitutional theories are derived from practice, not practice from theory. People were vitally interested in deciding whether the South should have its former place in the government or should be held in subjugation for a period of years, but they were not much interested in the theory of the right or wrong of either course, except as a justification in law for what they intended to do in practice. Lawyers and Congressmen, true to form, made lengthy speeches on matters of constitutionality, for this gave them an air of erudition, and satisfied the legalistic conscience of their constituents. Nevertheless constitutional discussions of the rights of the negro, the status of Southern states, the legal position of ex-rebels, and the powers of Congress and president determined nothing. They were pure shams.

We have already found that the condition and temper of the South, especially in the light of biased fabrication or deceptive half-knowledge, proved a favorite topic of political oratory in 1866. In a study of the issues this and the negro question and the Fourteenth Amendment must not be accepted at their campaign valuation. Other factors not recognized in the campaign literature as issues, must be considered because of their potential and actual importance. Politicians' tricks and machinery must be studied as the really determining factor. Claptrap and issues must be distinguished.

Economic Factors in the Abandonment of Reconstruction

WILLIAM B. HESSELTINE

This important essay of the mid-1930s sought to refine the Beard-Beale analysis of Reconstruction by asking the further question: If in fact the purpose of Radical Republicanism was to safeguard the wartime economic gains of Northern capitalism, was there a complete identity of purpose between professional politicians in the Republican Party and the businessmen who (according to the thesis) stood behind them and in the last analysis determined party policy?

Hesseltine answered, No. At first Republican politicians and Northern businessmen shared a desire to prevent the return to Congress of representatives from the Southern states (ironically, a representation more numerous because of the abolition of slavery, since after 1865 Southern Negroes were counted as whole men rather than as three-fifths men in apportioning Southern representation in the House of Representatives). But if the possibility of Democratic majorities in Congress seemed threatening to Northern businessmen, so too was the continued unrest in the South produced by Congressional Reconstruction which made orderly business activity there difficult. Hence, according to Hesseltine, about 1870 businessmen "who preferred the economic

The Mississippi Valley Historical Review, Vol. XXII (September, 1935), pp. 191–210. Reprinted with the permission of the Organization of American Historians.

to the political exploitation of the South" began to conclude that the return to power in the South of conservative Democrats who could create stability and order might best serve their interests. Greeley's Liberal Republican campaign in 1872 was the political expression of this tendency, the regular or "stalwart" Republican politicians supporting Grant.

C. Vann Woodward's *Reunion And Reaction* (1951) elaborated the Hesseltine thesis, arguing that Reconstruction was abandoned when in 1877 Northern and Southern propertied interests came to an understanding.

B Y COMMON CONSENT, PRESIDENT RUTHERFORD B. HAYES'S withdrawal of the federal troops from the South has been accepted as the end of reconstruction. The President's action, however, was but the outward and visible symbol of an already accomplished revolution in northern sentiment. For a number of years the northern voters had been coming to realize that the effort to force the South into the northern political mold was both costly and futile.

Commentators on the politics of the Reconstruction period have ascribed this reversal of opinion to the rise of new interests among the northern electorate, or have dismissed it with a remark that the people had grown tired of the southern question in politics. Such an interpretation fails to consider that reconstruction itself was an economic as well as a political problem, and that it was not until the political program failed to bring economic results that the control of the South was returned to the southern white man.

Fundamentally, reconstruction was the method by which the "Masters of Capital" sought to secure their victory over the vanquished "Lords of the Manor," and through which they expected to exploit the resources of the southern states. Long before the war was over cotton speculators, acting as the vanguard of an economic army, followed the advancing federal armies and annoyed commanders from the Red River to the Potomac by their persistent efforts to carry on trade with the South. Behind the lines, less mobile entrepreneurs calculated the possibility of carrying the northern economic system into the South at the close of hostilities. In the first months after Appomattox, business men in the North looked for immediate profits from the return of peace and endorsed General Ulysses S. Grant's leniency and President Andrew Johnson's plans for a speedy restoration of the southern states. One of Grant's aides-de-camp found that in the summer of 1865 "all the sober, substantial men" of New York, St. Louis, and Washington were in favor of Johnson's policy. Impressed with the necessity for southern industrial rehabilitation, the New York *Commercial and Financial Chronicle* ingratiatingly assured the South that the northern people contemplated no oppression but would accord the southern states an early readmission to the Union.

Totally ignoring the psychoses of the conquered southerners, northern financial circles seemed to believe that the South would "treat political questions as secondary" until industrial recuperation had been accomplished. This recovery, of course, would be the result of northern capital, in the hands of northern men, flowing into the South. "There can be no way so sure to make the late rebels of the South loyal men and good citizens," declared the New York organ of the financiers, "as to turn their energies to the pursuits of peace, and the accumulation of wealth." When goods from southern factories appeared in the New York markets, they caused this journal to remember that in 1860 there had been 350 woolen mills and 180 cotton mills in the South and that the total value of southern manufactured goods had been over $238,000,000! "Now," proclaimed the hopeful editor, "Northern men, accustomed to business, have gone South and will give a new impetus" to industrial development.

In order to encourage northern men to migrate to the South commercial newspapers began to advertise the South as the nation's new land of opportunity. The abundance of land, the manufacturing possibilities, the climate, soil, water-power, and timber of the South came in for extensive exposition, and the figures of the South's exports in 1860—over two hundred million dollars—were dangled before the eyes of the northern people. The South was assured that an immigration of new and energetic people would begin as soon as the Johnsonian governments were fully established.

Such roseate dreams of a golden harvest in the South were rudely shattered when the southerners began to take stock of their own position. In the first days after the war planters welcomed ex-officers of the Union armies who came to purchase cotton plantations, but few of these adventurers were successful either in handling negroes or in living harmoniously with their white neighbors. Political differences which engendered social ostracism and even physical violence soon developed, and the northerners returned to their homes none the richer for their experience. Instead of welcoming immigrants and making provisions to receive migrating capitalists, the provisional governments under Johnson's program showed more interest in attempting to solve the economic problems of an agrarian area.

Some efforts, however, were made by several of the states to attract immigrants, and boards of immigration were set up by the Reconstruction governments. But only in Tennessee was there a real enthusiasm for the task. There the East Tennesseans, who had never been a part of the cotton kingdom but had long nursed secret ambitions to become industrialized, controlled the state and made a serious effort to entice northern capital. Newspapers appealed to Tennesseans to advertise their lands, mill and factory sites, and mines in order to attract merchants, manufacturers, and bankers—"the very class of men . . . whose help is needed in developing the wealth of our great State." The legislature generously chartered a number of "immigration" companies in order to assist expected immigrants, and in December, 1867, a State Board of Immigration was established. The board employed an energetic commissioner to advertise the state's resources in the North and in Europe. In radical Missouri there was also a welcome to immigrants, but in other parts of the South a suspicion of the political motives of the migrants caused them to be either ostracized or mistreated.

The attitude of the southerners was not long in being reported to Congress. "Loyal" citizens, Unionists, and northern immigrants appealed to congressmen for protection against the "frightful spirit of lawlessness extant among the late rebels." From Virginia to Texas plaintive letters to congressmen told the story of bad treatment. Already the Radicals in Congress had determined to force negro suffrage on the South in order to maintain the Republican party in power. Under the added stimulus of the anguished cries of business men both North and South the congressional program of reconstruction was formulated. The Fourteenth Amendment would protect the property of Union men in the South and by disfranchising the leaders of the old agricultural South would enable "loyal" men and Negroes to enact the legislation which would protect the northern capitalist in exploiting the South. When the southern states rejected the amendment, Congress proceeded to carry its program into effect. Only radical Tennessee, whose arms were outstretched in welcome to invading capital, was admitted to representation in Congress.

The passage of the Reconstruction Act of March 2, 1867, renewed the hope of a migration of capital and labor to the South. Union men in Virginia looked forward to the migration of "Northern men with capital and enterprise to develop the resources of our fields and forests." Moreover a political purpose would be served for such people, wrote a citizen of Richmond, "by their social intercourse and votes . . . would do much to neutralize the prejudices and influence of parties inimical to the Government." When General James A. Longstreet renounced his Confederate heresies in favor of southern prosperity, Massachusetts' Ben Butler hastened to welcome him to the radical fold. If all southerners would take Longstreet's views, Butler foresaw that "harmony of feeling, community of interest, unity of action as well as homogeneity of institutions" would follow to produce national well being.

But Longstreet was almost alone in his decision to "accept the results of the war" and the military governments in the South could do little to further the North's exploitation of its southern colony. Men who had gone South for economic reasons took advantage of the changed situation to recoup their losses in politics, and others came from the North solely for the plums of office. But the Union men and northerners in the South continued to find themselves at a disadvantage. The property of loyalists was not safe in the courts, and Ben Butler soon heard appeals from the Unionists to turn the courts over to loyal men. "The Northern man will not come here unless his capital is safe," declared one of Butler's Georgia informants. From Texas it was reported that rebel leaders were growing rich but that there was no hope for Union men. On the advice of the "best financiers" Butler decided to abandon his own extensive investments in the South, although he contemplated, according to one newspaper, a bill which would prevent disfranchised rebels from holding office on railroads or chartered companies.

The New York *Commercial and Financial Chronicle,* a consistent supporter of Johnson's policy, soon found that Congressional Reconstruction was paralyzing business and unnecessarily prolonging southern industrial prostration. If Negro majorities controlled the state legislatures, the paper warned, capital would stay out of the section. Despite this analysis, the Radicals pursued their course and blamed bad conditions on President Johnson. When the Tennessee legislature met in December, 1867, Governor William G. Brownlow, the "Fighting Parson," reported that "men of capital and enterprise" had not come into the state in the expected numbers. This was due to Andrew Johnson's "insane policy" of holding out to "pestilential disloyalists" the hope that they would be restored to power. Butler agreed with this contention and declared that only a new president could insure the property rights of northerners in the South.

During the campaign of 1868 Democratic orators took pains to assert that peace and prosperity could only come through the abandonment of Congressional Reconstruction, but Republicans, saying little of the economic rehabilitation of the South, made much of the southerner's vindictiveness towards the Union men and loyal negroes of the South. Ku Klux outrages and Democratic murders constituted the main theme of the Republicans, despite the fact that these very stories would serve as a deterrent to capital seeking southern investments. In their belief, interest in manufactures and agriculture would "supersede the excitement of the caucus" and the South would "turn all her energies to . . . developing her immense resources" as soon as the election was over. When friction ceased, business would "spring to its feet . . . manufacture . . . unchain her idle wheels," and "the cotton and rice plantations of the South . . . vie - with the cornfields of the West." In the end, the business man of the North voted for the Republicans, not because he was convinced by this reasoning but because the party stood for the payment of the national debt in gold.

Republican success in the election of 1868 was widely interpreted as settling the disorders in the South. "The election of Grant and Colfax means peace," cried Tennessee's Brownlow. "It means that carpetbaggers are not to be molested in Tennessee; that capital, coming to us from abroad, whether of brains or hands, or money, is not to be spurned, proscribed, persecuted, because it comes from north of a given line." According to Horace Greeley, immigrants could now be safely invited into the country, and two-thirds of them would "go to build up the waste places of the South." Greeley also noticed that the election would insure the reconstruction of Virginia where northern capital was waiting for a favorable government before it advanced money for the completion of a railroad from the Ohio to the Chesapeake Bay. Even from ex-Confederates in the South there came echoes of the same conclusion. One Alabamian, who had served in the Confederate army and had voted against Grant, wrote to Butler that his state wanted to "induce men of capital and skill" to come in. "If you are desirous for the welfare of the South, and wish to be personally highly remunerated and at the same time become a public benefactor, you can accomplish these objects better than in any other manner by inducing your men of means and skill to invest their money and skill" in the South. John Letcher, erstwhile war-governor of Virginia, looked forward to a speedy settlement of the political controversies in order that the prosperity of his section might be assured.

President Grant entered office determined to end the conflict in the South. His first action on reconstruction was to submit the constitutions of Virginia, Texas, and Mississippi to a vote without the obnoxious clauses which disfranchised the Confederate leaders. This action was immediately hailed with satisfaction, and northern business men looked to the complexion of political reconstruction as the beginning of southern prosperity. In Virginia, the Conservatives of the state rapidly formed a party pledged to the acceptance of the Fifteenth Amendment, to the development of industry, and to the encouragement of immigration. "In short," commented Greeley, "Virginia, having had enough of Civil War and devastation, is about to subordinate political strife to industrial progress and material prosperity, and thus advance to a future of power and wealth undreamed of in her past." On the eve of the Virginia election, General J. D. Imboden, who had served his state from Bull Run to Appomattox, wrote to the *Tribune* that northern men were safe and welcome in Virginia. Millions of white men were needed to develop the state's resources. There was no doubt that Virginia was succumbing to the lure of profits. In May, 1869, General Lee visited Washington on railroad business, and called at the White House to assure Grant that Virginia favored the Fifteenth Amendment and Negro suffrage!

The Virginia elections were the quietest that had taken place in the South since secession, but the resultant Conservative victory struck terror into the ranks of the radical Republican politicians. On economic issues the newly elected governor, Gilbert G. Walker, was in thorough accord with the masters of capital who were backing the Republican party in the North. His party accepted Negro suffrage and stood for the industrialization of the state, yet there was little doubt that the Virginia Conservatives would unite with the northern Democracy in national elections. Faced with this certainty, Republican politicians sought for an excuse to keep the state under military government, while Walker hurried to Washington to lay his case before Grant and to promise that the Conservatives would not recant on their promises to ratify the Fifteenth Amendment.

The dissatisfaction of the politicians with this development was soon revealed. Although the politicians represented the masters of capital who were interested in tariffs, railroads, and the exploitation of the South, they were themselves more interested in the preservation of their party in power. The only member of Grant's cabinet who was a politician was Secretary of the Treasury George S. Boutwell, who immediately declared his unalterable opposition to the Virginia results. Publicly, he counselled caution, taking, according to the disgusted Greeley, "more account of the unity and coherence of the Republican party than of the triumph of its cardinal principle." Intent upon preventing a repetition of this miscarriage Boutwell condemned the Conservative party in Mississippi and persuaded Grant to repudiate his brother-in-law, Louis Dent, whom the Conservatives had nominated for governor. So great was the pressure of the politicians that Grant yielded to their wishes in Texas and threw the weight of the administration's influence into the scales against the Conservative candidate.

Boutwell's attitude foreshadowed the imminent separation between those who would exploit the South for political advantage and those who sought a field for economic expansion. Moderate Republicans, such as

James A. Garfield, deplored the violence that existed in Texas and Mississippi at the same time they commended the peaceful reconstruction of Virginia. Radicals of the Butler stripe, on the other hand, were convinced that Virginia had deceived the Republican party. The victory of the Conservatives in Tennessee in 1869 and the action of the Georgia legislature in expelling its Negro members seemed to them sufficient indication that the South was not yet reconciled to the Union. Butler's own losses in three southern investments had convinced him that capital was not yet safe in the South.

After the election of 1868 Horace Greeley had become the principal exponent of northern infiltration into the South. In much the same manner that he had formerly urged the male youth to seek the West, he now devoted the columns of the powerful New York *Tribune* to urging groups to settle in the South. Southern land which had been worth twenty dollars an acre before the war and would soon be worth that again could be bought for one or two dollars an acre. Advising settlement in colonies, Greeley estimated that three thousand colonists in Florida, five thousand each in Alabama, Louisiana, Arkansas, and Mississippi, and ten thousand each in Virginia, North Carolina, and Texas would make the South Republican and deliver it from "the nightmare which now oppresses . . . politics and industry." Within the South, said Greeley, there was a division between two classes on the issues of reconstruction. The "landholders, merchants and men of property, with all who are inclined to industry and thrift" were opposed by a "decreasing faction of sore-heads and malignants." In issue after issue of his paper, the expansionist editor carried articles by the first class of southerners setting forth the advantages of various sections of the South for immigrants and for capital investments. As the Virginia question arose, Greeley reiterated that the South was begging for immigrants and for northern capital and a *Tribune* correspondent wandered through the South gathering details of the wealth awaiting northern enterprise. North Carolina offered cheap land, docile laborers, ample timber resources, and political peace. In South Carolina there were woolen mills and cotton factories. Tennessee had blast furnaces already established by northern capital and there were rich opportunities for investment in mines of iron, coal, zinc, and copper. The South, editorialized the *Tribune,* had shown a general willingness to come back into the Union on the Greeley platform of "universal amnesty and universal suffrage."

The fundamental issues between the politicians and the business men were clearly brought out in an open letter from Greeley to Butler. Appealing to Butler's practical sense, the editor showed that the Radical program of proscription and disfranchisement had retarded business. In reply, Butler declared that Greeley's course had encouraged the rebels so that they had gained the upper hand in Tennessee and Georgia. In these states, the people had deceived the Republican party. Conditions would have been better if a half dozen leading rebels had been hung at the end of the war.

In the winter of 1869–70 these divergent views were advanced in the debates over the admission of Virginia and over the treatment to be accorded to recalcitrant Georgia. In the end, Virginia was admitted, although the Radicals had many misgivings. Georgia was remanded to military rule. Not even Greeley could defend the action of the "rebel element" in Georgia and both Moderates and Radicals were agreed that outrages against Republicans in the South should stop. As a means of stopping them, both elements heralded the ratification of the Fifteenth Amendment and supported the "Force Bill" of 1870 which would guarantee the right of suffrage to the negroes. To the Radicals the martial law in Georgia and the Enforcement Act were means of getting Republican majorities in the South; to the Moderates, the hope of eventual peace carried with it the promise of a prosperous infiltration of northern business in the South. In Greeley's opinion, it was time to "have done with Reconstruction." "The country is . . . sick of it," he added. "So long as any State is held in abeyance, it will be plausibly urged that the Republicans are afraid to trust the People. Let us give every State to herself, and then punish any who violate or defy the guaranties of public and personal rights now firmly imbedded in the Constitution."

Although Moderates and Radicals had agreed on the Fifteenth Amendment and the Enforcement Act there were differences between them on the method to be pursued in the future. Radical politicians of the school of Conkling, Morton, Chandler, and Butler looked to the power of the president to enforce the law, while Greeley and the Moderates continued to appeal to the South's hopes of prosperity as a means of producing peace. The advantages of immigration, the possibility of industrial development, and the potentialities of the South's mineral wealth were constantly kept before the southerners.

Despite Greeley's appeals, the majority of the southern states offered few inducements to northern migrants. The competition of western lands prevented new agricultural groups entering the South while cases of violence were constantly reported which discouraged those who might have thought of carrying their capital into southern industry. Greeley's Washington correspondent suspected that most of the outrage stories were "manufactured and published in the North to further the personal designs of unscrupulous and ambitious men." Yet a *Tribune* agent in the

South in the summer of 1870 found the Ku Klux in undeniable operation. Throughout the congressional campaigns the North was flooded
with atrocity stories, and a congressional investigation in the succeeding
winter gave ample evidence that the Klan was terrorizing the South.
The results of these outrages was the passage of two more acts which
would keep the South orderly: the Federal Elections Act of February
28, and the Ku Klux Act of April 20, 1871.

In contemplating the southern scene, Moderates found themselves
forced to admit that violence and political murders prevented business
recovery and impelled the government to take action. Greeley, however,
continued to advise moderation and amnesty as a more suitable means
of inducing the southerners to accept a real economic reconstruction. In
Congress, Garfield doubted the constitutionality of the "Force Acts" and
declared that the legislation was "working on the very edge of the
Constitution." Nevertheless, he found that a "kind of party terrorism"
forced all Republicans to vote for the measures. To J. D. Cox, Grant's
former secretary of the interior, it seemed that Congress was pursuing the
wrong course in attempting to conquer the South. "Capital and intelligence must lead," he told Garfield. "Only Butler and W. Philips would
make a wilderness and call it peace." The party should organize and
appeal to the "thinking and influential native Southerners"—the "intelligent, well-to-do, and controlling class" of southern whites.

Soon after the passage of the Ku Klux Act, Greeley sent correspondents
into the South to study conditions. The reporters found that the Klan
was overrunning South Carolina, but that the carpetbaggers, who were
levying high taxes upon industry and wealth, were giving partial justification for the outrages. Late in May, Greeley himself traveled through
the Southwest to speak on the glories of industry at the Texas State
Fair. The New Yorker's speeches inspired the editor of the New Orleans
Price Current to comment that the industrial doctrines of Greeley and
Seward had conquered the South. "It is the true duty of the South,"
declared the New Orleans editor, "to cultivate all those industries the
want of which has enslaved her." But Greeley had concluded from his
observations that the South would not be prosperous until the carpetbaggers with their taxes and the Ku Klux with its violence had both
been driven out. The South, said Greeley, was suffering from "decayed
aristocracy and imported rascality."

From this time of his southern trip Greeley was a candidate for the
presidency. From what he had seen in the South, however, he changed
his earlier ideas that capital would enter the South. The high taxes which
the carpetbag and negro governments had imposed was sufficient to prevent the migration of capital, but the editor believed that prosperity

might yet come through the efforts of the southerners themselves. There were millions of acres in the South which might be sold to immigrants, and the proceeds devoted to the development of local resources. The primary needs of the South, as Greeley came to see it, were more people, more skill, more energy, and greater thrift. The South did not need more capital than would naturally flow into it if the people should use their available resources. To his earlier program of universal amnesty and universal suffrage, the editor added the proposal that the South should work out its own salvation by encouraging northern immigration and, by driving out carpetbaggers, make a land free from oppressive taxes upon industry.

Opposed to these ideas, which were politically adopted by the Liberal Republicans, the regular Republicans insisted upon the necessity of maintaining control of the politics of the southern states in order to protect migrating capital and people. Social ostracism and personal violence, said President Grant in his message of 1871, prevented "immigration and the flow of much-needed capital into the States lately in rebellion." The South, echoed the New York *Times* in the midst of the campaign, needed local governments which would protect citizens. Only the Republican party could assume solid achievement and national prosperity and "restrain with firmness any resistance to the new order of things." The South had always depended upon outside capital and the war had destroyed whatever accumulation might have existed. "Industry is sluggish, trade creeps from point to point, manufactures are feeble and few," cried the administration journal as it demanded a continuation of the policy which held out "every encouragement . . . to Northern and foreign capitalists." As the campaign went on Greeley's *Tribune* carried more items concerning available southern farm lands and showed that "had it not been for carpetbag mismangaement, this country today would be filled with millions of Northern or foreign yeomanry carving out farms, or working in . . . iron, copper, coal, and marble." At the same time, Secretary Boutwell went into North Carolina to sing the praises of the carpetbaggers, and assure the North Carolinians that neither immigrants nor capital could be safe in Democratic regions. "The business men of the South," wrote a carpetbagger to the Republican National Committee, "want stability in business, which the election of Greeley . . . will not insure."

Although other factors combined to prevent Greeley's election, his southern program had made considerable impression on the voters. The carpetbaggers had received much unfavorable publicity during the campaign, and the idea that the friction between the races in the South was caused by dishonest adventurers who drove out industry, was widely spread over the North. In the next few years the horrors of carpet-baggery were to be proclaimed by the "liberal" and Democratic press until the masters of capital were convinced that only the removal of this "swarm of locusts" would make possible the economic exploitation of the section.

At the close of the election, Greeley sadly turned to advise the southerners to accept the situation, and "set to work to build up their section's industrial and commercial prosperity." This advice, said the defeated candidate, would sound harsh to men who were unable to pay the enormous taxes imposed by the carpetbaggers. How little encouragement the South might receive from the government in such an effort was evident from the attitude of the administration press. The New York *Times* ridiculed Greeley's efforts to advise his supporters, and the administration organ in Washington announced that the South was responsible for any misfortunes which had come upon it. Acceptance of Republicanism, the paper implied, was the only hope for the section.

The country had not long to wait for the development of the Republican policy in the South. Following immediately upon the election there ensued a struggle between two groups of carpetbaggers for the control of Louisiana. Although President Grant attempted to remain impartial between the contending factions, the New York *Tribune*, continuing its rôle as the Bible of the industrialists, lost no opportunity to point out the intimate connection between Republican policies and the disordered commonwealth. It spoke feelingly about the "plundered community," showed that its government was founded upon fraud, and declared that the dispute "prostitutes the business of the State." Louisiana finances were kept before the eye of the northern people, and the "moneyed interests of the country" were warned against investments in a state whose governor could sell its railroad interests without consulting the legislature and which had a debt of twenty-four millions.

At the same time that Louisiana was troubling the political waters other points of the South were contributing testimony to the economic derangements attendant upon carpetbag governments. In Arkansas there were quarrels between factions of the Republican party comparable to those in Louisiana, whilst the debts and taxes of the state were rising. The *Tribune* published a traveller's account of the corruption and the absurdities of the "prostrate State" of South Carolina where a handful of unscrupulous whites controlled the negro legislature. If anything were needed to impress the lesson it was furnished by the condition in the District of Columbia. At the beginning of reconstruction, Congress had granted the suffrage to the negroes of the District. Designed as an experiment to show the capacity of the negro for citizenship, it soon showed the reverse. Under "Boss" Shepherd's direction the negroes voted for new bond issues and went to the polls to approve the valiant plans which the District governor was making to pull the capital city out of the mud. But the property holders and tax payers of the District outvoted by the negroes, ignored the improvements to gaze with horrible forebodings upon the mounting debt. This was sufficiently close to the northern voter and tax payer to clarify his view on the Radical program in the South. Perhaps an underlying fear, which few dared to express, was the danger which was involved in the rising movement of the lower classes throughout the country. The Granger movement in the West was assailing the citadels of private monopoly, and there was a conceivable connection between these elements and the "bottom rails" who had gotten on top in the South. Two years before, one observer had noticed that there were six thousand native adult whites in Georgia "who cannot read or write, and if to them were added the whole bulk of the negro population, so vast a mass of ignorance would be found that, if combined for any political purpose it would sweep away all opposition the intelligent class might make. Many thoughtful men are apprehensive that the ignorant voters will, in the future, form a party by themselves as dangerous to the interests of society as the communists of France."

Evidence of a growing reaction in the North came simultaneously with these troubles in the South. In May, 1873, Senator Matt Carpenter, long a supporter of the extreme Radical position, visited Louisiana with a congressional committee. To the people of New Orleans the Wisconsin Senator promised a better government and urged that they turn their attention from politics to trade and business. Eugene Hale, a member of Congress from Maine, presiding over his state's Republican convention, announced that he was "tired and sick of some of the carpet-bag governments." Generally, men were coming to the belief that the poverty of the southern states was due to the villainies of the carpetbaggers, and they were coming to perceive that this had a national significance. The "withdrawal of taxes, which the Southern States might pay under favorable circumstances, throws just that additional burden upon the tax-paying property of the North," announced the *Tribune*. Even George F. Hoar came to admit that the character of the carpetbaggers was such that they would not have been tolerated in the North.

With the development of a sentiment of opposition to the carpetbaggers, there came a new hope that a change of policy might throw the South open for migration of capital and for manufacturing. Surveying the situation, it was noticed that only South Carolina and Louisiana were still in 1873 oppressed by excessive taxes, while the other states might welcome northern mills and factories. Virginia, for example, had accepted reconstruction, avoided carpetbaggers, and proceeded forward steadily in industrial development. The lesson was obvious—if the government abandoned its policy of upholding carpetbaggers, prosperity would come to the South. Propositions for moving New England cotton mills to the South were reported and discussed in the press and on the floors of Congress. Even southerners took a new hope from the renewed discussion of capital moving South.

Standing in the way of a change of policy stood the fact that stories of southern outrages had been the stock in trade of the Radicals since 1866 and the politicians had no thought of abandoning so profitable a source of political ammunition. But even the "outrage business" received a death blow in the congressional campaign of 1874. In the midst of the campaign an Alabama congressman published a list of murders and acts of violence which had recently taken place in his state. Long suspicious of such stories, the New York *Tribune* immediately investigated and found no substantial basis for the congressman's charges. Thereafter the accumulating atrocity stories were received dubiously by the northern people. However, the southern carpetbaggers were merely goaded into action by this exposure and a hastily called convention of Republican politicians assembled in Chattanooga to prepare an authentic list of atrocities for the benefit of the northern voter and to convince Congress that further protection should be given at elections. But the convention proved abortive. While a number of the delegates came prepared to contribute atrocity stories and demand more federal interference, a larger number were found to have come to the convention to prevent a "new flood of misrepresentations" which would "frighten men and capital from their neglected fields and factories." This latter class was composed of men who had become identified with the material interests of the South. Delegates from North Carolina were ready to declare that they had not heard of a political assault in their state for more than a year. The convention appointed a committee on "Facts and Statistics" which never reported, and passed general resolutions asserting that violence toward loyal men was common, but the total effect of their meeting was to give the South a clean bill of health. With the "outrage" business played out, the Republicans were deprived of their leading arguments for continuing in power, while the Democrats and the Liberal Republicans insisted that business was injured by the plundering governments of the southern states. Testimony was sedulously gathered by the *Tribune* to show that their were no outrages in Tennessee or Kentucky and that migrating capital was safe in those states.

The eventual victory of those who preferred the economic to the political exploitation of the South was foreshadowed in the election returns. The Democrats won control of Congress, and Republican politicians turned to a new stock taking. "We have got a hard lot from the South," said Postmaster-General Marshall Jewell as he surveyed the carpetbag governments, "and the people will not submit to it any longer, nor do I blame them." To Jewell's mind the carpetbaggers did not have "among them one really first class man." A consul in Germany thought it "to d——d bad that our party should be ruined and have to go to the wall through the careless labors of such cattle" as the Louisiana carpetbaggers. But, said this observer, the people were "tired out with this wornout cry of 'Southern Outrages!!!' Hard times and heavy taxes make them wish the 'nigger' 'everlasting nigger' were in ————— or Africa. . . . It is amazing the change that has taken place in the last two years in public sentiment." Even Vice-President Wilson concluded that the Republican party would have to change its policy, and noticed, after a trip through the South, that business conditions had improved and a spirit of industry was spreading among the southern whites. Wisconsin's Senator Howe ruefully regarded the wreck of Republican hopes and suddenly remembered that the war was not "fought for the 'nigger'" and the negro was not "the end and aim of all our effort."

The congressional elections of 1874 marked the abandonment of political reconstruction by the northern voters. The repudiated Radicals continued their course until after they had delivered the presidency to Hayes, but the popular vote in the North was cast in 1876 for Tilden and for a different method of exploiting the South. With the withdrawal of federal troops from the South, the masters of capital embarked upon a policy of conciliating their former enemies and of slow infiltration into their conquered but stubborn provinces.

A single glimpse at the situation a decade later will suffice to illustrate the new technique which the North came to employ in dealing with the South. In 1885 young William McKinley went to plead with the people of Virginia to send a protectionist to the Senate. "Do you imagine that anybody coming to Virginia with his money to build a mill, or a factory, or a furnace, and develop your coal and your ore, bring his money down here, when you vote every time against his interests. . . .?" he asked. "If you think so, you might just as well be undeceived now, for they will not come. . . . Be assured that the Republicans of the North harbor no resentments—only ask for the results of the war. They wish you the highest prosperity and the greatest development." The change from the method of coercion to that of appeal was great, but the hope was still alive that in spite of the abandonment of political reconstruction the South would receive the master of capital with his promises of prosperity.

Survival of the Plantation System in Louisiana

ROGER W. SHUGG

If the Civil War was a "bourgeois revolution," what effect did it have on the large plantations which dominated the ante-bellum Southern economy? Thaddeus Stevens had advocated confiscation of the plantations of leading Confederates so that freedmen (and poor whites) could have forty acres and a mule, in the belief that if "[Ye] seek first for the Negro a little land, all other things will be added unto him." Confiscation legislation failed, yet until the publication of Shugg's article in 1937 historians tended to assume that economic forces had brought about the division of large plantations which political efforts had failed to effect.

Shugg was content to state the facts. Other Marxist historians used them separate properties farms that, although individually operated, were actually owned by one man. He suggested that ante-bellum owners typically divided their plantations among sharecroppers, thus reducing the scale of farm management but not the scale of farm ownership.

Shugg was content to state the facts. Other Marxist historians used them analytically, contending that the failure to confiscate large landed properties in the South made the failure of Congressional Reconstruction inevitable. Thus James S. Allen concluded: "Defeated on the key issue of the revolution, the Negro people were handicapped from the start in the struggle for democratic rights. 'Without confiscation, the result of Negro suffrage will slip through their fingers,' declared a sage bourbon editor. When the

The Journal of Southern History, Vol. III (August 1937), pp. 311–325. Copyright 1937 by the Southern Historical Association. Reprinted by permission of the Managing Editor.

bourgeoisie lent a deaf ear to the cry for land, the fate of the revolution was already sealed." In the 1960s this analysis, somewhat less stridently expressed, was accepted by many non-Marxist scholars.

THERE HAS LONG BEEN A POPULAR BELIEF THAT AFTER THE CIVIL War plantations all over the South broke up into small farms. Between 1860 and 1880, according to census reports, the number of Southern landholdings was doubled, increasing from 549,109 to 1,252,249, and their average size was cut in half, declining from 365 to 157 acres. Such evidence is still cited in historical textbooks to prove that the old plantation system was destroyed by an agrarian revolution. This exaggerated idea arose from the failure of census marshals to distinguish between tenants and proprietors, lease- and freeholds. Because land rented by share croppers was put in the same category as farms owned outright, and the several tracts held by a planter were not registered as a single unit, it appeared that peasants rather than peons had taken the place of slaves.

While there was beyond doubt considerable redistribution in the ownership of real estate, to an extent which the historian is unable to measure for want of accurate census records, nevertheless the plantation system was not obliterated. In fertile regions where colored labor was plentiful, the large estate remained the primary basis of agricultural production. Far from there being any agrarian turnover, change was confined to methods of labor and finance. Planters thought it best, like a South Carolinian, "to work *several farms* on the same plantation," allotting parcels of their land to freedmen and controlling them through a form of credit known as the crop lien. Fields once cultivated by gangs of slaves were now worked by families who shared the produce with landlords; but the subdivision of these estates did not change their ownership. There was less discipline of labor and consequently less profit for capital than under the black codes of slavery. But "the planter princes of the old time," as Henry W. Grady observed, did not vanish from the South; they were "still lords of acres, though not of slaves."

When this fact was at last recognized by the census officials in 1910, they made a special survey of black belt counties, and for the first time designated as a plantation any continuous tract of land which was controlled by an individual or corporation but subdivided for cultivation among at least five tenants. According to this criterion, over one third of the landholdings in the black belt were found to be organized in plantations. The average size of these estates was 724 acres, or more than six times the average previously reported for all properties without regard to their consolidated ownership.

Although this survey disclosed the preservation of plantations, it came too late to correct the contrary reports of earlier decades, or to explain how large estates survived the vicissitudes of reconstruction. For this twofold purpose the unexamined manuscript assessment rolls of Louisiana, the state which contained the greatest plantations in 1910, were canvassed. Unfortunately, these ledgers leave much to be desired: almost all rolls before 1873 have been lost or destroyed; returns during reconstruction were grossly defective; until 1891 no distinction was made between the races to which owners and tenants belonged; and the number of tenants on each plantation was never recorded. Yet these local tax lists are a better index to agrarian tenure than the national census reports because they show the size of properties according to their actual ownership.

A typical cross section of the distribution of real estate in the planting regions of Louisiana after the Civil War is to be found in the records of five parishes. Two, Concordia in cotton and Iberville in cane sugar, represent the great plantations and staple crops of the Mississippi River bottoms. Two more, Cathoula and Lafourche, illustrate conditions in the adjoining regions of mixed soil and varied topography, where small properties were interspersed among the large, again in each staple. The last parish, Natchitoches, is divided between the cotton-growing alluvium of the Red River and the farming uplands of the north, where agrarian discontent broke forth in Populism during the nineties. Two of these five parishes, Lafourche and Catahoula, contained a majority of white people; the others belonged to the black belt.

The following table presents a statistical description of landholdings in these representative parishes. Because the number of tenants on each estate was never reported, even by local assessors, the size of a property is the only available criterion for distinguishing farms from plantations. I have followed local usage in classifying as plantations all properties of more than 100 acres; but since larger estates might often be cultivated without tenants, I have segregated those over 500 acres, which were impossible to operate except as tenant plantations, and compared them with those under 51 acres, which could not support more than the family of the owner. Whatever doubt remains as to the validity of these somewhat arbitrary distinctions may be resolved by reference to the proportions of ownership and tenancy. The table is divided into two parts, a static description of the distribution of landholdings in each decade, and a dynamic analysis of the rate of increase or decrease by twenty and forty year periods.

AGRARIAN PATTERN OF LOUISIANA, 1860–1900
(According to Selected Parishes)

STATIC					
Per centum	1860	1873	1880	1891	1900
All landholdings	100	100	100	100	100
Farms	66	26	30	35	42
under 51 acres	51+	12+	16	18	20
51-100 acres	14+	13+	14	17	22
Plantations	34	74	70	65	58
101-500 acres	23	47	48+	49	47
over 500 acres	11	27	21+	16	11
All landholders	—	100	100	100	100
Proprietors	—	57	53	48	48
Tenants	—	43	47	52	52

DYNAMIC			
Per centum Increase or (—) Decrease	1860–1880	1880–1900	1860–1900
All landholdings	89	53	189
Farms	—14	117	86
Plantations	287	29	401

It is apparent from this table that the plantation system in Louisiana not only survived but also expanded after the Civil War. Between 1860 and 1900 there was a fourfold increase in the number of plantations, while the number of farms was not even doubled. This tendency of the larger properties to outstrip the smaller is further illustrated by the fact that the number of holdings over 500 acres was augmented 203 per cent, and those under 51 acres only 10 per cent. The multiplication of these domains was accompanied from 1873 to 1891 by a steady growth of tenancy, colored and white; and by the end of the century over half the landholders no longer claimed possession of the soil they tilled.

An important difference appears, however, between the periods before and after 1880. In the later years the increase of farms was four times that of plantations, and the number of estates over 500 acres declined nearly one fifth. In the earlier years from 1860 to 1880, with which we are concerned in this study, the opposite occurred. The number of land-holdings multiplied 89 per cent, and of plantations, 287 per cent, while the number of farms actually decreased 14 per cent. Until 1880, in short, the larger properties encroached upon the smaller, but after that date farming developed faster than planting. Yet the increase of great estates throughout the century had such cumulative effect that although Louisiana had contained more farms than plantations in 1860, it was dominated by agrarian monopoly in 1900, when its proportion of absentee ownership and overseer management was the largest in the South, and the highest, except for Wyoming, in the entire United States. The evolution of the agrarian pattern in Louisiana was obviously away from the Jeffersonian (and Nashville) ideal of freehold farming and toward the tenancy and insecurity which burden agriculture today.

But the plantation system did not survive in Louisiana without a strug-gle, bitter and prolonged. Planters were threatened first with confiscation during reconstruction, then with bankruptcy and foreclosure because of adverse economic conditions, and finally with subdivision of their domains at the behest of agrarian philosophers, whose program seemed to be the only solution for grave difficulties of labor and finance.

First to endanger landed property were the freedmen and their radical sympathizers at Washington, Republicans like Carl Schurz and Thaddeus Stevens. Rumor ran wild through the South that the Negro might obtain "forty acres and a mule" from the expropriation of his old master, and there was apprehension of a colored uprising at Christmas in 1865. In response to a petition from frightened Louisiana planters, General Joseph S. Fullerton of the local Freedmen's Bureau warned the Negro that he was free—free to work, but not to seize his employer's land. "The Government will not do more for you," Fullerton informed the colored folk, "than for the white laborers who are your neighbors." So the landless poor, whether black or white, were not to receive title to the fields they worked. Southern planters soon became confident that the agrarian ambitions of Stevens, to distribute Confederate domains among the freedmen, would be repulsed by Northern conservatives lest such a revolutionary example excite their own factory hands to demand a similar division of industrial property.

The specter of agrarianism appeared next in New Orleans, when military reconstruction was inaugurated. At the radical constitutional convention of 1868 there were some colored delegates who desired to break up plantations, especially in the black belt Sugar Bowl, by pro-hibiting the purchase of tracts larger than 150 acres at distress sales, and by taxing uncultivated land double the rate of land in use. But the steering committee, which had a white majority, defeated this threat to the plantation system; only land sold by order of the courts was to be broken up into small tracts. After a brief skirmish the more progressive Negro leaders abandoned all dreams of agrarian reform, and advised their race to work and save money enough to buy parcels of the great estates for homesteads. So ended the freedmen's short-lived and feeble attack on landed property.

Although planters were now secure in legal title to their domains, they sometimes lost them beneath the crushing load of taxes imposed by corrupt and extravagant reconstruction legislatures. From the election of Governor Henry C. Warmoth in 1868 to the downfall of Governor Stephen B. Packard in 1877, the tax rate doubled, and at its peak amounted to 21½ mills. While the value of property had been reduced nearly one half, individual taxes almost doubled. To avoid expropriation by an avaricious government, planters often pledged standing crops for money to meet their public obligations. The property of those who were hopelessly in arrears, when sold at depreciated auction prices, brought the state over a quarter of a million dollars. Fully as oppressive as this confiscatory taxation was the arbitrary and inequitable assessment on which it was based. When such injustice could no longer be borne, a Tax Resisting Association was organized in 1873, and its stubborn fight against the exploitation of private property by corrupt public officials contributed to the eventual collapse of reconstruction. In this revolt the Shreveport *Times* took a conspicuous part; its editorial propaganda demonstrated that the power of taxation was becoming an instrument of destruction to the capital of both planters and merchants. Their desperate situation was revealed by the constitutional convention of 1879, whose delegates complained that the landed interests had been nearly taxed out of existence, and cited in proof such parishes as Union, where 1400 people were in arrears; Lafayette, where a considerable proportion of land had been forfeited to the state; and Caddo, where it was claimed that taxes left the planter no margin of profit. The temper of outraged landlords found vent in many economic safeguards of the new constitution. Delinquent taxpayers were granted relief, the legislature was forbidden to contract future debts except to suppress insurrection, and the ordinary tax rate was reduced to six mills. Planters who weathered the storms of reconstruction made the new constitution a bulwark of their agricultural system.

Their ability to survive had been tested by the poverty resulting from a war which was lost and the economic misfortunes which followed in its train. Four years of fighting prostrated the planting aristocracy, upon whom fell the larger share af Louisiana's tremendous loss of wealth, estimated at half of all the assessed property. The countryside, observed a rural correspondent, was "ground to powder between contending armies," and the ruin of war was not salvaged by its aftermath, "overflows and cotton worms, rains and politicians." It was difficult to profit by the high postwar prices of cotton and sugar, because the levees needed expensive repairs and the sugarhouses required costly new machinery. Land which lay in waste, with fewer hands and less capital to restore it, depreciated so much—Louisiana and South Carolina suffering most in this respect—that mortgages on many plantations were foreclosed at a third of their prewar value.

How many estates changed hands, or how often, it is at present impossible to judge. The contemporary press made no mention of any drastic overturn in the proprietorship of cotton plantations. After the local crop failures of 1866 -1867, it was estimated that not one cotton planter in five could start the next year without giving a lien on his crop for seed and supplies. With money easy to borrow after the war, however, cotton planters who owned their land were able to keep it by going into debt. But the expensive and speculative nature of sugar cultivation, which combined a highly capitalized manufacture with a none too reliable agriculture, led to a revolution in ownership. Almost half the sugar planters in 1869 bore names that slaveholding families would not have recognized. More and more estates were bought by partnerships and corporations, often with the help of Northern capital, which equipped them financially to improve the machinery and endure the vicissitudes of sugar culture. The processes of credit and alienation operated to preserve the plantation, if not the planters.

Labor was perhaps the gravest problem to confront proprietors, for the extent of their domains depended on the hands available to cultivate them, and "land without labor [was] worthless." Many planters, reared in the tradition of slavery, could not bring themselves to believe that the Negro would till the fields voluntarily. Their skepticism was expressed by the *Picayune,* which advised "the white man [to] go to work is if he were Robinson Crusoe, without a man Friday." Looking forward to white immigration to replace the inefficient freedmen, this newspaper predicted that "farms will multiply and plantations will diminish."

From the difficulties of adapting ex-slaves to plantation tenantry sprang an agrarian philosophy which championed the subdivision of estates. Its most articulate and untiring advocate was Daniel Dennett, editor of the *St. Mary's Planters' Banner* in the Sugar Bowl, who later preached his gospel from the agricultural columns of the *Picayune.* He was at first supported by James D. B. De Bow, famous political economist of slavery, who declared that "the South must throw her immense uncultivated domain into the market at a low price; reduce the quantity of land held by individual proprietors, and . . . induce an influx of population and capital from abroad." "Small farms and white labor," as Dennett said, "or large farms and coolie labor may save the land."

First to be tried was the latter alternative. Strenuous efforts were made to preserve the plantation system and to discipline the Negro by importing Chinese to force the freedmen to choose between competition and starvation. Some Orientals were brought from Cuba in 1866, and in the following years, colonies of Catholic Chinese from the Philippines. But they soon deserted the plantations to become independent fishermen and truck farmers for the New Orleans market. The idea of keeping large estates intact by replacing Negroes with coolies proved to be a fantasy, if only because Louisiana planters could not compete with the wages offered Oriental labor in California and on the Pacific railroads.

Would Dennett's other alternative, "small farms and white labor," succeed? Upon such a policy of agrarian reorganization depended the efficiency and prosperity of agriculture in the South, according to De Bow. He was seconded by L. Bouchereau, compiler of the annual sugar reports, who advised cane growers to attract industrious Germans from the Middle West by giving them patches of land. Immigration was indeed the only prospective source of white labor, because native "poor whites" would not leave their hill farms for the plantation lowlands, which were thought to be sickly with yellow fever, hard to cultivate, and overrun by Negroes, with whom white farmers had little sympathy and even less desire to compete either as share croppers or wage earners.

To encourage foreign immigration, an official bureau was established by conservative Democrats and maintained by radical Republicans. Thousands of pamphlets, describing Louisiana as a Garden of Eden, were scattered abroad. Yet few foreigners rose to the bait. Immigrants continued to seek lands in the West and could not be diverted to the unfamiliar latitudes of the South, then an unhappy section devastated by war, afflicted with social and political disorder, suffering economic depression, and already pre-empted by Negro labor. But the fundamental reason why immigrants did not come pouring into Louisiana was the relative lack of economic opportunity for the common man. Plantations dominated the fertile lowlands, which their proprietors would not subdivide, even to obtain labor superior to the Negro, or to enhance the general value of real estate by increased settlement. "You want our Germans to take the place of your former slaves," observed the shrewd president of the German Lloyd Steamship Company. So the foreigner avoided Louisiana because it semed to offer him nothing better than a chance to displace the Negro by working and forever living "like a nigger."

But from the South Atlantic states, the Middle West, and the North came several thousand "poor white" families to farm the piney woods. The national freeland in this section of Louisiana was not available under the Homestead Act until 1869. During the next decade it was entered to the extent of half a million acres, not as actual homesteads but chiefly in fraudulent or dummy claims for the purpose of stripping the land of timber. Poor settlers continued as before the war to stake out their farms without going through the formality of law. In any case, neither homesteaders nor squatters disturbed the plantation system.

The Jeffersonian ideal of freehold farming remained a mirage to trouble the future. It was scorned by planters after the war. Their attitude was expressed by a sugar grower who complained that the advocates of subdivision "ought not to be so liberal with other people's property." Proprietors everywhere were loathe to part with the acres that had once yielded them luxury: to own a large estate was still to enjoy social esteem. Ex-slaveholders were sincerely persuaded that the plantation was the salvation of the colored people, and that without it the land could not support the Negro. To subdivide plantations would have required more credit than the proprietors possessed, because there was "no sale for large tracts of land, and the multitude who want[ed] small tracts . . . [had] no money to pay for them."

The social and economic folly of not having broken up these estates was never forgotten in New Orleans. "So long as there are wastes of idle and unproductive lands blotting the fair face of Louisiana, and starving workmen thronging the streets of New Orleans," it was said, "there can be no such thing as prosperity for the State." When the panic of 1873 threw thousands of laborers out of work, it was brought home to all men that in the city there was "an immense amount of idle muscle," and in the country a vast domain of idle or monopolized land.

What prevented their profitable union and consequently save the plantation system? The answer is threefold in nature, political, economic, and social. Among the political factors were the collapse of reconstruction, the failure to carry the revolutionary changes of the war beyond the abolition of slavery, and the frustration of all plans to subvert the laws of property, whether undertaken by Republicans or Populists. Bourbon Democracy, composed of an alliance of planters and merchants, stood guard over its property and controlled the government in its own interest throughout the nineteenth century except for the interlude of reconstruction.

Among the economic factors which operated to preserve the plantation system, the most important were the large scale necessities of staple agriculture, the subordination of freedmen to peonage, the credit afforded by crop liens, and finally the free play of economic forces which allowed estates to change hands by bankruptcy or alienation. Cotton and especially sugar have always been crops well adapted to cultivation on a large scale, and the stimulus of high post-bellum prices in these staples renewed the extensive tillage of slaveholding days. The expense of maintaining levees and drainage canals in the river bottoms, and of improving machinery in the sugarhouses, combined to make the plantation a capitalistic unit which farmers of small means could not easily break up. The labor essential to its operation was provided by the return of landless freedmen to the soil as they realized that they must work or starve. The ex-slaveholder learned to be landlord, merchant, and overseer, furnishing his tenants the food, clothes, tools and land necessary to grow staples, while the ex-slave went to work, first for cash, then for crop shares, and in the cane fields for a monthly wage. Although the difficulties of colored labor aggravated the process of reconstruction, and strikes were sometimes suppressed as racial insurrection, owners and tenants reached a *modus vivendi* long before the overthrow of Carpetbag government.

As the planters made it possible for Negroes to support themselves, so in turn the cotton and sugar factors, merchants and banks of New Orleans enabled the planters to resume operation of their estates. Without such credit, extended on the basis of crop liens and blanket mortgages, it is extremely doubtful if the plantation system could have sustained the ruin of war, the occasional crop failures and constant political burden of reconstruction, and the price and tariff fluctuations during the remainder of the century. Luckily for the larger landholders, however, sufficient capital was always available in New Orleans, where it accumulated from Northern and foreign investments and from the profits of expanding commerce. It is really extraordinary that after 1865 the local money market suffered no contraction except the periodic stringency which affected the entire nation at times of severe depression. While planters paid interest as high as twenty-five per cent for financial accommodation and soon found themselves bound hand and foot by the crop lien and blanket mortgage, it was this chain of credit which not only revived plantations after the war but also preserved them intact whenever the burden of debt pushed them into bankruptcy. The title to an estate often changed, but seldom its size, for every acre, all its equipment and crops, were collateral for the credit necessary to work it. Planters and merchants were therefore unable to subdivide their landholdings with any profit, and transfers of ownership precluded the disintegration of landed monopoly.

It was, in short, the planters, freedmen, and factors who preserved the plantation system in Louisiana after the Civil War.

AN AMERICAN TRAGEDY

Money, Class and Party

ROBERT F. SHARKEY

In the 1950s American historians attacked Charles Beard's economic approach to both the first and second American revolutions. Hesseltine in 1935 had argued that Republican politicians and Republican businessmen were not united in their stance toward Reconstruction. In 1959, Robert F. Sharkey and Stanley Coben went one step further, insisting that businessmen were at variance among themselves on such issues as the tariff, contraction of the currency, and desirable policy toward the defeated South.

Sharkey said that he had no quarrel with the "overall dimensions" of Beard's conception of Civil War and Reconstruction. However, the conception of a monolithic capitalist class would have to be abandoned. Starting

Robert F. Sharkey, *Money, Class and Party: An Economic Study of Civil War and Reconstruction* (Baltimore, 1959), pp. 290–293, 299–306. Reprinted by permission of the author and The Johns Hopkins Press.

from the discovery that Thaddeus Stevens favored monetary inflation rather than the hard-money policy Beard ascribed to capitalists as a class, Sharkey went on to delineate two widely divergent Northern economic groups. One comprised the textile manufacturers of New England and the bankers of New York City, who generally favored a low tariff and monetary contraction. The second group included iron and steel manufacturers (such as Stevens himself) and trade unionists, who on the whole supported a high tariff and inflation. Sharkey took both Beard and Beale to task for exaggerating the unity of Northern business interests, as well as for predating the emergence of significant agrarian opposition to Republican policies. And he emphasized that the business interests of New York City, far from supporting Radical Reconstruction, had feasted Andrew Johnson at Delmonico's after his "swing around the circuit" in 1866.

"It seems clear," Coben concluded in his comparable presentation, "that factors other than the economic interests of the Northeast must be used to explain the motivation and aims of Radical Reconstruction."

IN THE PRECEDING PAGES THE MOST IMPORTANT CONCLUSIONS REACHED in this study have been briefly summarized. The task which remains is that of demonstrating in what respects these conclusions differ from those contained in what may be considered the prevailing interpretation of the history of the Civil War and Reconstruction. This necessarily involves an excursion into the historiography of the eighteen sixties. Two demurrers must be entered at the outset. No attempt has been made to consider all the works in which the prevailing economic interpretation appears. Only the works in which this interpretation was originally developed as well as a few works which demonstrate its current acceptance have been treated. Secondly, it must be emphasized that I have tremendous respect for the scholars whose works are analyzed here. This analysis has been made purely in the interest of obtaining a better understanding of the real meaning of a most controversial and perplexing period of American history.

In the opinion of the present author basic responsibility for the prevailing view of the economic meaning of the Civil War and Reconstruction must be assigned to the great American historian, Charles A. Beard. Beard must be included along with J. Allen Smith and Vernon L. Parrington in that select group of American scholars who in the first quarter of the twentieth century first assaulted the almost exclusive preoccupation of American historians with political, military, and constitutional history. By placing great emphasis upon social, cultural, technological, and particularly economic forces in historical development, Beard lay bare for all to see the real red meat of history. After the publication of his works on the Constitution and Jeffersonian Democracy, historians would neglect only at their very great peril the vital importance of economic factors in historical interpretation.

In 1927 with the publication of *The Rise of American Civilization* Charles and Mary Beard impressed their method and predilections upon the whole course of American history. Perhaps no other aspect of this path-breaking work was more startling or iconoclastic than the Beards' now famous interpretation of the Civil War and Reconstruction which they lumped together as the "Second American Revolution." This interpretation discounted the fondly held notion that the importance of the Civil War was to be sought in the movements of vast armies or in the interminable list of battles and skirmishes. "To be sure," wrote the Beards, "the battles and campaigns of the epoch are significant to the military strategist; the tragedy and heroism of the contest furnish inspiration to patriots and romance to the maker of epics. But the core of the vortex lay elsewhere. It was in the flowing substance of things limned by statistical reports on finance, commerce, capital, industry, railways, and agriculture, by provisions of constitutional law, and by the pages of statute books—prosaic muniments which show that the so-called civil war was in reality a Second American Revolution and in a strict sense, the First." The war was in essence "a social war, ending in the unquestioned establishment of a new power in the government, making vast changes in the arrangement of classes, in the accumulation and distribution of wealth, in the course of industrial development, and in the Constitution inherited from the Fathers." If indeed, "the operations by which the middle classes of England broke the power of the king and the aristocracy are to be known collectively as the Puritan Revolution, if the series of acts by which the bourgeois and peasants of France overthrew the king, nobility, and clergy is to be called the French Revolution, then accuracy compels us to characterize by the same term the social cataclysm in which the capitalists, laborers, and farmers of the North and West drove from power in the national government the planting aristocracy of the South. Viewed under the light of universal history, the fighting was a fleeting incident; the social revolution was the essential, portentous outcome."

With the overall dimensions of this interpretation I have no quarrel. To the historian who considers essential meanings rather than the sound and fury of events, the ultimate significance of the Civil War and Reconstruction lies in the fundamental fact of social upheaval, the process by which the power of the planting aristocracy in the South was broken and the hegemony of other economic groups established. The core of my disagreement with Professor Beard lies not in the overwhelming emphasis which he placed upon economic forces but rather in the fact that he failed to disentangle the interests of the various triumphant economic groups and to show that they were frequently contradictory. It will be noted that Beard has the "capitalists, laborers, and farmers of the North and West" accomplishing the defeat of the planting aristocracy. The spoils of the victory which accrued to the laborers and farmers are hurriedly sketched. For the former the benefits were virtually non-existent and are consequently passed over with scarcely a comment. For the latter the fruits of victory consisted essentially of the passage of the Homestead Act and the high farm prices which ensued because of inflation. With these elements of the coalition Beard is actually concerned very little. It is the "capitalists" who really gain the choicest spoils of war, and it is with this group that Beard is primarily concerned. It is on the question of the meaning of the term "capitalists" and its use in the Beardian interpretation that this study takes issue with the concept of the "Second American Revolution."

In treating "capitalists" as the chief beneficiaries of the social upheaval of Civil War and Reconstruction, the Beards have created a conceptual monolith. They have failed to recognize the cleavages which existed within the capitalist group itself on various questions of economic policy. . . .

. . . Essentially the Beards make the mistake of confusing the divergent interests of industrial and finance capitalists. Whereas the former group tended to profit from wartime inflation, the latter group tended to suffer. Whereas industrialists generally favored high protective tariffs and a policy of easy money, finance capitalists tended toward free trade and sound money. The touchstone of self-interest was present in both cases, but the Beards have failed to understand that the interests of these two groups were entirely different. When the divergent interests of financial and industrial capitalists, of bankers and manufacturers are understood, the conceptual monolith of the interests of "capitalists" which the Beards have created falls to the ground, and it becomes apparent that the economic history of the Civil War and Reconstruction must be approached from the standpoint of the conflicting interests of various economic groups.

It will be noted that in the passages quoted above the Beards refer twice to the Republicans as the party of sound money. In another place they are referred to as "the party of industrial progress and sound money." Just what the Beards mean by "sound money" is difficult to elicit from the text, but to the present author it is impossible to imagine as the champion of "sound money" that party which passed the First Legal Tender Act against strong Democratic opposition in 1862, which supported the policy of contraction in the House by a bare margin of five votes in 1866 while the Democrats were supporting it twenty-seven to one, and which decisively opposed further contraction in 1868 by a vote of one-hundred and three to eighteen. If the Beards mean to imply that the Republicans donned the mantle of "sound money" by their establishment of the National Banking System, it should be pointed out that the real "sound money" advocates of the time (including the New York Clearing House and the economist Amasa Walker) regarded the system, which placed its greatest emphasis on the note-issuing function, as little better than the "wildcat" banking of earlier years. If indeed the national bank currency can be regarded as an improvement over the old state bank issues, it should be understood that the new system was still a long way from fulfilling the demands of the most ardent advocates of "sound money." In any event it is impossible to see how the Republicans can be regarded in these years as the patrons of "sound money." Until 1867 the Democrats would have far sounder claim to this distinction.

The Beards' concept of the "Second American Revolution" has been of basic importance in recent American historiography. The persuasiveness, (if not the logic), the panoramic scope, as well as the general iconoclastic nature of the thesis have recommended it to readers of history as well as to historians. The concept has been of such great significance that it has formed the framework within which a whole school of historians has interpreted the economic meaning of the Civil War and Reconstruction. From the standpoint of historiographical influence perhaps the most influential member of this school has been Professor Howard K. Beale whose scholarly work, *The Critical Year,* has impressed the general Beardian frame of reference upon the economic history of Reconstruction.

Beale accepts the Beards' thesis that "capitalists" were the chief beneficiaries of the economic *fait accompli* of the Civil War and Reconstruction. Like the Beards he also fails to distinguish between the divergent interests of industrial and finance capitalists. Beale carries the conspiracy concept of the Beards one step further, for he sees conspiracy on the part of the Radical Republicans, representing the interests of "big business," to keep Southern representatives from regaining their seats in Congress. The motive for this conspiracy was economic as he points out:

If Southern economic interests had coincided with those of the rising industrial groups of the North, there would have been no Radical reconstruction. The real danger from 'a return of rebels to power' was not overthrow of the Union, but ousting of the new industrial forces from control in Washington through a renewed union of Southern planters and Western farmers. In an alignment on the new industrial questions, the Radials would have been outnumbered even in the North. If Johnson had staked his fortunes on them instead of on the indeterminable condition of a remote South, his chances of success would have risen.

Again in another passage Beale gives his impression of the economic factors at work and the possible consequences of readmitting the South to the Union.

Contraction of the currency was already a subject of heated controversy, though the opposition to it had not yet gained the momentum necessary to the launching of a political party. Still, most of the factors that in subsequent years underlay Greenbackism, the Granger movement, Populism, Progressivism, and the Farm Bloc were at work in 1866. It is significant that it was while in retirement on his farm from May of 1866 to the following May that Kelley in conversation with his Minnesota friends worked out the details of the Granger organization suggested to him by what he saw on a Southern trip early in 1866. Therefore, while the first Grange was not organized until 1867, its need was based on conditions of 1866. Had the South been back in the Union, similar economic conditions would have united the Northwest and the South in advocacy of an inflated currency. Realization of this fact was one of the reasons for Radical determinations to keep the South out of the Union.

Let us analyze these passages in light of the conclusions reached in the present study. In the first place Beale assumes that the farmer's discontent with his economic lot played an important part in Oliver Kelley's early attempts to organize the Grange. As has been pointed out above, this was simply not the case. Farmers were prosperous in the years following the Civil War. There is no evidence in Kelley's writings to support the notion that the discontent of farmers with their economic lot played a part in his organizational efforts. The original objectives of the Grange were, as Solon Buck has written, "to advance agriculture and bind the farmers together." Social and cultural betterment was the goal, not political agitation based on economic hardship. There is little evidence available to support the thesis that the farmers as a group favored expansion of the currency or even a halt to contraction. Their prosperous condition until about 1869 left them relatively unconcerned with financial questions.

If we accept the premise that the farmers were as a group uninterested in the outcome of the contraction-expansion controversy, Beale's thesis is vulnerable. If agricultural opinion was apathetic on this issue then it is misleading and incorrect to assert that had the South been back in the Union "similar economic conditions would have united the Northwest and the South in advocacy of an inflated currency" through a "renewed union of Southern planters and Western farmers." But the thesis is not vulnerable on this ground alone, for Professor Beale assumes that "Realization of this fact was one of the reasons for Radical determination to keep the South out of the Union." In making this statement Beale is creating the same type of conceptual monolith that the Beards engendered in their use of the idea of the group interests of "capitalists." He is assuming that the Radical Republicans represented a cohesive group of politicians possessing well defined aims in the economic sphere on which there was essential agreement. A large part of this study has been devoted to disproving that notion. There was actually no agreement whatsoever on financial policy between such Radicals such as Thaddeus Stevens, Benjamin F. Butler, William D. Kelley, and Ben Wade on the one hand and Radicals such as Roscoe Conkling, Justin Morrill, James A. Garfield, and William P. Fessenden on the other. As a matter of fact the most radical of the Radicals were the group which tended most definitely toward the soft-money philosophy. Those who held "sound money" views were often essentially moderates both on economic and political issues. Beale's thesis is thus vulnerable on another count. Radicals could hardly have conspired to keep the South out of the Union because of fear that Southerners would unite with Westerners to inflate the currency, because there was absolutely no unity on this point among the Republicans themselves.

At various points Beale seems a little embarrassed by his own theory. He cites at least as much evidence that Radicals opposed contraction as that they favored it. For example, he says, "Even that inveterate Radical, George L. Stearns of Boston, feared a panic would result from contraction." At another place he writes regarding the contraction bill that "so strong was the opposition even among Radicals, that they had to accept a compromise proviso. . . ." Again he writes: "Even in the East the bill faced bitter opposition."

Inasmuch as Beale accepts the proposition that the Radicals, on balance, favored contraction as well as the general thesis that they represented the "business" interest, he is led to declare that "Manufacturers generally sought contraction of the currency along with an increase of tariff rates." So far as the present author has been able to determine, he cites not one jot of evidence to support this thesis. Now the opinion of manufacturers on the contraction issue present a very complex problem as we have been at pains to point out, but it is quite clear that manufacturers did not generally seek contraction of the currency. The most vocal of their number sought just the opposite, namely a cessation of contraction. The high protectionists, with which Beale is especially concerned, were the most powerful single element in opposition to Hugh McCulloch's policy of contraction of the currency.

In his treatment of the National Banking System Professor Beale once more assumes that the interests of "business" formed some sort of monolithic unity.

Around the new national banks centered continual controversy. A strong tradition of opposition to the idea of a national bank remained from Jackson's day. The new banks were different, but they bore the onus of the popular distrust of the "monied monster" of the 'Thirties. In truth the new banks *were* a potent influence; they were intended to be. They aroused Western opposition by intensifying the concentration of financial control in the Northeast—in New York, Philadelphia, and Boston. Endowed with greater resources than the old state banks, they wielded great power. "Business" stood solidly behind them as it had behind the Bank of Jackson's day, and urged their extension. These new national banks it was that later helped Big Business in the extraordinary financing of the last years of the century. Small banks, Western state banks, debtors, hated them as early as 1866 for their very stabilizing activity, and for their apparent favoring of Easterners and business men.

This treatment involves some oversimplifications. Like the Beards, Beale holds that "business" including finance as well as industrial capitalists presented a solid phalanx of mutual self-interest to the "Small banks, Western state banks, [and] debtors" who hated the National Banking System. Now this characterization may be accurate for a later period, but it is misleading for the year 1866. In that year "business" was by no means so greatly enamoured of national banking. It has been pointed out above that only in some states of the West where the excesses of "wildcat" banking were best remembered was there any real enthusiasm in banking circles for the legislation of 1863 and 1864. Among the powerful bankers of the eastern seaboard cities, national banking continued to be suspect for years. It was only the punitive act of March 3, 1865, placing a ten per cent tax upon the note issues of state banks, which hastened the conversion of large eastern banks. In October, 1865 the new system was described by James Gallatin as "an odious system of plundering the people by a double interest process." Such a statement might well have been expected to come from a western agrarian. Actually, it came from one of the most powerful and conservative of New York bankers. The known hostility to the new system of the country's most powerful bankers leads the present author to seriously question Beale's statement that "Business" stood solidly behind them [the national banks] as it had behind the Bank of Jackson's day, and urged their extension." On balance, "business" (if such a conglomerate term has any meaning at all) may have stood behind the new banking system, but there were important elements within the realm of finance capital who distrusted and opposed it.

In their treatment of the interests of "capitalists" and of "business" the Beards and Professor Beale have created a conceptual monolith ill adapted to the purpose of explaining the real meaning of the economic history of the Civil War and Reconstruction. I have no quarrel with the Beard-Beale concept that the economic play within a play constitutes the

hard core of meaning which can be elicited from the drama of Civil
War and Reconstruction. For purposes of analysis, however, the Beard-
Beale thesis has provided us with a meat cleaver instead of the more
useful scalpel. Only by understanding the interplay and contest of forces
within the "capitalist" or "business" group itself can the historian begin
to arrive at a sound and comprehensive interpretation of this formative
period of American history.

An American Crisis (Economic)

W. R. BROCK

Sharkey's implicit challenge to salvage Beard's "overall" approach to Reconstruction while rejecting his specific economic analysis was accepted in
1963 by the English historian W. R. Brock. Brock conceded the force of
the Sharkey-Coben contention that Northern businessmen were divided in
their attitudes toward Reconstruction. But, he said: "Economic interpretations may . . . have been applied to Reconstruction at the wrong level; a confusion of economic aims when men calculate their interests in the immediate
future is compatible with the determination of basic political attitudes by the
economic character of a society. If one goes beneath the superficial arguments
over means one may well find a uniformity over ends."

In defense of this perspective Brock argued, first, that "the impetus in
Reconstruction came not from what Northerners wanted to do with the
South but from their fear of what the South might do to them." Businessmen might differ as to what policies a Republican majority in Congress
should favor while agreeing that the return of a Democratic majority would
be disastrous.

Brock went on to portray what he considered a typical Republican constituency and the life cycle of a typical Republican politician. He found a
rising lawyer or small businessman in a medium-sized Middlewestern community bent on rapid economic growth. From these circumstances (according

W. R. Brock, *An American Crisis: Congress and Reconstruction, 1865–1867*
(London, 1963), pp. 239–248. Reprinted by permission of St. Martin's Press, Inc.,
Macmillan & Co., Ltd.

to Brock) there arose "a coherent view of what America ought to be," a concern that there develop in the South a pattern of institutions similar to the North's so that national government would rest on a homogeneous foundation. "Here was the dynamic force which unified the Republican party behind Radical leadership and endorsed Radical Reconstruction."

THIS BRIEF AND SELECTIVE REVIEW OF ECONOMIC CONTROVERSIES AND influences during the Reconstruction period is, perhaps, sufficient to confirm the verdict of a close student of the problem that 'The Reconstruction program of the Radicals cannot be explained as an organized attempt by the business interests of the Northeast either to preserve and promote their own economic advantages or to obtain protection for the economic exploitation of the South. Actually northeastern businessmen had no unified economic program to promote'. In any complex economic society it is unlikely that the leaders of business will agree upon policies when confronted with a novel situation, and even less likely that they will succeed in persuading the politicians and the electorate to adopt such a policy if conceived. Occasionally the economic consequences of a policy may appear to businessmen to be so clear that they unite in support of or in opposition to it—such, for instance, has been the modern businessman's reaction to socialism—but no such clear and over-riding considerations presented themselves in the Reconstruction crisis. The majority of business interests would probably have been well served by a speedy return to business as usual; a minority with vested interests in high protection hoped to get their tariffs through before the Southerners were able to resume their traditional opposition, but many others had lived profitably in the past under Democratic tariffs with Southerners in the Union; a good many were concerned and divided over the currency question, but it was impossible to forecast how this might be affected by Reconstruction. Economic interpretations may, however, have been applied to Reconstruction at the wrong level; a confusion of economic aims when men calculate their interests in the immediate future is compatible with the determination of basic political attitudes by the economic character of a society. If one goes beneath the superficial arguments over means one may well find a uniformity over ends.

Though economic controversies had figured prominently in all the major political conflicts of the American people there was little fundamental difference of opinion about the kind of economic society which they desired. Most Americans believed consciously or unconsciously in a natural economic order and, though the use of economic power might be attacked, the nature of that power was a part of the divinely ordained plan. They believed that the right of property was one of the basic rights which government existed to protect, that the general welfare was best served by private enterprise, that the motive force in economic life was and ought to be individual decision, and that these decisions should be left as free from restraint as possible. They believed that society could not exist without the unremitting labour of the majority of its members, but they also believed that their system provided the opportunity by which those labourers possessed of prudence and ability could escape from dependence upon others. From this fundamental agreement two traditions had developed which placed different emphases upon its implications, and this led to different views of the role of government, and particularly of the national government, in economic affairs.

The emphasis of the Democrats was upon freedom, and they regarded government intervention as its necessary enemy. If the public interest required action it should be made by the government which was closest to the individuals concerned. They believed that the economic functions of the national government were few, strictly defined in the Constitution, and ought not to be enlarged by interpretation. The theory of State rights was the traditional bulwark against unconstitutional activity by the national government, and this negative view was reinforced by the laws of political economy—by free trade and by hard money—which reduced the discretionary power of government or of moneyed men. The Democrats were not hostile to business provided that it had established its position by 'natural' means, without privilege conferred by government, and in the few cases in which it was necessary to confer privilege by incorporation this should be done exclusively by State government. They resisted the argument that men could be made happier by giving them economic advantages which nature had not conferred, and they believed that a man could be happier in a backward society, provided that he was his own master, than in an advanced society if dependent upon somebody else. This attachment to freedom stopped short at the negro who was happier under control because of his child-like and inferior character.

The Republicans inherited the old Whig doctrine which had grown out of the experience of developing communities during the early nineteenth century. They believed that moral and material progress were intertwined, and, though men could be good without economic success, communities required a measure of prosperity in order to provide churches, schools, cultural activities and charitable institutions. For them 'general welfare' meant the development of the separate communities but they believed that the needs of these communities could be treated as a national problem and not in isolation from each other. Localism was an obstacle to progress, and State rights had been interposed between the people and the material development which they deserved. They did not believe in unlimited national government or in the annihilation of local authority, but they believed that limited government and divided sovereignty were the means and not the ends and should yield when they obstructed useful economic development. While Democrats opposed all national economic action which was not positively sanctioned by the Constitution, the Republicans believed that when the utility of an action was demonstrated it was legitimate unless positively prohibited. The great contested points had been the tariff and Federal aid for internal improvement, and these two test cases were the symptoms of different attitudes towards the role of the national government. The Democrats believed that the government must do no more than permit the development of economic life along lines chosen by the people in their States; the Republicans believed that the national government had a positive function to perform as the architect of beneficial growth and as the regulator of economic harmony. To these cardinal tenets the Republicans had added the abolitionist doctrine of free labour. Most Republicans were not prepared to give the negro equal status in their own communities, but they did believe that he should have the same opportunities of development as the white man. Moreover they believed that the existence of servile labour degraded labour everywhere.

For Republicans the South had been, in the past, the main obstacle to economic growth along the desired lines. Southerners had opposed the tariff and internal improvements; they had imposed the concept of negative government upon the nation, but had also supported a system of land monopoly and servile labour which was the negation of free enterprise and free labour. The experience of war had confirmed the picture of the Southerners as the enemies of human betterment, and as a consequence of their secession it had been possible to enact a protective tariff, to pass a homestead law, to grant land for transcontinental railways, and to abolish slavery. 'Southern aristocracy', 'State rights' and 'slavery' had become symbols which evoked strong negative responses amongst Northern Republicans, and during the Reconstruction period this image of the South as the enemy of healthy economic progress had a powerful influence upon Northern minds. Thus the threat of a restored and unreconstructed South was in part an economic threat; but the impetus in Reconstruction came not from what Northerners wanted to do with the South but from their fear of what the South might do to them. This picture of the South in peace and war was more powerful than the prospect of gain, and imagination was more potent and pervasive than calculation.

The economic aspects of Reconstruction must be seen in this context, and one passes immediately from economic aims narrowly conceived as expected profits to fundamental social aims. What was at stake was the kind of society which was to exist in America, and the 'blood-stained hands of traitors', the black codes, the denial of civil rights, the persecution of loyalists were the symbols of a society which the Northern majority wished to reject. It had been proved by the secessionists themselves that the two societies could not co-exist, and it became necessary to remodel the defeated society on the lines laid down by the victorious. The Union must be indivisible and this implied social homogeneity.

To understand the power of these ideas in the Republican party it is necessary to imagine the kind of constituency which its members served. The typical constituency is perhaps a fiction, but it is not beyond the bonds of reasonable fiction to construct a constituency which has the largest number of possible common factors. This typical constituency was largely rural but included one or two small towns which served as market and commercial centres, perhaps as railway junctions and certainly as the place of business for bankers, real estate dealers, and lawyers. There might be a little manufacturing industry and probably a good deal of agricultural processing. At a distance was the metropolitan centre through which passed most of the strings which controlled the local economy, and somewhere beyond the metropolis were the distant markets and distant suppliers. If the constituency was not in New England it would probably have a strong flavour of New England transported. If the Church was not Congregational it probably had the same emphasis upon communal organization, and only very poor villages did not have their schools. It was not improbable that the town centre of the constituency would have a college or other establishment for higher education. It probably depended much upon communications which owed more to artifice than to nature and was linked by railway with the outside world.

In such a constituency the emphasis was upon development, and development was the result of energy and enterprise. In all constituencies west of the Appalachians there still lived pioneers of early settlement, the rise from small beginnings was a part of living traditions, and so was the knowledge that growth had followed upon the application of the instruments of capitalism to virgin resources. The successful farmers had not been content with subsistence agriculture but had aimed at increasing land values by commercial production; the businessman had not come into the agricultural community as representative of an alien civilization but in response to indigenous needs, and nowhere in the world did he enjoy higher prestige. There was little class antagonism or class consciousness because the idea of community development embraced the interests of all sorts and conditions of men. The idea of the harmony of interests appeared as a real statement of fact and not as a theoretical abstraction, for the fruit of productive labour was multiplied by the services of an advanced business system. By contrast the typical Democratic constituency was either a large city with a mass of low-paid and immigrant labourers, or a rural area of scattered farms and backward agriculture. In these city or rural Democratic constituencies the poor in worldly possessions were strong in votes and felt themselves alienated from the dominant trends in Northern society.

The Republican congressmen had usually made their early career either as small business entrepreneurs or, more commonly, as lawyers. They belonged to the community which they represented; if businesmen they were conscious of the part which they had played in its progress and anxious to promote its interests on the national stage; if lawyers they represented their communities as they had once represented their clients and the two were often indistinguishable. The political magnates—the senators or the more powerful members of the House of Representatives— might have acquired an outlook which transcended the interests of a particular community, but when they thought of the State or the nation it was as the community enlarged.

The kind of community which has been sketched was an amazingly successful institution; nowhere else had pioneer societies produced so high a standard of material and educational achievement, and nowhere else was so general a level of contentment compatible with so advanced an economic organization. The constraints, tensions and stratification of Old World societies had been by-passed, and the Old World transplanted to the New (which was how they viewed the South) had been rejected and defeated. Nowhere else was it possible to combine intense individualism with a realization of mutual dependence within the community and, beyond the community, upon the outside world. Yet success had exacted a price, and men who were not indigenous to this society could be shocked by the self-righteousness of its members, by their apparent hypocrisy in the combination of high moral sentiment with sharp business practice, by the contempt bred of ignorance with which they regard all other peoples, and by the dull conformity of their thought and custom. All their virtues combined to make them the last people in the world to understand the difficulties of others or to tolerate the existence of those whom they regarded as harmful. These limitations had not been removed but reinforced by the experience of war; lives and material had gone to preserve the society of the North, moral indignation had sprung readily to the support of military effort, and participation in an epic struggle had sublimated the quest for material betterment.

A description of the social aims of the Northern Republican community cannot be couched solely in material terms. The social and economic environment made certain beliefs attractive and relevant to experience, but the beliefs themselves had an independent history which made them more potent as factors of union in the Republican party than economic aspirations. The principles of the American resolution, finding a fertile soil in regions where there was no ready-made ruling class, had fused with the older traditions of New England Puritanism. The exclusion of slavery and abundant land had prevented the formation of an upper class based on large estates, while the emphasis upon communal development and the dependence of individual fortunes upon the prosperity of regions as a whole had made businessmen the natural leaders of society. At the same time dependence upon commercial agriculture had prevented any sharp division of interest between the countryside and the towns. In the West settled from New England and Northern Europe it had been necessary to rely upon the developed capitalism of the East, and the mutual interest of the two regions became one of the axes upon which American politics revolved. The fact that this community of interest depended upon man-made communications had led through the history of internal improvements to an expectation that the national government must act as a positive factor in national growth. In New England itself, in western New York, and in western Pennsylvania these attitudes had been ingrained at an early stage and persisted with the stimulation of manufacturing and mining. Here the tariff emerged as the leading popular economic issue. Finally the Philadelphia region retained the imprint of early Quakerism with its anti-slavery tradition in a city which was one of the emporiums of Western trade.

Working in these regions there had been, since the early thirties, the strong ferment of the anti-slavery movement, which had identified the slave power as the fount and origin of all those policies and ideas which the Republican North had come to dislike. The anti-masonic movement, with its strong reaction against the idea of privileged groups, also formed a background to Eastern Republicanism; but anti-slavery had proved the stronger influence because it gave men a positive ideal as well as a negative response. Anti-slavery also forged an abiding link between the popular democracy of the community and the men of letters and intellect, and the prejudices of humble men were voiced in elevated language by Emerson, Whittier, Lowell and Whitman, in penetrating oratory by refugees from European oppression such as Carl Schurz and in the sermons from a thousand Northern pulpits. Widespread popular emotions, powerful economic forces and a committed intelligentsia made the Republican party one of the strongest political combinations of modern times, and unlike most American parties it had an ideological backbone.

It is as ideology that one must interpret the real force behind Radical

Reconstruction. Prejudice and emotion was there in strong measure; but so also was a coherent view of what America ought to be and an appeal to ideals which transcended while they expressed popular aspirations. As with other ideologies it arose from the needs and experience of the society which accepted it; and as with other ideologies it was blind to the merits of differing systems. To the Northern Republican the logic and the justice of his society seemed to be self-evident, and it was the peculiar triumph of old abolitionist and new Radical propaganda to convince him that negro freedom was an intrinsic part of this logic. The proposition was easier to accept because few Northern communities contained many negroes, but those who are not in the immediate presence of a problem can often appreciate best the principles involved. Fear of restored Southern domination was a spontaneous result of the war and the commitment to protect the rights of the negro as a citizen was reached by more subtle means; but as the passions of war slowly subsided fear of the Southerners took second place to the obligations arising from the abolition of slavery.

The progress of an ideology is not to be stopped in mid-course, particularly when it has been blessed by the heroism of war. The premise of the revolution had been stated and largely accepted, and thereafter conservative objections were likely to come tumbling down. Opposition and checks did not argue men out of their beliefs, but led them on to insist upon their realization. Northern opinion, faced with the choice between sacrificing through compromise some of the gains of the war and pushing forward to find new ways of securing them, almost inevitably chose the bolder course; and in general the people at large moved faster than the politicians. Here was the dynamic force which unified the Republican party behind Radical leadership and endorsed Radical Reconstruction. . . .

Peace for the South

ERIC McKITRICK

In the 1960s, as the federal government began to resume an active responsibility for the enforcement of the Civil War amendments to the Constitution, the attention of historians shifted to the question: Why has the national will to see civil rights become a reality in the South been so faltering and weak?

With this question in mind Eric McKitrick reopened the problem of Andrew Johnson's role in Reconstruction. McKitrick's view was essentially that Johnson's policy was right, but his manner of execution was altogether inept. *Andrew Johnson and Reconstruction* scrutinized the President's conduct in the summer of 1865, when Congress was not in session and Johnson had a free hand. McKitrick argued that Johnson's greatest failure lay simply in not making clear to the governing class of the South what in fact he expected of them. In Mississippi, for example, the President gave way "before his provisional governor in the face of his own military commander and his own special envoy."

According to McKitrick, Johnson's vacillations cut the ground from under influential Southerners such as Wade Hampton who in the summer of 1865 might have been prepared to grant limited Negro suffrage. Such enlightened leaders were left at the mercy of the prejudiced majorities of the Southern uplands. "Besides leading the South into realms of fantasy regarding the true location of Northern authority, the nature of majority sentiment, and the support which he himself could command for whatever policies he deemed proper, the President at the same time had thrown away most of the vast bargaining power with which he had started out."

THE FIRST THING THE SOUTHERNERS NEEDED TO KNOW WAS WHICH conceptual framework, among several possible ones, the North would use in defining the nature of reconstruction. They needed some notion of their own status, which was anything but clear; they had to have some indication of the kinds of actions that would be required of them and possibly even some cues to how they ought to behave. Even the most general nod in this direction, before anything at all was done, would clear the air tremendously. It would eliminate the need to dwell upon any number of alternatives, each equally conceivable and each requiring quite different sets of responses and different styles of behavior.

The President's first move here, after issuing his proclamations, was to invoke the Constitution. Not only were the principles of the Constitution self-evident, he told the South, but also, among the several versions of those principles that men might be tempted to consider, the self-evident version was his version. Every Southern delegation that visited the President was treated to discourses on the nature of the Constitution and states' rights. "A State cannot go out of the Union," Johnson announced to the South Carolinians before appointing a provisional governor for them, "and therefore none of them having gone out, we must deal with the question of restoration and not of reconstruction." He was "a better States rights man," he suspected, "than some of those now present," and proceeded to say why. Now that the rebellion had been suppressed it would be the policy, in line with constitutional principles, "not to restore the State Government through military rule, but by the people." (The gentlemen "seemed to be well pleased with the proceedings," according to report.) The same thoughts were communicated to a large group of leading citizens from several Southern states later in the summer:

> While I think that the rebellion has been arrested and subdued, and am happy in the consciousness of a duty well performed, I want not only you, but the people of the world to know, that while I dreaded and feared disintegration of the States, I am equally opposed to consolidation or concentration of power here, under whatever guise or name; and if the issue is forced upon us, I shall still endeavor to pursue the same efforts to dissuade from this doctrine of running to extremes. But I say let the same rules be applied. Let the Constitution be our guide.

This, then, was Johnson's most general step toward letting the Southerners know where they stood: "Let the Constitution be our guide." They were thus encouraged—if not commanded—to think of reconstruction in its general nature as a constitutional and legal problem rather than primarily a political one, and this in itself must have relieved their minds of much uncertainty. Since constitutional thinking was quite congenial to the Southerners anyway, we may suppose that their submission to Johnson's views must have been more or less cheerful and that squaring their own hopes—full restoration—with those views could be managed with a minimum of strain. As for "behavior," it seemed to follow that the definition given to this very vague notion was also being narrowed to essentially legal rather than political terms; conceivably, in this closer setting, many of the overtones in behavior which might otherwise influence undisciplined popular passions would not be subjected to excessive scrutiny.

A major elimination of alternatives had been made. Yet the South needed to have its problem defined in still another way. Nobody had to be told that the South must adjust to Northern power, but the Southerner who eyed the North with any alertness, any sensitivity at all, would not have been satisfied very long to think simply of generalized and undifferentiated "power." He would have wanted to know more specifically where that power was located. To which aspect of Northern power must the South accommodate itself? Which centers of prerogative must be watched most carefully? If all must look to the Constitution as their guide, who then was the true guide to the Constitution? By whose authority, in short, would reconstruction proceed? The President said, in effect, to those most concerned not to misconstrue his meaning, "It shall proceed by my authority, and mine alone."

When Johnson made it known in a variety of ways that he considered reconstruction solely an Executive function, so far as federal authority was needed to set it going, he was performing an act of communication whose effects would be diverse and far-reaching. He enabled the Southerners—indeed, he compelled them—to fasten their attention upon himself with a peculiar sharpness, while they might at the same time selectively ignore many a potential anxiety-point which had now been defined for them as having but secondary importance. The power to which they had primarily to adjust was the Executive; so far as their position was concerned, the legitimate authority variously resident in Northern opinion and in the other branches of the federal government was all being duly expressed and represented to them through the Executive. Should there be new developments and complications, political or whatever, then the Executive might be expected, in the proper course of things, to give the South due indication of them.

Not only did the President define for the South all those legitimate areas of authority which he in his person might safely be taken to represent; he also let them know where the illegitimate areas were—areas of opinion and feeling from which he dissociated himself and which were thus not entitled to be counted in the eventual settlement. Through his own words, he gave to "radicalism" a definition which the Southerners had no choice but to take as official and formal. When Mississippi organized its convention, for example, Johnson's telegram to Governor Sharkey was so conspiratorial in tone that it probably could not have exerted much leverage for getting what he seemed to be asking; but to the South it had much value just for the substantial morsels of information that might be con-

strued out of it. The President deprecatingly suggested that the convention might "with perfect safety" extend suffrage to certain heavily qualified
classes of Negroes in such a way as would "completely disarm the adversary." The "adversary" was named: ". . . the radicals, who are wild upon
negro franchise, will be completely foiled in their attempt to keep the
Southern States from renewing their relations to the Union by not accepting their senators and representatives." That is, there were men of evil
intentions who were not nearly so well disposed as Johnson himself to
permit a speedy restoration. On the other hand, given a reasonable cir-
cumspection, the presidential plan could be relied upon to provide the
necessary protection. "There may be speeches published from various
quarters," Johnson told the Southerners, "that may breathe a different
spirit. Do not let them trouble or excite you, but believe that it is . . . the
great object of the Government to make the union of these United States
more complete and perfect than ever. . . ." It was almost as though he had
defined as "radical" all sentiment, present or potential, that should make
any kind of objection to the course he himself had laid down. With such
official certification, at any rate, the South might have been excused for a
growing sense of reassurance:

It may safely be said [according to the Charleston *Daily Courier*] that the
views of Sumner, Thad Stevens, Wilson, and some other Northern Radicals
have been considered too unworthy to be seriously commented upon by
members of the convention. It is well known that the sentiments of these
gentlemen are extremely unpopular in the North.

Along with Johnson's concept of the presidency as the reconstructing
power, it was probably unavoidable that certain suppositions regarding the
legislative branch, and the extent of its authority in such matters, should
also be communicated to the South. On suffrage, he appears to have told
Governor Perry with great emphasis, "It must be left to the Legislature
of each State to decide who shall be allowed to vote in that State." He
also said, as Perry reported to the people of South Carolina, "Any attempt on the part of Congress to control the elective franchise of a State
would be an unwarrantable usurpation." Johnson's message to Sharkey
was only one of many in which the President expressed his conviction
that the South would be entitled by winter, barring radical sabotage, to
have its representatives in Congress. After the governors and conventions
had done their work, all that the states needed to do, in their organized
capacity as states, was to ratify the Thirteenth Amendment (though even
that, apparently, could not be absolutely insisted on), in order to "make
the way clear for the admission of senators and representatives to their
seats in the present Congress." This conviction was repeated before the

entire country in the President's annual message. The right of Congress to judge of its own membership was admitted by the President, but he chose to construe that right in the narrow procedural sense: members were to be admitted or rejected on their individual qualifications, not on any other basis. In other words, Congress had legally nothing to say on reconstruction: the process was complete by the time the states could present delegations for admission, and thus the power to pass on qualifications of members-elect would be a power improperly and unconstitutionally usurped should Congress presume to use it as an instrument of reconstruction.

This angle of the case, to say nothing of the many other implications concerning the President's own vast prerogatives, was apparently accepted in full faith by the South. Herschel Johnson of Georgia, hearing of the embarrassments which might be made for the Southern delegations at the opening of Congress, thought that a splendid way to settle the thing once and for all would be for the President simply to issue a proclamation announcing that they *were* entitled to representation. "It would not only delight the Southern States," he wrote enthusiastically to Watterson, in a letter intended for the President's eyes, "but, in my judgment, it would be a stroke of masterly policy. For being *constitutionally* qualified, no party in the North can be sustained who will advocate rejection." One might almost think that men of judgment had been pushed into something of a fool's paradise when it became possible for them to demand, in answer to doubts about the President's power in this connection: "Hasn't he the army?" The New Orleans *Picayune* thought that the President, to effect his full purposes, might actually require a military force during the first sittings of Congress—"but if so, the bayonets will be there!"

It might still be supposed that the Southerners were acting not primarily upon the cues they were getting from the President but simply out of perversity and unreason. Yet somewhere between the feelings of their own people and the things the President told them, they were understandably, and perhaps correctly, working out for themselves the limits of the possible. Since their primary responsibility was after all the repairing of Southern fortunes, there was a sense in which they were hardly doing wrong by applying themselves with great care to the work of discovering just where their liberty of action lay. Again, communication should be considered the primary key to this, and it should be recognized that for their purposes the communication process was critical. The point may be illustrated by a specific case study.

Though the Sharkey-Slocum affair has already been mentioned in other connections, the most instructive aspect of the episode may perhaps lie in its character as a sequence in communication. All the correspondence is available; moreover, the significant items were published in the newspapers at the time, and public men not only in Mississippi but everywhere in the South were thus given a peculiar opportunity to scrutinize and assess for themselves a series of dispatches that could tell them much of what they most needed to know in charting their own course. Governor Sharkey, greatly desiring to muster local militias throughout the state of Mississippi, told the President of his wishes, but then, without awaiting a reply, on August 18 he proceeded to issue a proclamation authorizing them. Johnson in his reply of the twenty-first (unaware of the proclamation) advised Sharkey not to take this step—reminding him of the efforts being made "by the extreme men of the North" to thwart Southern restoration—but instead to call on General Slocum for any military assistance that might be needed in suppressing disorder. Sharkey replied on the twenty-fifth, protesting that this would leave the state "in a helpless condition." "General Slocum," he said, "has no cavalry, and has not force enough to protect us. His negro troops do more harm than good when scattered through the country." Johnson, replying the same day, was still not disposed to accept Sharkey's view of the case but assured him that "the government does not intend to irritate or humiliate the people of the south, but will be magnanimous and remove the cause of your complaint at the earliest period it is practicable to do so."

Meanwhile, on the twenty-fourth, Slocum issued his "General Order No. 22." He declared that such an organizing of the young men would create greater difficulties than it would solve and ordered all those so engaged to cease and desist. Sharkey now called for a showdown between himself and Slocum. He wired Johnson on August 30, in language of exceptional belligerence (considering the personage he was addressing), and resurrected his version of some matters apparently touched upon in a prior talk with the President: "In our last interview you distinctly stated to me that I could organize the militia to suppress crime if necessary." He further declared,

General Slocum has thought proper to issue an order to prevent any such organization, and to arrest those who attempt it. His chief reasons seem to be because I did not consult him. Here is a collision that must be settled, and it rests with you to do it. I wish to be able to vindicate myself when trouble comes, as we apprehend it will.

It was two or three days before this that Carl Schurz, the President's special commissioner, had come upon the scene. Schurz's dispatch of the twenty-ninth to Johnson briefly but approvingly reported Slocum's order, and deplored what "would have been a fatal step," had it not fortunately been prevented. Johnson's first knowledge, then, of Slocum's order came not from Sharkey but from Schurz, and before he even received the

Sharkey dispatch of the thirteen (on the afternoon of the thirty-first) he had already sent his blistering telegram to Schurz, rebuking both him and Slocum:

I presume General Slocum will issue no order interfering with Governor Sharkey in restoring the functions of the State government, without first consulting the government, giving the reasons for such proposed interference. It is believed there can be organized in each county a force of citizens or militia, to suppress crime, preserve order, and enforce the civil authority of the State and of the United States, which would enable the federal government to reduce the army and withdraw, to a great extent, the forces from the States, thereby reducing the enormous expenses of the government. If there was any danger from an organization of the citizens for the purposes indicated, the military are there to detect and suppress on the first appearance any move insurrectionary in its character. One great object is to induce the people to come forward in the defense of the State and federal government. . . .

The main object of Major General Carl Schurz's mission to the south was to aid as far as practicable in carrying out the policy adopted by the government for restoring the States to their former relations with the federal government. It is hoped such aid has been given. The proclamation authorizing restoration of State governments requires the military to aid the provisional governor in the performance of his duties as prescribed in the proclamation, and in no manner to interfere or throw impediments in the way of consummating the object of his appointment, at least without advising the government of the intended interference.

Johnson, when he received Sharkey's telegram the next day, sent an identical copy of this message to him. It may be imagined that the Governor was filled with the sweetest satisfaction. He moved quickly to take the fullest possible advantage of the dispatch, and asked Johnson if he might publish it. "It will do great good; it will soothe a troubled public mind, it will give implicit confidence in you." Johnson promptly granted the desired permission, and the whole affair with all its particulars was spread across the newspapers of North and South.

Aside from the reaction which this episode produced in the North (to say nothing of its effect on Schurz and Slocum), it is important to consider what sort of enlightenment may have been given to Governor Sharkey himself, and to other persons in the South who were in any way concerned with public matters. The pertinent documents contained a wealth of what appeared to be the most official kind of information, and there were specific classes of inference that the South was fully entitled to draw. In the first place, Johnson was committed in the deepest personal way to a program of restoration, whose completion he was singularly impatient to see and with which he would brook no interference. In the second place, Johnson was convinced that whatever dangers to that program existed lay not in the South but in the North. Moreover, he felt his own position sufficiently correct, and sufficiently secure, that he could afford to move ruthlessly against any "radical" meddling, even at the expense of sanctioning Southern actions whose propriety had by no means been settled in his own mind. His sympathies appeared to be such that he was actually less tender of Northern feelings than of Southern: he had no wish "to irritate or humiliate the people of the south." To avoid it, he was quite willing to humiliate two of his own generals instead, and to do great damage to their effectiveness and influence, all with the fullest publicity. Furthermore, Johnson made it clear that already he regarded military occupation itself as an affair so strictly temporary that in any local conflict of jurisdiction he would be almost automatically predisposed in favor of the local civil authority: in short, he had more fully identified himself with the latter than with the former. And finally, in giving way before his provisional governor in the face of his own military commander and his own special envoy (who thereupon became no envoy at all), Johnson gave significant clues to the liberties with federal authority that Southern officials might take generally, without his insisting on anything to the contrary.

* * *

The Southerners could not know, of course, that whereas they were learning much about the President and his ambitions and intentions, they were at the same time being demoralized. The process of communication was in a positive sense revealing a great deal to them; the very same process, however, had a dark and negative side. There were matters of the most vital importance being concealed and obscured from them.

This negative aspect was somehow bound up with the President's failure —indeed, his refusal—to insist on terms. For all his assumption of prerogative, he would not put himself in the posture of an agent whose government required a specific settlement. Agents of no legal status—but agents nonetheless—awaited his pleasure, only too anxious to know the conditions under which they might bury their pretended "government" forever. That establishment was moribund, but it was still an entity of some kind and would remain so despite all legal fictions to the contrary until its affairs might with emphasis be liquidated once and for all. The South knew, in its way, as did the North, that such liquidation would have to occur rather more palpably and more visibly than by the mere waving aside of the war as an odd delusion which had really changed nothing. Virtually everything, in fact, had changed. Let it be called anything—

rebellion, organized treason, or whatever—but let it be something, simply that men might lay hold of the thing and dispose of it: let it be settled. Andrew Johnson did much to baffle this impulse when he refused to specify clear terms, communicate them to the concerned parties, and then insist that they be met. "The President . . . said that as Executive, he could only take the initiatory steps to enable them to do the things which it was incumbent upon them to perform."

Such was the position which Johnson had defined for himself that the whole process of reconstruction had to be called a voluntary one. True, there did have to be a "voluntary" aspect of this peacemaking. But conceivably to place so much of that responsibility on the defeated power as Johnson did, was to impose burdens beyond what the South was in a position to bear. It is in the nature of peace terms to a defeated enemy that they must partake, no matter how lightly, of the punitive; and there is something a little eerie about asking a helpless foe to prescribe his own penalties.

There would be terms, and there would not be terms. Johnson might hint to the Southerners of "things which it was incumbent upon them to perform," and yet deny that he was dictating to them. He could nod in a general way toward the kinds of acts which would be acceptable, but his own position—that all was being done through the free will of the people—denied him the resources, the graded standards, whereby he could say with assurance that such acts were or were not being performed acceptably. The free will of the people and the self-evident Constitution: here was something of a closed circle, a sacred grove wherein oracles might be consulted and from which omens might emerge, but nothing seemed to come out of it that resembled a hard and fast understanding among men of responsibility.

Thus, while men might imagine they heard Andrew Johnson saying, "Let there be terms," what were they to think when he not only shrank from spelling out the terms, with that precision and assurance which a dazed people needed, but provided no sanctions against their being met or not met—nothing that he was ready to stand back of in the name of his government, nothing for which *he* was prepared to be responsible? The President had assumed immense powers while shunning others that properly accompanied them; and having taken his position, he depended not upon the North but on the South—an impotent, disorganized, and prostrate entity—to sustain him in it. Just how much—more than one Southerner, in his second thoughts, might have asked himself—did the President really comprehend of their dilemma? How much did he care? How much attention was the President really paying to the efforts they were making? Could it be that Johnson wanted his restoration project so badly, was he so anxious, so irritably impatient to get it over with, that in his preoccupation it did not too much matter in the meanwhile what they did?

In any case, it was almost as though Johnson were goading the Southerners into taking liberties even with the things they knew he wanted. The most notable of such instances were Mississippi's nonratification of the Thirteenth Amendment and South Carolina's nonrepudiation of the Confederate debt. Here again, nothing is so instructive as Johnson's own message to the governors.

The pertinent sequence, in the case of Mississippi, is as follows:

Johnson to Sharkey, Aug. 15 [Hopefully]:
I hope that without delay your convention will amend your State constitution, abolishing slavery . . . also that they will adopt the amendment to the Constitution of the United States abolishing slavery.

Johnson to Sharkey, Aug. 21 [Still hopefully; perhaps if they do not care to do it one way, they might prefer the other]:
Your convention can adopt the amendment to the Constitution of the United States, or recommend its adoption by the legislature.

Johnson to Sharkey, Nov. 1 [Now wheedling; they still have not done it]:
It is all-important that the legislature adopt the amendment. . . . The argument is, if the convention abolished slavery in good faith, why should the legislature hesitate to make it part of the Constitution of the United States?
I trust in God that the legislature will adopt the amendment, and thereby make the way clear for the admission of senators and representatives to their seats in the present Congress.

Johnson to Sharkey, Nov. 17 [Downright plaintive; it would really be in their own interest to do this]:
Let the amendment to the Constitution of the United States abolishing slavery be adopted. . . .
I do hope the southern people will see the position they now occupy, and avail themselves of the favorable opportunity of once more resuming all their former relations to the government of the United States, and, in so doing, restore peace, prosperity, happiness, and fraternal love.

At no point does Sharkey, in any of his replies, acknowledge these hints. But on December 8 a copy of the legislature's committee report on the amendment, together with a resolution adopted December 2 regarding the same, is transmitted to the President:

The first and main section of the article has already been adopted by Mississippi, so far as her territory and people are concerned.
It was substantially . . . incorporated into the State constitution by the late convention. Now is it possible for the State by any act, or in any mode, conventional or otherwise, to change the status fixed by the convention?

. . . The second section is subject to more grave objections. It confers on Congress the power to enforce the article by "appropriate legislation." Slavery having been already abolished, there is really no necessity for this section, nor can the committee anticipate any possible good that can result from its adoption. On the contrary, it seems to be fraught with evils. . . .

If there be no danger now, the committee fear the time may come that the public mind might be influenced on this subject to the degree of endangering the reserved rights of the States.

The committee are also of the opinion that the present is not a propitious time to enlarge the powers of the federal government. The tendency is already too strong in the direction of consolidation. . . .

It would be unwise and inexpedient to open a subject which your committee had believed extinct, as themes for radicals and demagogues to use to the detriment of the best interests of the country. Mississippi cannot give her deliberate consent to leave open any question from which agitation can arise, calculated to disturb the harmony so happily being restored among the States and the people. . . .

Resolved, therefore, by the legislature of the State of Mississippi, That it refuses to ratify the proposed amendment to the Constitution of the United States.

"There is nothing," announced the *Picayune* triumphantly, ". . . to confirm the view that President Johnson holds the ratification of the amendment to be an indispensable duty, and as a condition precedent to their restoration to their functions as States in the Union."

In the case of South Carolina, the President addresses Governor Perry in general terms, as the convention is about to meet.

Johnson to Perry, Sept. 2:

I hope you will proceed with the work of restoration as rapidly as possible, and upon such principles as will disarm those who are opposed to the States resuming their former relations with the federal government. This is all-important.

Either the President has not made the debt question clear, or Perry thinks he may safely ignore it, for the latter telegraphs on September 20, after the convention is finished, still not having repudiated the debt: "I hope the action of our convention is satisfactory." And three days later, on September 23, to the Secretary of State:

I am happy to have it in my power to inform you that the State convention of South Carolina have done well, and shown a perfectly loyal spirit throughout all their proceedings. . . .

. . . They have, in fact, carried out all of my recommendations which were important. . . .

I enclose you a copy of my message. [Perry in his message does not mention repudiation of the debt among the "recommendations" he deems it necessary to have carried out.]

At this point the Secretary of State takes up the correspondence, speaking for the President:

Seward to Perry, Nov. 10:
He [the President] observes with regret that neither the convention nor the State legislature has pronounced debts and obligations contracted in the name of the State for unconstitutional and even rebellious purposes to be void.

Seward to Perry, Nov. 20:
Upon reflection, South Carolina . . . would not care to come again into the councils of the Union incumbered and clogged with debts and obligations which had been assumed in her name in a vain attempt to subvert it. The President trusts that she will lose no time in making an effective organic declaration, disavowing all debts and obligations created or assumed in her name in aid of the rebellion.

Perry to Seward, Nov. 27:
Your telegram of the 20th instant was not received in due time, owing to my absence from Columbia. The convention having been dissolved, it is impracticable to enact any organic law in regard to the war debt. That debt is very small, as the expenditures of South Carolina were reimbursed by the confederate government. The debt is so mixed up with the ordinary expenses of the State that it cannot be separated. In South Carolina all were guilty of aiding the rebellion, and no one can complain of being taxed to pay the trifling debt incurred in his own account in perfect good faith. The convention did all that the President advised to be done, and I thought it wrong to keep a revolutionary body in existence and advised their immediate dissolution, which was done. There is now no power in the legislature to repudiate the debt if it were possible to separate it from the other debts of the State. Even then it would fall on widows and orphans whose estates were invested in it for safety.

Seward to Perry, Nov. 30:
I have the honor to acknowledge the receipt of your telegram of the 17th instant informing me that, as the convention had been dissolved, it was impossible to adopt the President's suggestion to repudiate the insurgent debt, and to inform you that while the objections which you urge to the adoption of that proceeding are of a serious nature, the President cannot refrain from awaiting with interest an official expression upon that subject from the legislature.

Nothing at all, however, was done about the debt, and the Columbia *Phoenix* praised what everyone knew to be Perry's own stubborn opposition to any action on it. The *Picayune* had already predicted: "As the President, however, endorsed the action of Mississippi, so will he doubtless endorse also that of Alabama and South Carolina; and it matters not a straw whether the fanatics like the programme or not. Let them rave." Meanwhile Secretary Seward, in his message of December 23 relieving Perry, serenely took leave of the truculent provisional governor by saying: "It gives me especial pleasure to convey to you the President's acknowledgement of the fidelity, the loyalty and the discretion which have marked your administration."

In the Mississippi election, Benjamin G. Humphreys, an unpardoned Confederate general, was a candidate for governor, and it was well known not only in Mississippi but all over the country that Johnson did not want him elected. But Humphreys would not withdraw, and he was subsequently elected. Johnson's reaction to this rebuff has been cited by one writer as an example of the President's firmness: "Humphreys was not recognized as Governor of Mississippi until Johnson saw fit to pardon him. . . . Johnson knew how to be firm when he chose." It is unlikely, however, that anyone in Mississippi so construed it. Humphreys was elected on October 2, had himself inaugurated on the sixteenth, and was handed his pardon on the twenty-sixth. Johnson's displeasure consisted in telling Sharkey (as, for that matter, he told all the others) that he was to remain as provisional governor until duly relieved; if the President really considered not recognizing Humphreys, it must have been awkward in the meanwhile to have to instruct Sharkey—as he did—to show certain presidential dispatches to the governor-elect. Sharkey was relieved on December 14 (sooner than any of the other governors except Holden) and told to turn over the state's affairs to Humphreys. The Baton Rouge *Tri-Weekly Advocate* hooted at the New Orleans *Star* for advising men who had been prominent in the rebellion not to "force themselves upon the people":

President Johnson has "forced" a number of men "prominent in the rebellion" into high positions since he became President. . . . The long and short of it is, this cry about men not running for office who have fought heroically for the past four years in a cause they loved, is all nonsense. . . . Their past bravery and their frank submission to the Government is the best guarantee of their future fidelity, a fact known and already recognized by the President.

When it came to the black codes—so wrathfully denounced in the North and so often cited as the prime instance of Southern tactlessness —it might at least be said on behalf of the Southerners that not only had they received no hint from the President concerning the inadvisability of such codes but there was actually little evidence in Johnson's prior or subsequent behavior that he himself disapproved of them.

There was even evidence that he considered the legislatures to have been quite within their rights. He had ample foreknowledge of what these legislatures were preparing to do. Governor Perry wired on October 29 that he had submitted to the South Carolina legislature "a code of laws on this subject, prepared by order of the convention." He thought it would be passed. Two days later he sent the President a copy of the convention journal, together with the proposed code in its entirety.

In Mississippi, Governor-elect Humphreys, though not recognized by the President, immediately took over the duty of advising the legislature on laws regulating the freedman. In his inaugural address on October 16, published everywhere, he said that the Negroes should be protected in person and property, and should be compelled to fulfil their labor contracts. He also declared, "It is due to ourselves . . . to maintain the fact that ours is and it shall ever be a government of white men." He sent a message to the legislature on October 20, again urging the passage of a code. A committee had in fact already been working on the matter (as in South Carolina) since the convention, and its report was submitted a few days later, with a proposed series of laws.

> While some of the proposed legislation may seem rigid and stringent to the sickly modern humanitarians, they can never disturb, retard or embarrass the good and true, useful and faithful of either race, . . . while the wayward and vicious, idle and dishonest, the lawless and reckless, the wicked and improvident, the vagabond and meddler must be smarted, governed, reformed and guided by higher instincts, minds and morals higher and holier than theirs. . . .

All these items received the fullest publicity.

In each case, the governors supposed such legislation to be part of the process that would bring them closer to full restoration. They imagined that it would hasten the removal of the military, and particularly of the Freedmen's Bureau (strongly denounced by Humphreys in his message), by taking over the functions which the Bureau was currently performing. Both Perry and Humphreys said as much to their legislatures, and even the President had uttered thoughts which might be construed as encouragement:

> There is no concession required on the part of the people of Mississippi, or the Legislature, other than a legal compliance with the laws and Constitution of the United States, and the adoption of such measures giving protection to all freedmen and possession of property without regard to color, as will entitle them to assume their constitutional rights in the Federal Union.

No sooner had the Mississippi code been passed than General O. O.

Howard, head of the Freedmen's Bureau, took the initiative and tele-
graphed orders to his assistant commissioner on November 30 suspend-
ing much of the new code in that state. Similar action was taken a month
later in South Carolina when General Sickles declared that state's entire
code to be "null and void." But all that Johnson himself did was to
refrain from reversing what his commanders had done, thus simply allowing the codes' non-enforcement. As a matter of fact, the governor of
Mississippi immediately sent to Washington a committee of two, protesting Howard's action, and the committee was assured by the President that "none of the acts should be nullified except by courts of law."

What had happened? Besides leading the South into realms of fantasy
regarding the true location of Northern authority, the nature of majority sentiment, and the support which he himself could command for whatever policies he deemed proper, the President had at the same time
thrown away most of the vast bargaining power with which he had
started out. Having placed an extraordinary amount of faith in the
non-coercive side of his role—a side which by definition put extra stress
upon techniques of persuasion and negotiation—he had then proceeded
to breach all the most basic principles of advocacy, diplomacy, and bargaining. As advocate for the plaintiff, he had in effect conspired with
the defendant; as representative of a sovereign nation, he had cut himself off from the power of his government; as bargaining agent, he
had kept shifting the terms of the bargain so that nobody could be
sure what he was asking for. Even as judge, as mediator, as go-between
—to whatever extent his role partook of those functions—he had got
himself and his emotions openly involved in the claims of the one side,
at the expense of those of the other. Such behavior would certainly have
sabotaged the business of any courtroom, chancellery, or bargaining table;
as for the affairs of an entire nation, the disruption which may have been
effected there, and the extent of its consequences, can only invite speculation. That the primary victim of those consequences—the defeated
South—should have been in any position to point out the President's
errors, to resist them, or to aid him in repairing them, is a likelihood
that cannot be taken with very great seriousness. For once the President's
attitude had been fully revealed, the South, by the very nature of its
position, could not for a minute afford to see things through eyes other
than his.

But if the President had done disservice to Southern claims—to say
nothing of Northern—in his negotiating character, it is just as conceivable in a curious way that from the coercive side of his role he may
have done them even deeper mischief. To say that the problem had its
negotiating aspects is most important, but it should never carry us too

far from the primary thing, which was that the South had been defeated in war; no amount of words could talk away the fact that the South was being confronted by its conqueror. Nor was there any use pretending that the South was not in some sense being asked to pay; no fact, for the South, could have been more immediate. Thus no matter what the beaten enemy might be asked to do, no matter how little, it would be idle to imagine that he should derive the least pleasure from it —except for the relief, once it was done, of having it cleanly and honorably over with. Moreover, it is much to be doubted that there was any real mercy in telling the enemy that his punishment, especially if never made fully clear, must be undergone voluntarily—or much realism in expecting, on that basis, that he would go about it in any but a confused and afflicted state of mind. In those areas in which the South was, indeed, without choice, it was conceivably better to say so, and to order that the thing be done—coolly, sparing the Southern gentlemen those words about "forgiveness" and "fraternal love" which could not sound in their ears without some ring of mockery until a later, happier day. Some things are easiest to do when there is no choice at all.

On those rare occasions when President Johnson, in his dealings with the South, did come in any way close to laying down the law, those concerned responded immediately, almost with alacrity. Contrasted with the oddly inhibited character of most of the President's dispatches, there is something of the coiled spring in his message to Holden on the North Carolina debt:

> Every dollar of the debt created to aid the rebellion against the United States should be repudiated finally and forever. The great mass of the people should not be taxed to pay a debt to aid in carrying on a rebellion which they in fact, if left to themselves, were opposed to. Let those who have given their means for the obligations of the State look to that power they tried to establish in violation of law, constitution, and the will of the people. They must meet their fate. . . . I repeat [etc.]. . . .

He spoke to Georgia in similar language, and in both cases the thing was done. In Alabama, the relative ease with which the Executive wishes were carried out was doubtless due in some measure to the fact that there happened to be in Washington men of influence communicating those wishes to Governor Parsons in terms stronger and more precise than those used by the President himself. In South Carolina, at the same time, Governor Perry's success in convincing the convention delegates that he could be counted on to represent reliably to them what the President would and would not stand for was what gave him such extraordinary influence. Sidney Andrews, who was present at the time of the convention, wrote of Perry that his position, in the peculiar circumstances of the hour, makes his word and wish of very unusual significance. . . . it is an almost every-hour occurrence, in the debates, that the question is asked, "Is that view approved by the Provisional Governor?" or that the remark is made, "I think we had better consult the Governor first." So it may be said that he is the leader of the Convention.

Indeed, there were repeated occasions on which the Southerners themselves had to beg Johnson to make himself clear on a thing if he really wanted them to do it. A member of the South Carolina legislature wrote, regarding the unrepudiated debt: "Make the *requirement absolute*, the state will meet it." Indeed, Johnson's strong words to North Carolina and Georgia on that same subject were not forthcoming until the governors themselves, in each case, urged the President by telegraph to declare himself. Even in Tennessee, when difficulty arose in November over the enactment of a Negro testimony bill, the Tennessee secretary of state, recognizing that the bill would not pass unless the legislature were convinced that its failure to do so would have a bad effect on Tennessee's chances of readmission, implored the President to telegraph an "opinion" for his use in the matter. A question of some delicacy in Georgia was the election of United States senators. The preference in the legislature was for such men, prominent in the Confederacy, as Alexander Stephens and Herschel Johnson, and the election of a Unionist like Joshua Hill would only be possible through the express influence, unmistakably exerted, of the administration. Hill himself informed the President to this effect. "I tell you," a prominent man of Richmond said to Whitelaw Reid, "President Johnson can name his Senators and they will be straightway elected. He can say what he wants, the Virginia legislature, so-called, will register his edicts in legislative enactments."

There was much evidence that men of influence in the South initially understood their own position a good deal more clearly than did the President. There was much quibbling in the early sessions of the Mississippi convention over abolishing slavery in the state constitution, and a series of resolutions was introduced by one of the ablest delegates, casting doubts upon the validity of emancipation. Three prominent judges, men of conservative views, thereupon took the occasion, one by one, to lay things on the line and remind the convention exactly where it stood, and in terms Johnson himself would never have dreamed of using. J. W. C. Watson reminded the delegates that they were a conquered people, that their freedom of action was impaired by the very circumstances under which they met, and that they had no right to dictate to Congress the terms of their readmission. "Gentlemen talk as if we had a choice," Judge Amos Johnston then declared, "but we have no choice, and it is no humiliation to admit it. The only course we can pursue is that dictated to us by the powers at Washington." Judge William Yerger spoke of the Northern people's determination not to be "trifled with." "As men of sense," he admonished them, "let us endeavor to remedy what we cannot alter, and gather together whatever may tend to palliate our misfortunes." The speeches made quite an impression on the convention, and by a large majority the resolutions were tabled forthwith.

The "men of sense" whom Judge Yerger invoked had declined in influence by November, but there were enough of them, even then, who were appalled at the passage of the black code. The laws were denounced by some of the foremost newspapers of the state, including the leading one, the Jackson *Clarion.* The Columbus *Sentinel* said that the legislature had been controlled by

a hard and shallow-headed majority, that were far more anxious to make capital at home than to propitiate the powers at Washington. They were as complete a set of political Goths as were ever turned loose to work destruction upon a state. The fortunes of the whole South have been injured by their folly.

Nowhere in the South, any time, could more than a tiny minority have been assembled to enact of its own free will even a qualified Negro suffrage. But it is important to note that things were still open enough in the summer of 1865, all through the South, that men of standing could discuss with surprising freedom even this subject as a possibility. Professor Fleming, writing in 1905, said that in Alabama political leaders talked a great deal about suffrage in 1865, and that even before the Reconstruction Acts, Negroes were allowed to vote in a few local elections. General James L. Alcorn of Mississippi, one of the two senators elected by that state in 1865, was convinced that if the whites did not make the Negroes their friends through the franchise, their path would be "red with blood and damp with tears." A few of the leading men in South Carolina felt that it would be wise and proper to enact a limited Negro suffrage; among them were A. Toomer Porter, Wade Hampton and his brother Christopher, Joseph LeConte, and Judge Edward Frost (who had headed the delegation that visited the President on June 24). "I insisted," wrote LeConte, "that the convention should adopt a franchise *without distinction of color,* but with a small educational and property qualification. My friends admitted the wisdom of the suggestion but said that it was impossible, as the leaders had not 'backbone' enough to propose it, and the people were not ready to indorse it."

Here we may revert once more to the early aftermath of the surrender, with the themes it contained, and make a final effort to appreciate the crushing effects of defeat, the ruin which lay in all hearts and minds, the South's apprehension of unnamable penalties, and the mute petition of the South for any kind of settlement. "The months of May and June," wrote Whitelaw Reid, "were the chaotic period of the returning Rebel States. All men were overwhelmed and prostrated under the sudden stroke of calamity which the fewest number had anticipated." The theme of irreconcilability—of rage, bitterness, and hate—was mingled and balanced with that of submission, and of exposed sensitivity, and readiness to do what had to be done.

The first feelings were those of baffled rage. . . . Then followed a sense of bewilderment and helplessness. Where they were, what rights they had left, what position they occupied before the law, what claim they had to their property, what hope they had for an improvement of their condition in the future—all these were subjects of complete uncertainty.

. . . They expected nothing; were prepared for the worst; would have been thankful for anything.

In North and South Carolina, Georgia, and Florida, we found this state of feeling universally prevalent. The people wanted civil government and a settlement. They asked no terms, made no conditions. They were defeated and helpless—they submitted. Would the victor be pleased to tell them what was to be done?

But things had apparently begun to happen when the President started imposing himself on Southern feelings. J. R. Dennett, much impressed by the orderly state of sentiment in South Carolina in midsummer (the people of that state having gone into the rebellion "more earnestly and honestly" than anywhere else, had acquiesced in their defeat "more honestly and promptly than any others"), thought it just possible by late August that a "reaction" may have occurred, "caused by the premature establishment of civil government, unsettling their minds, and interrupting a healthy progress of opinion." Reid, who had been in the South from early May to midsummer, took another trip in November and found the people's temper much changed. "Yesterday they cringed for pardon at the feet of 'the boorish and drunken tailor' they had denounced; today they are harder to satisfy than ninety and nine just men who have no need of repentance." About this time Johnson's own provisional governor in North Carolina, William W. Holden, wrote to the President in rather pathetic words that betrayed something close to a failure of nerve:

I regret to say that there is much of a rebellion spirit still in this state. In this respect I admit I have been deceived. In May and June last these rebellious spirits would not have dared to show their heads even for the office of constable; but leniency has emboldened them, and the Copperhead now show his fangs. . . .

I communicate these corrections with regret. It may be that the policy of the government has been too lenient; or it may be that I have seriously erred in the discharge of duty, or that I was not the proper person for Provisional Governor. . . . I am ready and willing at any moment to retire from this position; and if you have the shadow of a wish that I should do so, I pray you as a friend to let me know it.

Johnson had encouraged the Southern people to think of him as their protector against the Black Republicans of the North. He himself had so defined the picture for them, and such were the illusions he had given them of his power that even a year later, when any remnants of that power had all but collapsed, they could still look forward to the fall elections of 1866—which would actually bring Republican landslides—expecting a triumphant vindication for the President and themselves. Their shock may well have been all the worse, since they had come to know that the President would not use his power to coerce *them*. Meanwhile the President, all unwittingly, may have worked a still subtler mischief with the feelings of two whole peoples as they emerged from conflict. Standing in the ambiguous position which he had taken up between them, he had with the best of intentions cut himself off from the deepest needs of both. It may be supposed that these enemies, when the fight was over, wanted at least to respect each other, so that they might the more respect themselves for the exertions they had made, and to put aside their arms at least in the honorable knowledge of pride well served. This may be the point at which the "balm of time" idea is actually most relevant. A certain decent punctilio of reserve was needed, a due season of correctness and repose not to be interrupted by too many exhortations to "fraternal love" from a man whose title to the place he held could never be quite above doubt—a man whom neither North nor South, with all good will, could quite help regarding as an outsider. In such a setting as this, and with Johnson's special position vulnerable just on general principles, one can imagine that the President's resources might have been much augmented by a greater willingness to share his authority.

In the interests of the South's own pride, it might possibly have been as well that the basic terms of the settlement, if there was going to be one, should initially be concluded with a minimum of reference to the people—though for maximum success the parties to it would have had to be men whom the people trusted, men fully identified with the cause. The possibilities of secret diplomacy, if such it might be called, were about at an end by December, 1865. One of the reasons was that the presidential power, to which Southerners had been so ready to adjust earlier, was not being put to coercive uses. Since by winter this was more or less clear to all, the new power to which Southern political leaders were now having to adjust, in ever increasing degree, was the power of their own constituencies—that is, the will of the people. Democracy in such circumstances is of course the enemy of diplomacy. All this placed ever greater limits on these men's freedom of action, so limited already—a kind of freedom indispensable for complying with demands bound to be distasteful no matter what. Moreover, they needed sanctions of coercion at their backs, for their own protection, so that they might tell the people, as Judge Johnston told the Mississippi convention, "we have no choice, and it is no humiliation to admit it." Every "political Goth" (as the Columbus *Sentinel* might have put it) that came down from the Mississippi hills to sit in the legislature spelled that much less influence for the likes of Judge Johnston, Judge Yerger, and General Alcorn. . . .

Triumph of the Conservatives

KENNETH STAMPP

Whereas McKitrick stresses the failure of President Andrew Johnson to use the powers available to him in 1865 on behalf of a moderate Reconstruction program, Kenneth Stampp's emphasis falls on the failure of Johnson's successor, President Grant, to act energetically so as to salvage the Radical Reconstruction policy ten years later. The end of Republican efforts to remake Southern society, described by Dunning early in the century as "the undoing of Reconstruction" (no. 6), appears to revisionist Stampp as "the triumph of the conservatives."

The reader will note that Stampp, like Sharkey, revises rather than rejects Beard's fundamental contention that the Civil War was a capitalist

Kenneth Stampp, *The Era of Reconstruction 1865–1877* (New York, 1965), pp. 186–192, 204–215.

revolution. He explains how the idealist wing of the Republicans fell away through death—as with Stevens and Sumner—or disillusionment, and how the direction of party policy passed to political bosses and spokesmen for economic interests. By the early 1870s neither group considered a continuation of Congressional Reconstruction essential to its ends. Republican politicians, having consolidated new constituencies in the Northwest, "no longer needed the votes of Southern Negroes." Northern economic leaders, as Stampp says following Hesseltine (no. 8) and Woodward, discovered that "the conservative Democratic leaders of the New South were no longer enemies but allies."

For Du Bois, writing at the turn of the century, the end of Reconstruction was unqualified tragedy. Now that the verbal pledges of the Fourteenth and Fifteenth Amendments have begun to be redeemed, it can appear (in Stampp's words) that "it was worth a few years of radical reconstruction to give the American Negro the ultimate promise of equal civil and political rights."

THE YEAR 1876, THE CENTENNIAL OF AMERICAN INDEPENDENCE, had special meaning for southern white Democrats. This was the year when they fought the last great battle with the radical Republicans; when, in the folklore of the white South, a new generation of Minute Men engaged in another heroic struggle to throw off the yoke of tyranny and oppression. Eight of the southern states had already fallen to the Democrats,[1] but three of them—South Carolina, Florida, and Louisiana— were still in the hands of the coalition of carpetbaggers, scalawags, and Negroes. In the elections of 1876, the Democrats claimed to have won these remaining states; and the new President, Rutherford B. Hayes, though a Republican, was not inclined to dispute the point. In April 1877, Hayes withdrew the last federal troops from the South and surrendered political control of South Carolina, Florida, and Louisiana to the Democrats.

The South was "redeemed." This favorite euphemism of the white Democrats meant that the federal government had renounced responsibility for reconstruction, abandoned the Negro, and, in effect, invited southern white men to formulate their own program of political, social, and economic readjustment. These developments were by no means the least of the tragedies of the so-called "tragic era." How they came about remains to be explained.

[1] The Democrats won control of Tennessee in 1869; of Virginia and North Carolina in 1870; of Georgia in 1871; of Alabama, Arkansas, and Texas in 1874; and of Mississippi in 1875.

The first sign of what might ultimately happen was the decision of the Republicans in 1868 to nominate Ulysses S. Grant for the presidency—to pass over all of the recognized Republican leaders in favor of a popular military hero who would appeal to the less committed and more practical elements in the party. Grant lacked the moral dedication that was so vital an element in Republican radicalism; in fact, he had been a conservative until Johnson had pushed him into the arms of the radicals. He failed to provide the firm leadership that was essential in a period of profound social change. In spite of his good intentions, he contributed little but political ineptitude. Worst of all, he filled his Cabinet with mediocrities and party hacks, some of whom helped to give the Gilded Age its shabby reputation.

The inauguration of Grant marked the approaching end of the Republican party's creative role as the political instrument of what Charles A. Beard has called "The Second American Revolution." [2] Since its birth in the 1850's this party had been a dynamic force in the political, social, and economic life of the United States. It had sponsored the policies which hastened the triumph of an urban-industrial social order over the already declining rural-agrarian interests centered in the South and West: the protective tariff; a new national banking system; a sound paper currency in national bank notes secured by government bonds; a prohibitive federal tax on the note issues of irresponsible state banks; federal subsidies for internal improvements, especially for the railroads; the sale of mineral and timber resources on the public domain to private enterprise; and finally, in 1869, an act providing that federal securities, most of which had been purchased during the war with depreciated paper money, were to be redeemed in gold. Having achieved all this, the Republican party's economic role became less dynamic—more one of consolidation, of defending policies already in force against the criticism of discontented groups, especially farmers and urban workers. Thus, on questions of economic policy, Republicans began to find themselves on the defensive rather than on the attack.

Their southern policy, too, was now almost completed. They had crushed the secession movement, restored the Union, and vindicated American nationality. They had destroyed the Calhoun conception of state sovereignty—never again would a group of disaffected states contemplate disunion as a potential remedy—and the trend toward expanding federal power went on relentlessly. Republicans had permanently reduced the enormous political influence that the South had enjoyed before

---

[2] The label that Beard gave to the years of the Civil War and reconstruction is quite appropriate, but it implies more than his narrow concentration on economic change.

the war. They had achieved the abolition of slavery, written guarantees of civil and political rights for Negroes into the federal Constitution, and fully developed a program of political reconstruction. By 1869 land reform was a dead issue, and the Freedmen's Bureau began to wind up its affairs. Thus Republicans disavowed further federal responsibility for the Negro's economic future, or for providing him with educational opportunities. Here, too, future Republican policy would be one of retrenchment, of consolidation, not one of continuing development. Practical Republicans still found the votes of Negroes useful, and until the mid-seventies they continued to support the southern radical governments as best they could. But radical reconstruction was clearly entering a period of decline, and the constructive role of the Republican party in the remaking of the South was nearly finished.

These changes in the character and function of the party were accompanied by the decay and rapid disappearance from public life of the old radical leadership. Thaddeus Stevens died in August 1868, and his death brought joy to the hearts of conservative white Southerners. "The prayers of the righteous have at last removed the Congressional curse!" wrote one southern editor. "May his new ironworks wean him from earth and the fires of his new furnaces never go out!" Many of Stevens's Republican colleagues in the House sighed in relief, too, as they were freed from his stern parliamentary leadership; and so did the bankers and bondholders who distrusted this monetary heretic.

Stevens was only one of many radicals who were removed from public life by death or retirement. Joshua R. Giddings, Edwin M. Stanton, and Salmon P. Chase joined Stevens in the hell to which conservatives had consigned them; in 1869 Benjamin F. Wade lost his seat in the Senate, and the next year George W. Julian lost his seat in the House. Charles Sumner and Carl Schurz broke with Grant early in his first administration, and Grant's henchmen completely destroyed Sumner's power in the Senate. Horace Greeley, editor of the New York *Tribune,* and Edwin L. Godkin, editor of the *Nation,* both repudiated Grant and the Republican policy in the South. Many former abolitionists showed little understanding of the free Negro's postwar problems. In short, the force of a great movement for social reform seemed to be spent, and its leadership was being lost.

To replace the old Republican radicals a new set of leaders emerged and soon won a dominant position in the Grant administration. These new leaders were appropriately called stalwarts, for in conformance with the party's changed role they favored not radicalism, not reform, but the *status quo.* Some of the stalwarts were ruthless bosses of state political machines; some were almost paid retainers of railroad, oil, textile, and steel interests. They were the men who completed the institutionalization of the Republican party; who, more than ever before, made the quest for office an end in itself; and who, through the spoils system, prostituted the federal civil service. Among the more colorful of the stalwart leaders were several of the state bosses: Senator Oliver P. Morton of Indiana, Senator Roscoe Conkling of New York, Senator Simon Cameron of Pennsylvania, and Representative Benjamin F. Butler of Massachusetts.

The remnants of the old crusading radicals found this new Republican leadership appalling, and they began to wonder whether their party had outlived its usefulness. "Like all parties that have an undisturbed power for a long time," wrote Senator James W. Grimes of Iowa, the Republican party "has become corrupt, and I believe it is today the most corrupt and debauched political party that has ever existed." George W. Julian, one of the most dedicated radicals of the 1860's, revealed his disillusionment when, in 1884, he wrote his political recollections. To begin with, he recalled, the Republican movement had been "a political combination, rather than a party. Its action was inspired less by a creed than an object, and that object was to dedicate our National Territories to freedom, and to denationalize slavery. . . . The organization was created to deal with this single question, and would not have existed without it." By the 1870's many regarded the Republican party "as a spent political force, although it had received a momentum which threatened to outlast its mission." Julian then spoke of the "new problems" of the postwar years; and, significantly, he did not count the plight of the southern Negroes among them. He had turned his attention to other things: "Our tariff legislation called for a thorough revision. Our Civil Service was becoming a system of political prostitution. Roguery and plunder, born of the multiplied temptations which the war had furnished, had stealthily crept into the management of public affairs." But the Republican party, "led by base men," ignored all these issues and sought to retain its power "by artful appeals to the memories of the past." What the country needed, Julian concluded, "was not . . . the fostering of sectional hate, but oblivion of the past, and an earnest . . . endeavor to grapple with questions of practical administration."

It was sentiment such as this that caused many of the old reformers to repudiate Grant in 1872, to help form the so-called Liberal Republican party, and to support its candidate, Horace Greeley, for the presidency. Schurz, Julian, Sumner, Theodore Tilton, David Dudley Field, and many other one-time radicals were among the rebels in that campaign. Their platform was a plea for civil service reform and for honesty and efficiency in government. Though accepting the Fourteenth and Fifteenth Amendments, the platform also demanded universal amnesty and an end to military rule in the South. To these disenchanted men the radical governments had failed, the Negro as a freedman had been a disappointment,[3] and home rule under the old white leadership was the only way to restore honest government.

Ironically, it was the pro-Grant stalwart faction of the Republican party that continued to stand by the southern Negroes and to demand that their civil and political rights be protected. The stalwarts still hoped to maintain a southern Republican party with Negro votes; and as political realists who did not expect too much of frail humanity, they were not so easily disillusioned with the radical governments as were the moral reformers. Since the Grant Republicans won the election of 1872, the federal government stood by the carpetbaggers, scalawags, and Negroes a while longer. But the party split—the disaffection of the Liberal Republicans and their concentration on other issues—was a clear sign that the crusade for Negro rights had lost its vitality.

• • •

[There were] various forces operating against the radicals within the South. But if violence and intimidation were the weapons of the conservatives, why was there no effective federal intervention? Why did President Grant and Congress permit the Mississippi Plan to succeed? Why were the Fourteenth and Fifteenth Amendments, the Force Acts, and the Civil Rights Acts not enforced? Why were more federal troops not sent into the South to protect the Negroes? In answering these questions some additional reasons for the collapse of the radical governments may be discovered.

In the first place, it should be obvious that once the Republicans rejected land reform and abolished the Freedmen's Bureau, their political alliance with southern Negroes was at best an uneasy one. Negroes joined the Republican party because it had given them civil and political rights and because southern white Democrats were hostile to them, not because they found Republican policies on other postwar issues particularly attractive. As small farmers, tenants, sharecroppers, and unskilled rural and urban laborers, their interests were far removed from those of the leaders of northern business enterprise to whom most Republican legislators usually deferred on matters of economic policy. Here and there Negro farm laborers tried to organize, and occasionally they attempted through strikes and collective bargaining to achieve a minimum wage. In the early 1870's, when the Granger movement spread into the South, Negroes began to organize their own Granges and to discuss the plight of the American farmer. Such activities were well calculated to cool the ardor

[3] Sumner and some of the old abolitionist leaders, however, did not lose faith in the Negro.

of stalwart Republicans for the Negroes as political allies. In 1871 a northern Republican, observing that in Georgia some six thousand adult whites were illiterate, warned that "if to them were added the whole bulk of the Negro population, so vast a mass of ignorance would be found that, if combined for any political purpose it would sweep away all opposition the intelligent class might make. Many thoughtful men are apprehensive that the ignorant voters will, in the future, form a party by themselves as dangerous to the interests of society as the communists of France."

Meanwhile, at the time that the Liberal Republicans were denouncing their party's southern policy, a number of regular Republicans began to toy with Lincoln's scheme of appealing to the Whiggish propertied elements in the South. Jacob D. Cox of Ohio, Grant's first Secretary of the Interior, was one of the earliest to advocate such a course. Never enthusiastic about radical reconstruction, Cox had described it privately as "one of those revolutionary excesses which play most powerfully into an adversary's hands." In 1871 he suggested, again privately, that the Republican party ought to make peace with, and bid for the support of, the "thinking and influential native southerners," the "intelligent, well-to-do, and controlling class." The following year a Virginia conservative told Schurz that many white Southerners "take the Democratic party as the choice of evils. Many who now vote with the Radicals, a large number of old Whigs, and all who call themselves conservatives . . . want to defeat both Radicalism and Democracy." Even some of the carpetbaggers broke with the Negroes and became "independent" Republicans in alliance with conservative southern whites. These were the seeds from which eventually grew the Compromise of 1877 and the subsequent Republican abandonment of the Negro.

Northern businessmen, who became increasingly concerned about continued turbulence in the South, were especially eager to have the Republican party come to terms with conservative Southerners. Capitalists with an interest in the South as a field for investment had at first given their support to the Johnson program; but they were soon disillusioned with the President and turned to the radicals. What businessmen sought were conditions favorable to northern economic penetration of the South, and the radicals aided them, especially the railroad promoters, in a number of ways. However, they were distressed by the violence and, in some cases, financial instability that were a part of southern politics during the radical regimes; for these conditions were bad for trade and frightened capital away.

By 1870 the New York *Commercial and Financial Chronicle,* the New York *Tribune,* and the *Nation* were demanding an end to radical reconstruction, because it was paralyzing southern business and discouraging those who had capital to invest in that section. In May the *Nation* reported that "businessmen of the highest character" from New York and Boston had been examining conditions in the South "with reference to investments" and that they had found the state of affairs quite discouraging. Five years later, William E. Dodge, a New York capitalist and Grant Republican, returned to the same theme. "What the South now needs," he said, "is capital to develop her resources, but this she cannot obtain till confidence in her state governments can be restored, and this will never be done by federal bayonets. . . . As merchants we want to see the South gain her normal condition in the commerce of the country; nor can we hope for a general revival of business while things remain as they are." As for the southern Negroes, Dodge concluded that it had been a mistake to make them feel "that the United States government was their special friend, rather than those with whom their lot is cast, among whom they must live and for whom they must work. We have tried this long enough. Now let the South alone."

Thus Republican politicians found less and less sympathy among northern businessmen for their southern program. It appeared that only southern conservatives could restore order and political stability and thus create conditions favorable to economic development with northern capital. Moreover, since southern conservatives were being converted to the gospel of a "New South" which would emphasize commerce and industry, they could now be relied upon to give northern businessmen a friendly welcome. Radical reconstruction was then not only not essential, it was a nuisance.

Republican politicians also found that Northerners in general were growing tired of the reconstruction issue, that appeals to them on behalf of southern Negroes were greeted with massive indifference. Waving the bloody shirt to revive the passions of the Civil War eventually reached the point of diminishing returns; for, by the 1870's, most Northerners were as little concerned about the alleged disloyalty of southern white men as they were about reports of continued outrages against southern Negroes.

Then came the business panic of 1873, followed by four years of severe depression and the exposure of scandals in the Grant administration. These events dealt the American people a series of shattering blows. Grant, once the great military hero and the embodiment of numerous national virtues, though personally honest, was now associated with corruption and the debasement of the civil service. Jay Cooke, the most powerful banker in America, presumed to be a model of business probity, went bankrupt because he speculated recklessly in railroad securities.

Even the Reverend Henry Ward Beecher of Plymouth Church in Brooklyn, the best-known preacher in America, to whom many middle-class Protestants looked for moral guidance, became involved at this inopportune time in a private scandal that culminated in a trial for adultery. If men such as Grant, Cooke, and Beecher, Republicans all, had feet of clay, the country was in a sorry state. To the *Nation* the remedy was clear: give the South home rule, and the country would "once more resume the path of careful and orderly progress from which the slavery agitation and its consequences have during the last generation driven us. It were better that all the blacks and whites now living south of Mason and Dixon's line were sunk in the sea than go on as we are going now, for we are forming habits and establishing precedents which can only lead to a result over which many generations would mourn and wonder."

As they became concerned about business stagnation, unemployment, collapsing farm prices, and the decay of public and private morals, Northerners not only lost interest in reconstruction but temporarily lost faith in the Republican party. The bloody shirt could no longer control the outcome of an election, and in 1874 the Republicans lost control of the House of Representatives—their first political defeat in a national election since the Civil War. After the Democrats gained a majority in the House, there was no chance that additional federal protection would be given to southern Negroes. Instead, the House Democrats, in 1876, refused to pass an army appropriation bill in order to force the President to withdraw federal troops from the South. It was then that one Republican politician concluded that the people were bored with the "worn-out cry of 'southern outrages' "; another now remembered that the Civil War had not been fought primarily to free the slaves—that the Negro was not "the end and aim of all our effort."

Under these circumstances the absence of federal intervention when the Mississippi Plan went into operation is understandable. In 1875, Governor Ames begged Grant's Attorney General, Edwards Pierrepont, to give protection to the Negroes of his state during that violent election. But the federal government took no action. A delegation of Republicans from Ohio, where an election was also being held that year, warned President Grant that if he sent troops to Mississippi his party would lose Ohio. Grant decided to save Ohio and sacrifice the Negroes of Mississippi. His Attorney General's reply to Governor Ames was that the people were "tired of these annual autumnal outbreaks in the South." With this "flippant utterance," Ames later recalled, "the executive branch of the National government announced that it had decided that the reconstruction acts of congress were a failure."

During the state and presidential elections of 1876, when violence broke out in South Carolina, Florida, and Louisiana, President Grant would do nothing more than issue a sanctimonious proclamation. Indeed, when the outcome of that election was in dispute, Republicans had to bargain hard with southern Democrats in order to secure the peaceful inauguration of Rutherford B. Hayes. In one last sectional compromise, that of 1877, the Republicans promised to remove the remaining federal troops in the South, to be fair to Southerners in the distribution of federal patronage, and to vote funds for a number of southern internal improvements. In return, southern Democrats agreed to acquiesce in the inauguration of Hayes and to deal fairly with the Negroes.

The Compromise of 1877 signified the final end of radical reconstruction, for with the removal of federal troops, the last of the radical regimes collapsed. Soon after his inauguration President Hayes made a goodwill tour of the South. Conservative Democratic leaders, such as Governor Wade Hampton of South Carolina, greeted him cordially and assured him that peace and racial harmony now reigned in the South. Hayes tried hard to believe it, because he hoped so much that it was true.

"What is the President's Southern policy?" asked ex-Governor Chamberlain of South Carolina. Judged by its results, "it consists in the abandonment of Southern Republicans, and especially the colored race, to the control and rule not only of the Democratic party, but of that class at the South which regarded slavery as a Divine Institution, which waged four years of destructive war for its perpetuation, which steadily opposed citizenship and suffrage for the negro—in a word, a class whose traditions, principles, and history are opposed to every step and feature of what Republicans call our national progress since 1860."

It was in the 1870's, then, and not in 1865, that the idealism of the antislavery crusade finally died. Along with the loss of the idealism that had been one of the prime motivating forces behind radical reconstruction, the practical considerations also lost their relevance. Whereas in 1865 the urban middle classes still regarded the agrarian South and West as a serious threat, by the 1870's their position was consolidated and their power supreme. By then the leaders of business enterprise had so far penetrated the Democratic party and had so much influence among the so-called "redeemers" of the South that they no longer equated Republican political defeat with economic disaster. Samuel J. Tilden, the Democratic presidential candidate in 1876, was a wealthy, conservative New York corporation lawyer, thoroughly "sound" on monetary, banking, and fiscal policy, in no respect unfriendly to business interests. Whichever way the presidential election of 1876 had gone, these interests could hardly have lost. Grover Cleveland, the only Democrat elected President between James Buchanan before the Civil War and

Woodrow Wilson in the twentieth century, was also "sound" and conservative on all the economic issues of his day.

As for the Republican party, it too felt more secure than it had before. In 1865 it was still uncertain whether this party, born of crisis, could survive in a reunited, peaceful Union in which the slavery issue was resolved. But by the 1870's the party was firmly established, had an efficient, powerful, amply endowed organization, and had the unswerving support of a mass of loyal voters. True, the Republicans lost the congressional elections of 1874 and almost lost the presidency in 1876, but this could be attributed to the depression and abnormal conditions. Normally, in order to exist as a major national party, Republicans no longer needed the votes of southern Negroes. The reason for this was that during and since the war they had won control of the Old Northwest, once a stronghold of agrarianism and copperheadism.[4] Indeed, a significant chapter in the history of reconstruction is the political and economic reconstruction of this flourishing region. The Civil War, the identification of the Republican party with nationalism and patriotism, the veteran vote, the Homestead Act, and federal appropriations for internal improvements all helped to make the states of the Old Northwest Republican strongholds. Moreover, the westward advance of the industrial revolution—the growth of urban centers such as Cleveland, Detroit, and Chicago—identified powerful economic groups in the Old Northwest with the industrial interests of the Northeast.

How these western states voted in the eleven presidential elections between 1868 and 1908 is significant when it is remembered that they had consistently gone Democratic before the Civil War. In eight elections the Old Northwest went Republican unanimously. Of the seven states in this region, Indiana voted Democratic three times, Illinois and Wisconsin once, the rest never. Thus, with the Old Northwest made safe for the Republican party, the political motive for radical reconstruction vanished, and practical Republicans could afford to abandon the southern Negro. With the decline of the idealism and the disappearance of the realistic political and economic considerations that had supported it, radical reconstruction came to an end.

Viewing radical reconstruction with its three chief motivating forces in mind, are we to call it a success or a failure? Insofar as its purpose was to consolidate the position of American industrial capitalism, it was doubtless a striking success. During the last three decades of the nineteenth century, social and economic reformers subjected irresponsible business entrepreneurs to constant attack, but they won no significant

[4] The states of the old Northwest include Ohio, Indiana, Illinois, Michigan, Wisconsin, Minnesota, and Iowa.

victories. In fact, they met constant defeat, climaxed by the failure of the Populists in the 1890's. With William McKinley, the conservative son of an Ohio industrialist, installed in power in 1897, American capitalism rode to the end of the nineteenth century with its power uncurbed and its supremacy not yet effectively challenged. Above all, the conservative Democratic leaders of the New South were no longer enemies but allies.

Politically, radical reconstruction was also a success. Even though Republicans failed in their effort to establish an effective and durable organization in the South, they nevertheless emerged from the era of reconstruction in a powerful position. Most of their subsequent political victories were narrow; sometimes they lost a congressional campaign. But until Wilson's election in 1912, only once, in 1892, did the Democrats win control of the presidency and both houses of Congress simultaneously. And if conservative Republican Congressmen counted almost no Southerners in their caucus, they found a large number of southern Democrats remarkably easy to work with. The coalition of northern Republicans and southern Dixiecrats, so powerful in recent Congresses, was an important fact of American political life as early as the 1880's. The coalition had to be an informal one and had to endure a great deal of partisan rhetoric, but it was real nonetheless.

Finally, we come to the idealistic aim of the radicals to make southern society more democratic, especially to make the emancipation of the Negroes something more than an empty gesture. In the short run this was their greatest failure. In the rural South the basic socioeconomic pattern was not destroyed, for share-cropping replaced the ante-bellum slave-plantation system. Most of the upper-class large landowners survived the ordeal of war and reconstruction, and the mass of Negroes remained a dependent, propertyless peasantry. After reconstruction, in spite of the Fourteenth and Fifteenth Amendments, the Negroes were denied equal civil and political rights. In 1883 the Supreme Court invalidated the Civil Rights Act of 1875; in 1894 Congress repealed the Force Acts; and in 1896 the Supreme Court sanctioned social segregation if Negroes were provided "equal" accommodations. Thus Negroes were denied federal protection, and by the end of the nineteenth century the Republican party had nearly forgotten them. In place of slavery a caste system reduced Negroes to an inferior type of citizenship; social segregation gave them inferior educational and recreational facilities; and a pattern of so-called "race etiquette" forced them to pay deference to all white men. Negroes, in short, were only half emancipated.

Still, no one could quite forget that the Fourteenth and Fifteenth Amendments were now part of the federal Constitution. As a result, Negroes could no longer be deprived of the right to vote, except by extralegal coercion or by some devious subterfuge. They could not be deprived of equal civil rights, except by deceit. They could not be segregated in public places, except by the spurious argument that this did not in fact deprive them of the equal protection of the laws. Thus Negroes were no longer denied equality by the plain language of the law, as they had been before radical reconstruction, but only by coercion, by subterfuge, by deceit, and by spurious legalisms. For a time, of course, the denial of equality was as effective one way as the other; but when it was sanctioned by the laws of the Johnson governments and approved by the federal government, there was no hope. When, however, state-imposed discrimination was, in effect, an evasion of the supreme law of the land, the odds, in the long run, were on the side of the Negro.

The Fourteenth and Fifteenth Amendments, which could have been adopted only under the conditions of radical reconstruction, make the blunders of that era, tragic though they were, dwindle into insignificance. For if it was worth four years of civil war to save the Union, it was worth a few years of radical reconstruction to give the American Negro the ultimate promise of equal civil and political rights.

An American Crisis (Ideological)

W. R. BROCK

It has long been clear that the failure of Reconstruction must be ascribed not merely to the role of capitalists in the Republican Party, the indecision of President Johnson, or the failure to divide plantations in the South, but also to an evaporation of concern on the part of the Negro's Northern friends. White America, even abolitionist white America, lost interest. Why?

Radical Republicanism was (in the words of Kenneth Stampp) "the last great crusade of the nineteenth-century romantic reformers." Hence it shared the weaknesses of nineteenth-century liberalism along with the strengths. This meant a recurring temptation to abandon the Negro to the operation

W. R. Brock, *An American Crisis: Congress and Reconstruction, 1865–1867* (London, 1962), pp. 284–304. Reprinted by permission of St. Martin's Press, Inc., Macmillan & Co., Ltd.

of "natural" economic forces, on the theory that the state's responsibility ended when each man had been given an equal start in life's race. But what did "equality" mean? Which were the natural "inalienable" rights which government was bound to guarantee? In words recalling Du Bois' 1903 position, Brock declares: "The Radical solution to the dilemna of rights which were natural but which could be secured by artificial means was negro suffrage."

Synthesizing many of the strands of interpretation included in this volume, Brock concludes: "The failure of Radicalism is a part of the wider failure of bourgeois liberalism to solve the problems of the new age which was dawning." Ideally, what should the federal government have done? Brock suggests: "If it is believed that nothing should have been done the responsibility of the Radicals for having done something is clear . . . [but] though one may blame them for their determination to have a revolution it is a little unfair to blame them for being forced to stop half-way."

IT IS COMPARATIVELY EASY TO EXPLAIN THE WANING OF RADICALISM IN terms of personal failure, evaporating enthusiasm, the urgent demands of business, and the tendency of all political organizations to fall into the hands of professionals. It is easy also to see how the challenge of the new age, with its manifest problems of the relationship between private business and public authority, had a divisive effect upon the Radicals—turning Kelley into a fanatical protectionist, Schurz into a free trader, Butler into a Greenbacker, and Donnelly into an agrarian radical—while drawing together the main body of Republicans around the citadel of American capitalism. But the break-up of Radicalism may also reflect more profound weaknesses in the position which it maintained.

It has been argued that much of the Radical success was explained by the pressures from below which drove cautious politicians even further than they had intended, and that this pressure must be explained in ideological terms and not as the product of mere interest groups. The ideology had expressed in abstract but attractive terms certain propositions about man in society which, for a moment in time, seemed to epitomise the aspirations of the Northern people. Racial equality, equal rights and the use of national authority to secure both were living ideas in the Reconstruction era as they have since become, in some quarters, in the mid-twentieth century. For the first time these concepts were cast in the form of a political programme which could be achieved; but their success depended upon the response which they aroused from the Northern people. After Reconstruction the ideas persisted but failed to rouse the same enthusiasm; their formal acceptance was a very different thing from the popular emotion which could push them forward despite the usual obstacles to policies which disturb complacency and refuse to let men rest in peace. The question remains whether the slackening of the pressure behind the Radical ideology should be explained by rival distractions and changing interests or by a weakness in the ideology itself. Examination will show that the generalities of the Radical ideology—so attractive at first sight—could not stand pressure. The weapons bent and broke in the hands of those who used them.

A belief in racial equality has never won universal assent and to the majority of men in the mid-nineteenth century it seemed to be condemned both by experience and by science. The literal equality between men of obviously different physiological characteristics was an abolitionist invention and it rested upon emotional conviction rather than upon rational proof; the comparison between intelligent negroes and retarded poor whites proved little because the civilization of a few blacks did not redeem the mass from docile ignorance and the degradation of some whites did not detract from the high standards of the majority. The abolitionist argument was based largely upon pure *a priori* statements or upon experience with fugitive slaves; a mass of argument could be produced against the one, while the defiance of the occasional runaway did not prove that the mass of his fellows were not fitted by nature for a subordinate position. The behaviour of the negro was obviously different from that of the whites and, though those who knew him best granted him some admirable traits, they would also maintain that he was sadly deficient in the capacity for industry, thrift, self-reliance, enterprise, sexual restraint and the whole galaxy of virtues esteemed by nineteenth-century civilization. The abolitionist argument that the negro appeared 'inferior' because he had lived in slavery for generations failed to carry weight because no free negro society could be found to prove the proposition. Moreover there was an added complication in the mixed ancestry of so many of those who, like Frederick Douglass, were quoted as evidence of innate negro intelligence. This is not the place to enter upon the tangled problem of racial characteristics; it is sufficient to state that in the later nineteenth century racial equality was a hypothesis which was generally rejected. It was not accepted in the North any more than it was in the South and even abolitionists were anxious to disclaim any intention of forcing social contacts between the races and all shied away from the dread subject of racial amalgamation. An initial weakness of the Radical ideology was therefore its dependence upon a concept which was not self-evident, lacked scientific proof, and offended popular susceptibilities.

The usual weakness of equalitarian theory lies in demonstrating that people ought to be treated as equals in spite of natural inequalities, and this difficulty is acute when dealing with people of different races. While it is possible to argue, among men of the same race, that it is necessary to treat men as though they were equal, it is far harder to do so in the face of popular prejudice that men of a different race are marked at birth as 'inferior.' The conventional Republican argument was that men were unequal in capabilities but equal in rights, and in the American context this proposition rested mainly upon an appeal to the preamble of the Declaration of Independence; but the assertions of the Declaration were not 'self-evident' to most white Americans when applied to negroes. Moreover there were some particular difficulties in equalitarian theory when applied to a mass of people, concentrated in a single region, and occupying from time out of mind a subordinate position in society. Equality demands protection of the weak against the strong and positive law to afford it; but it usually involves the assumption that given certain legal rights the due process of law will enable men to maintain their equality. With the negroes this assumption could not be made: what was required was protection, maintained by enforceable law, at every point where the power of the dominant race was likely to impinge upon the weaker. With tradition, economic power, prejudice, social custom and, in most Southern districts, numbers all entrenched on one side, protection could not be provided merely by changing the law and leaving its administration to the local authorities and courts. The concept of negro equality demanded interference with the processes of local government on a scale never before contemplated in America or in any other nation. Would the Northern majority be prepared to exert continuously this kind of pressure and provide this kind of protection? In the answer to this question lay the second great weakness of the Radical ideology.

Further difficulties lay in the complexities which sheltered behind the simple word 'equality.' Whatever the moral arguments the negro was not, and could not be in the immediate future, an equal to the white man in economic life, in competition for the scarce education facilities of the South, or in winning public office. Racial equality would have to be an artificial creation imposed upon Southern society; the negro would have to have guarantees which were not given to the white man, and the quest for equality would demand unequal incidence of the law. No other minority required special legislation to ensure equal status in the courts, or the care of a Federal bureau, or the use of force to protect the right to vote. Negro equality implied that something must be taken from the whites, and this was explicit in two features of Radical policy: confiscation and disqualification. Stevens never wavered in his belief that negro democracy must have an economic basis in negro landownership; confiscation and redistribution were therefore cardinal points in his programme. Yet the most passionate advocates of equality could not persuade the Republican majority to embark upon such a disturbance of property. Negro democracy would also be a sham if the former ruling class retained its grasp upon local and national office, and disqualification was necessary. This policy succeeded because it was supported by Northern fear of restored Southern domination at Washington, but it proved to be the most vulnerable and perhaps the least wise aspect of Reconstruction. Both confiscation and disqualification demonstrate the formidable difficulties which attend the imposition of equality upon a society in which it did not exist, and in which the beneficiaries of equalitarian policy were too weak, socially and economically, to stand upon their own feet. The price of equality was revolutionary change, vigilance and constant pressure, and who would pay the price when enthusiasm grew cold and the suspicion grew that the negroes were not yet ready to exercise rights which could not be secured without the coercion of their fellow citizens.

It is in this context that the work of John A. Bingham assumes great significance. In his fight for the civil rights clause of the Fourteenth Amendment he cut equal rights free from negro protection and made them national. The later perversion of this clause to protect the rights of corporations tended to obscure the significance of a measure which protected all citizens and all persons under the jurisdiction of the States, but once the importance of nationalized right was recognized the Fourteenth Amendment grew in stature. Conversely the Fifteenth Amendment was weak from the outset because it linked suffrage with race; it was a law for negro enfranchisement and could be enforced only so long as some people had an interest in doing so. If the Fifteenth Amendment had declared in unequivocal terms that all males over the age of twenty-one who were citizens of the United States had the right to vote it might have been recognised as a cornerstone of democracy and attracted popular support. As it was the Fifteenth Amendment enacted "impartial" suffrage which meant that the States could impose any qualification they chose provided that it was not based on race; this meant that the white majority of the nation had no particular interest in its enforcement.

Beyond the major problem of equality by enforcement lay the vast and ramifying difficulty of definition. Was equality indivisible or if divisible which aspects were essential? The three classic definitions of equality—*in* the eyes of God, *under* the law, and *of* opportunity—each carried different implications. Equality in the eyes of God might well be an excuse for inequality on earth: Dives and Lazarus had both lived under the judgment of God, both received their deserts after death, and their inequality on earth was dramatic but irrelevant to their condition in eternity. Equality in the eyes of God implied some limitation upon the principle of subordination for it had been an essential part of the abolitionist case that the children of God should not be treated as less than human beings, but it provided no definition of the place of man in society. Many pious Northerners saw no inconsistency between Christian conviction and racial discrimination, and the brotherhood of man in Christ was no barrier to the belief that equality on earth was no part of God's purpose. It was therefore necessary to supplement the Christian concept of equality in eternity with the purely secular arguments for equality on earth.

Equality under the law had deep roots in the Anglo-Saxon tradition but in its mother country it had not proved incompatible with aristocratic privilege, an established Church, denial of suffrage to the masses, and the exploitation of low paid labour. The guarantee of equal status in the courts was a great and important addition to the rights of negroes, but it would not of itself create a political and social revolution. Beyond the formal guarantee of equality under the law lay the intractable question of who should administer the law. The legal rights of negroes might be recognized in Southern courts but they were likely to be strictly interpreted; one could be confident that the white Southern judge would administer the law scrupulously, but between the negro and equal justice stood the white Southern jury. Equality under the law was a grand sweeping theory, without which no other form of secular equality was possible, but it did not erase the notion that the negro was an inferior man to whom only a grudging recognition was extended. It might be argued that, once the groundwork of legal equality had been laid, the progress towards equality in other fields would follow, yet one might doubt the certainty of this hypothesis. It was only in 1867 that the British Parliament was to decide after centuries of equality under the law that the agricultural labourer was entitled to a vote, and millions of simple Englishmen still went unlettered to their graves.

Equality of opportunity seemed to be a more positive demand. If the racial barrier could be removed from access to education, occupation and public office the negro would have the right to compete on equal terms with the whites in most of the fields to which his aspiration might lead him. Yet equality of opportunity implied inequality of achievement and in the South its immediate result might be the confirmation of white supremacy. If the negro was to be given a real chance of equal achievement he must be given positive aids which were not given to the white man, and one was brought back once more to the basic problem of equalitarian theory: that positive government was required to correct habitual inequality. This led on to the political difficulty that, in the climate of nineteenth-century opinion, sustained and purposeful government intervention was unpopular and improbable. The comparatively modest aims of the Freedmen's Bureau aroused intense hostility in the South and many doubts in the North; any further attempt to translate the commitment to equality into governmental responsibilities might wreck the whole structure of Reconstruction, yet without this the purpose of equalitarian Radicalism could not be achieved.

Many Republicans contended that it was unnecessary to embark upon the troubled sea of racial equality if one could stop in the safe haven of guaranteed rights. The negro was a man, and as a man he had certain inalienable rights; if these could be secured the vexed question of equality could be deferred or perhaps dismissed. This theory of inalienable right had better prospects than any theory of equality. American tradition had long accepted as its cornerstone the idea of man as an atom in society, entitled to do all that was within his power provided that it did not impinge upon the rights of others. But American tradition had usually failed to recognize the fact that rights were not 'inalienable', that the exercise of legal rights depended upon the consent of the majority, or that some rights of some men could always be denied by the sovereign power of the people. In Reconstruction Americans were brought face to face with the problem of free men whose 'rights' were denied by the local majority and could be secured only by external coercion. Moreover the whole attitude of Americans towards rights had been governed by their implicit acceptance of the idea of checks and balances. The rights of the people were a check upon the enlargement of authority, and to give some rights to some people at the expense of others had been damned by association with the idea of privilege. What was the intrinsic difference between rights conferred upon a chartered monopoly and rights conferred upon a weak minority? This conundrum had always been implicit in American political discourse but Reconstruction made it explicit.

Even if these pitfalls could be avoided there remained the knotty problem of which rights should be protected and how they could be distinguished from rights which were unprotected. The Declaration of Independence referred to the rights of life, liberty and the pursuit of happiness, but these were *among* the inalienable rights and not an exclusive list; and even if one stopped short at the classic three the pursuit of happiness was so elastic an idea that it was little guide to an enumeration of rights which could be protected by law. There were three main attempts to distinguish the categories of right and to determine which could, and which could not be protected. The first was the distinction between civil rights and political rights, the second between those which were fundamental and those which could be left to the discretion of political authorities, and the third was that between public and private rights. The first proposal made by Thaddeus Stevens—that all laws, state and national, should apply equally to all persons—attempted to cut through this maze of difficulties. Later Sumner was to express the same idea when he said 'Show me . . . a legal institution, anything created or regulated by law, and I will show you what must be opened equally to all without distinction of color.' This was the true Radical argument. It recognized that private prejudice could not be legislated out of existence, but maintained that discrimination could be prohibited in every activity touched by the law. Stevens and Sumner would have left people to do what they liked in their homes or in private associations, but they would have outlawed discrimination at the polls, in public places, on public transport, and in education. Sumner even hoped to add churches, cemeteries and benevolent institutions to this list. He resisted the argument of 'separate but equal' by asserting that 'Equality is where all men are alike. A substitute can never take the place of equality.' At the other end of the Republican spectrum was Lyman Trumbull who said the civil rights' (which should be guaranteed by law) were 'the right to his liberty, to come and go as he pleases, have the avails of his own labor, and not to be restricted in that respect.' In other respects the legal rights of negroes must depend upon the discretion of their political sovereign for these were 'all matters of privilege.' This attempted to treat the negro as a free man without treating him as an equal man, and Trumbull even regarded the right to serve on a jury as one of these matters of privilege.

Before the Reconstruction controversy ended moderate Republicans including Trumbull himself, had moved significantly nearer to the Radical view of rights which ought to be guaranteed, but there remained a distinct cleavage between those who believed that wherever the law flowed it should carry with it equality of right, and those who believed that one soon reached a frontier at which a 'right' became a 'privilege' and could be withheld at the discretion of the legal sovereign. The extreme Radical position was unequivocal and relatively uncomplicated, but would require a large invasion of the traditional areas of State authority; the 'moderate' position was clouded with difficulties of definition and separation but in the nature of things it was more likely to appeal to the majority of men who disliked sweeping logic and preferred to believe that the minimum of effort would produce the best results. Under the circumstances the best which the Radicals could obtain was probably the imprecise but traditional phrases which Bingham wrote into the Fourteenth Amendment. The 'privileges and immunities' of citizens of the United States, 'the equal protection of the laws,' and 'due process of law' were all expressions which could mean as much or as little as lawyers were prepared to read into them. They did not prevent the Supreme Court from legalizing segregation but they also provided ammunition for the Court's later attack upon segregation. It is possible that Bingham's first suggestion, which would have given to Congress the responsibility for initiating measures to protect rights, would have obviated some of the difficulties inherent in judicial legislation; but Congress, even more than the Court, would be unwilling to act until there was sufficient public interest to support action. Once the Northern majority had refused to accept the principle that wherever the law operated race must be forgotten, and had accepted the distinctions between rights which were rights and rights which were privileges, the whole idea of equality under the law was lost. Natural right became neither more or less than the right which the majority was prepared to recognize and to protect.

Charles Sumner realized the dangers inherent in the attempt to split up the rights of man into various categories, and devoted the closing years of his life to a struggle for a measure which would have embodied the Stevens principle of equal incidence of national and State laws on all citizens. When he was accused of occupying the time of the Senate with arguments over access to hotel rooms or the exclusion of negroes from benevolent institutions he replied that 'Every question by which the equal rights of all are affected is transcendant. It cannot be magnified, But here are the rights of a whole race, not merely the rights of an individual, not merely the rights of two or three or four, but the rights of a whole race.' A year after Sumner's death Congress enacted some of the provisions of the bill for which he had fought and guaranteed to the negroes equal rights in hotels, places of public entertainment, and public transport, but did nothing about education. In 1883 the Supreme Court found this Act invalid on the ground that it was intended to protect 'social' and not 'civil' or 'political' rights. In 1896 the Supreme Court upheld a State law requiring segregated facilities on railroads, and the tide of Radicalism which had once lashed so furiously against the ramparts was at its lowest ebb. Only a bold man could have predicted that the stone which the builders rejected was to become a cornerstone of liberal orthodoxy in the second half of the twentieth century.

The Radical solution to the dilemma of rights which were natural but which could only be secured by artificial means was negro suffrage. With the vote the negro would be equipped to protect his own rights, and there were Jeffersonian echoes in the idea that the cultivator of the soil would not only defend his personal rights but also act as a repository for political virtue. The voting negro would protect himself against injustice and the Union against its enemies, but this concept of suffrage as a protective device proved inadequate when Reconstruction govern-ments were compelled to assume the tasks of modern administration in a region where the best government had always been that which governed least. So long as the vote was merely protective the ignorance of the negro was not a relevant argument because a poor man could understand what had to be defended as well as the best educated; but when negro suffrage became the basis for an economic and social revolution guided by positive government it was relevant to ask whether the former slave was yet equal to his responsibilities.

The Radicals argued the case for the negro suffrage in the context of nineteenth-century liberal thought, and they can hardly be blamed for not having transcended the ideas of their age. Moreover they were inhibited by the political cirumstances in which they had to operate. It was hard enough to convince Northern public opinion that negro suffrage was safe and just without complicating the question. In the summer of 1866 a Radical member of the Reconstruction Committee told Congress that 'we may as well state it plainly and fairly, so that there shall be no mis-understanding on the subject. It was our opinion that three fourths of the States of this Union (that is of the loyal States) could not be induced to vote to grant the right of suffrage, even in any degree or under any restriction, to the colored race.' Between this time and the passage of the Fifteenth Amendment a remarkable change took place in public opinion, but in order to foster it the Radicals were forced to rely less and less upon appeals to abstract justice and more and more upon the utility of the negro vote to the party and to the Union. This stress led them to pass lightly over the tasks which negro democracy might be called upon to perform, and to treat their votes merely as a counterweight in the political balance of the nation.

Radicals themselves hesitated at times over the problem of the vote. Was it one of the inalienable rights, or was it, as everyone else said, a political right which could be granted or withheld at the discretion of the political sovereign? Among the conservative Republicans, and par-ticularly amongst the better educated, there was genuine hesitation about mass democracy, and if they turned one eye towards the negroes of the South they turned the other to the foreign-born city vote which formed the electoral basis of Boss Tweed's New York ring. Reformers could join hands with the merely fearful in urging the case for universal literacy tests, and old Know-Nothings could make common cause with new Re-publicans against universal suffrage. Yet literacy tests which would exclude the mass of the Southern negro people, and could be manipulated by the ruling State authorities, were useless as a political solution in the South, and Radicals were pushed from their early caution on the suffrage question to an outright avowal of belief in universal suffrage. In a letter written for communication to a Republican meeting in New York in January 1868 Thaddeus Stevens insisted that the right to vote was inalienable, and put natural right ahead of the argument from utility, but he went on to stress the other arguments in favour of universal suffrage. 'True, I deemed the hastening of the bestowal of that franchise as very essential to the welfare of the nation, because without it I believe that the Government will pass into the hands of the loco-focos, and that such an event will be disastrous to the whole country. With universal suffrage I believe the true men of the nation can maintain their position. Without it whether their suffrage be impartial or qualified I look upon the Republic as likely to relapse into an oligarchy which will be ruled by coarse Copperheadism and proud Conservatism. I have never insisted that the franchise should be unjustly regulated so as to secure a Republican ascendancy but I have insisted and do insist that there can be no unjust regulation of that franchise which will give to any other party the power if the Republicans are true to themselves and do not fall into their usual vice of cowardice. The Republicans once beaten into a minority by the force of Negro prejudice will never again obtain the majority and the nation will become a despotism." Six months before his death Stevens explained that after long reflection he had "finally come to the conclusion that universal suffrage was one of the inalienable rights intended to be inserted in (the Declaration of Independence) by our Fathers at the time of the Revolution and that they were prevented from inserting it in the Constitution by slavery alone." His reflection owed more to the exigencies of contemporary politics than to a knowledge of history, but there is no need to doubt the sincerity of his conclusion. Universal suffrage was the logical and complete answer; "impartial" suffrage was not. With Stevens dead, however, there was no one with the same influence who could put the case so clearly and the Fifteenth Amendment enacted impartial and not universal suffrage. The Radicals failed in the first instance because they did not or could not spell out what negro democracy was to do, and the second instance because they could not resist the modification of the right to vote which let in literacy tests, grandfather clauses, and poll taxes.

Paradoxically some of the Radical arguments for negro suffrage tended to rebound. The idea that the vote would enable the negro to protect himself provided an excuse for non-intervention, and for the belief that the Southern question could now be treated as a local question. In 1880 James G. Blaine, writing in the *North American Review*, justified the grant of negro suffrage by saying that 'had the franchise not been bestowed upon the negro as his shield and weapon for defense, the demand upon the General Government to interfere for his protection, would have been constant, irritating and embarrasing. Great complaint has been made for years past of the Government's intereference, simply to secure to the colored citizen his constitutional right. But this intervention has been trifling compared to that which would have been required if we had not given suffrage to the negro.' It was thus easy to infer that having instituted negro suffrage as an automatic regulator of the Southern political mechanism Northerners could turn their eyes away from what actually went on in the South. To be fair one should add that when Blaine wrote the extensive disenfranchisement of the negroes had not taken place, and that in some districts he could vote freely provided that he voted for the Democratic ticket.

It is not suggested that equal participation by the negro in Southern politics would have been automatically secured if the Radicals had succeeded in establishing the suffrage as an "inalienable right," but an unequivocal statement that all adult males had the right to vote would have been easier to enforce and more difficult to evade. Nor is it suggested that universal suffrage would have done anything to solve the vexed and unexamined qusetion of what the negro was to do with his vote. What is suggested is that the Fifteenth Amendment was a weak compromise which failed to achieve the Radical aims and, in the long run, helped to discredit that freedom of State action which moderates wished to preserve. Under the Reconstruction Acts all "loyal" males had voted; the Fifteenth Amendment allowed States to retreat from that position while the belief that the suffrage was secured on equitable terms allowed the Northern majority to relax pressure at the point where it was most needed. The keystone of the Radical arch proved too weak to hold up the edifice. In a sense negro suffrage was premature—though it could have been written into the law at no other time—but this was only in part the result of negro immaturity. Beneath the surface of the suffrage question lay larger problems of the role of government in a democratic State and these American society as a whole was unwilling or unready to contemplate. By 1880 *The Nation,* which had earlier given somewhat lukewarm support to negro suffrage while insisting that it should be impartial and not universal, was emphasizing that the *quality* of voters should be the primary consideration. For the intelligentsia who had, for the most part, thrown their influence behind Radical Republican-isf, the great national problem was no longer the protection of negro rights but the defense of public morality, social respectability and economic orthodoxy against demagogues, bosses, agitators, agrarian Radicals, and mass ignorance.

It has been argued in the preceding pages that an essential weakness in the Radical programme lay in its demand for national intervention to secure equality and protect rights, exercising a power which was unfamiliar and depending upon the support of public opinion which might well be apathetic or even hostile to its objectives. The arguments for enlarged national power were made clearly and forcibly, and there was no failure on the part of the Radicals to realize that their policy demanded the use of national authority not only on a greater scale than ever before but also upon new principles. The idea which had been presented in Sumner's 'Freedom National' speech of 1852 had germinated and grown until it was possible to see the nation newly based upon equal right and abandoning the divided sovereignty of the past. 'It certainly seems desirable,' said the moderate Luke Poland in 1866, 'that no doubt should be left as to the power of Congress to enforce principles lying at the very foundation of all Republican government if they be denied or violated by the States.' This was a constant theme of the Republican party and one which brought forth the most bitter cries of anguish from their opponents. 'The time was,' said one Democrat in 1869, 'when the suggestion of grave doubts of constitutional warrant would cause the advocates of pending measures to hesitate, to reflect. . . . Innovation and reform, however specious and desirable, were rejected at once and finally unless clearly sanctioned by constitutional authority.' Six years later another Democrat expressed the common view of his party when he charged that Republican interpretation of the Constitution 'freed from all verbiage and ambiguity . . . amounts simply to the assertion of a supreme power in Congress over every subject that concerns the life, liberty and property of any person within the United States; in other words over everything that is the subject of the law.' The detached observer may well ask what was wrong with the exercise of such power, and why the national government should not remedy the deficiencies of the States. The Radicals did not wish to scrap the Constitution, but they thought that its failure in 1861 demonstrated the need for greater flexibility in interpretation and greater concentration of power at the centre. This may appear to have been not unreasonable, but by and large the Democrats have had the best of the argument, and modern historians have echoed their criticisms though approving an extension of national authority during the New Deal which went far beyond the wildest expectations of the Radicals. It remains to ask why the concept of strong national government, which has proved so attractive to so many men in the twentieth century, did not gather the support which might have sustained it during the later nineteenth century.

Some of the explanations are obvious. The weight of tradition was against strong national government, and the word 'centralism' was bogey enough to frighten large numbers of people who would not stop to ask what was being centralized, by whom, and for what purpose. Increased national authority might put power into the hands of those who were distrusted by the would-be reformers, and the professional politician might be the beneficiary from an attempt to provide the national government with a moral purpose. Roscoe Conkling had a telling point against the opponents of 'centralism' when he said that 'Every civilized government may protect its citizens in the uttermost ends of the earth, but when the United States interposes to check murders, and burnings, and barbarities at which humanity shudders, perpetrated by thousands, and overawing all local authority, it is suddenly discovered that we are in danger of "centralism." ' Yet for many people the argument against 'centralism' was epitomized in the fear that it might increase the power of men like Roscoe Conkling; they could not ignore the fact that his vehemence against civil service reformers was as great as that against the perpetrators of Southern atrocities.

In their presentation of the case for national power the Radicals were inhibited by conventional American and nineteenth-century political thought. While the old Whigs, whose ideas they inherited, had believed in more positive action by the national government than their Democratic opponents, they had never thought of writing a blank cheque for government intervention. What they wanted was Federal responsibility for the performance of certain economic functions defined by the economic interests concerned, and since that time the concepts of *laissez-faire* had tended to narrow the sphere of action which business interests were likely to prescribe for government. Northern intellectuals who were attracted by the political aims of Reconstruction were precisely those who were equally attracted by the utopian elements in *laissez-faire*, by the theory of natural harmony, and by the faith in betterment through individual enterprise. The government was therefore being asked to 'secure the blessings of liberty' at the very time when it was being asked to contract its responsibility for 'promoting the general welfare,' and the hope of securing civil justice for the Southern negro was not coupled with the expectation of securing social justice for the Northern farmer and worker. Thus the Radicals' concept of national power was too wide to satisfy conservative men but not wide enough to gather support from the nineteenth-century movements of protest.

Even if the concept of national power had not suffered from these inherent weaknesses it would still have had a precarious hold upon the nation. Radical Reconstruction declared certain principles of national responsibility but it did nothing to create the institutions of government which could give these principles a permanent place on the national stage. The Freedmen's Bureau was such an institution but even its friends recognized that its life must be limited. The Fourteenth Amendment left the door open for Congress to make laws which would enforce the civil rights clause, but it did not make it mandatory for Congress to do so and the assumption was that the law would be self-enforcing through the existing machinery of government and courts. The initiative remained with the traditional instruments of government—with the President, with the judges and with the States themselves—and no new instruments of government were brought into being. One can contrast this with the experience of the New Deal with its proliferation of governmental agencies; when enthusiasm receded the administrative achievement remained, and many Americans (ranging from highly paid government servants to the very poor) had acquired a vested interest in these new institutions. When Radical enthusiasm withered away it left behind it no such institutional bulwarks, and when the Freedmen's Bureau expired there remained no new government departments, no new government agencies, and no administrative doctrine to carry out those obligations to citizens of the United States of which so much had been heard.

* * *

The arguments which have been presented in the preceding pages have attempted to show why the ideology of Radical Republicanism, which appeared so powerful during the crisis of Reconstruction, failed to gather that momentum which could have carried it forward in the years which followed. It is of course exceedingly improbable that the Radicals of the Reconstruction period could have conceived their problems in any other way or that they could have gone on to produce the ideas and institutions which would have corrected the weaknesses in their edifice. Radicalism shared the weaknesses of all liberal bourgeois movements of the nineteenth century, and it would have required a far more profound revolution in thought and action to make them view their situation through the eyes of twentieth-century liberals. In their equalitarian sentiments, in their realization that individual rights might be incompatible with local self-government, and in their attitude towards national power they were prophets of the future; yet they remained children of their age and were bound by its assumptions and inhibitions. And even if their vision occasionally transcended these limitations they were unlikely to persuade the majority of their countrymen that the revolution which they had initiated ought to proceed to further innovation. The failure of Radicalism is thus a part of the wider failure of bourgeois liberalism to solve the problems of the new age which was dawning; but having said this it is important to remember that if the Radicals shared in the weaknesses of their age they also had some achievements which were exceptional.

First among civilized nations the United States had met the problems of a bi-racial society, and first among civilized nations they had committed themselves to the proposition that in such a society human beings must have equal rights. If the definition of 'rights' was confused the idea that they must be recognized was clear. The civil rights clause of the Fourteenth Amendment was in many ways unsatisfactory, but it contained explosive material which could shatter the lines of racial discrimination. The United States had committed themselves to the statement that suffrage should be colour-blind, and if the phrasing of the Fifteenth Amendment invited evasion the principle which it enunciated would outlive attempts to defeat it. Americans may well differ upon the wisdom of these equalitarian ideas, but it is impossible to deny their importance for the future. The Fourteenth and Fifteenth Amendments could have been enacted only during the period of Reconstruction, and without them the subsequent history of the United States would have been very different. Not least important has been their effect upon the negro race in America, for the knowledge that the goals of negro aspiration are already written into the Constitution has had the powerful consequence of turning American negroes aside from thoughts of revolution. In his quest for equality the negro appeals to established national law and not against it, and one of the most striking developments of twentieth-century history has been the failure of Communists amongst a people who had many reasons for disaffection. The constitutional amendments had an equally powerful effect upon Northern thought. If Northern opinion, in the later years of the nineteenth century, was not prepared to implement the principles of the amendments, they were not removed from the Constitution and were to become the basis for further thought about the problem of race in America and in the world at large. It is possible to attribute the modern American hostility to 'colonialism'—which so often embarrasses the European allies of the United States—to memories of the Revolution, to ingrained suspicion of Great Britain and to mere calculation about the changing balance of power in the world; but it is equally significant that during Reconstruction Americans rejected the idea that law should recognize the 'inferiority' of non-European races. These are not unimportant consequences and may serve to lighten the gloom with which Americans have been accustomed to regard the crisis of Reconstruction.

The great failure of Radical Reconstruction lay in its attempt to remould Southern society. Hypothetical arguments may be produced to show that the attempt should never have been made, or that it was not made thoroughly enough, that too much or too little pressure was applied to the white people of the South; all that the historian can do is to record that the attempts as made did not produce the immediate results for which Radicals hoped. If it is believed that nothing should have been done the responsibility of the Radicals for having done something is clear; if it is believed that not enough was done it has been argued that moderate pressure not Radical initiative laid the ground for a Southern counter-revolution. Radicals argued at the outset that compromise and conservatism were not the principles with which to meet an unprecedented situation, and though one may blame them for their determination to have a revolution it is a little unfair to blame them for being forced to stop half-way. On the other hand if the revolution was going to stop half-way it is fair to blame the Radicals for insisting upon the alienation of the Southern ruling class whose support was vital for any compromise solution. It can be shown—and it is likely that the evidence will gather weight—that the Reconstruction governments in the South were not so bad as they have been painted in the Southern picture, but no amount of argument is likely to convince anyone that they were successful governments. This book has been concerned with the ideas and motives of Northern Reconstruction policy and not with the consequences of that policy in the South. It is true that the policy cannot be divorced from its consequences but motives cannot be judged from results. The authors of Reconstruction policy did not intend that it should perpetuate racial antagonism in Southern society, discredit colour-blind democracy, and provide further ammunition for Southern attacks upon the North. They were not disunionists, as Andrew Johnson called them, but they believed that the old Union, containing elements which could not combine, must be reconstructed. They hoped that the preamble to the Declaration of Independence should become the new formula for national existence, and they hoped to endow the national government with the power to ensure this result. These ideas were not negligible, absurd or unworthy. Their presentation was marred by a bitterness which was the legacy of war but was sometimes redeemed by the idealistic impulses which war had released. They left a record of failure in the South and permanent alterations in the law of a great nation. They faced intractable problems which still vex the modern world and they anticipated many of the assumptions with which men now tackle these problems. There was tragedy in the crisis of Reconstruction, but the tragic element transcends the particular circumstances of the post-war era and belongs to the whole condition of modern man.

SELECTIVE
BIBLIOGRAPHY

The difference between the old and the new in Reconstruction historiography can be readily grasped by comparing William A. Dunning, *Reconstruction, Political and Economic, 1865–1877* (1907, reprinted in 1963; paperback*) with John Hope Franklin, *Reconstruction after the Civil War* (1961; paperback). The contrast is also evident when James W. Garner, *Reconstruction in Mississippi* (1901, reprinted in 1964), one of the best state monographs of the Dunning school, is read together with Vernon Lane Wharton, *The Negro in Mississippi, 1865–1890* (1947; paperback), one of the best state monographs of the revisionists.

Hopefully, the reader surfeited with secondary interpretations will want to turn next to primary sources. Recent collections are: *Reconstruction, 1865–1877*, ed., Richard N. Current (paperback); *Reconstruction and the Freedmen*, ed., Grady McWhiney (paperback); *The Reconstruction: A Documentary History of the South after the War: 1865–1877*, ed., James P. Shenton (1963; paperback); and *Reconstruction in the*

---

* Dates in parentheses are original publication dates. The word "paperback" indicates that the work is now available in paperback. If only the word "paperback" appears after the work cited, its original publication was in paper.

South, 1865–1877, ed., Harvey P. Wish (paperback). One way to get a sense of the national mood toward Reconstruction at the time Dunning's work appeared is to contrast the novels of Tourgée with turn-of-the-century novels such as Joel Chandler Harris, *Gabriel Tolliver; A Story of Reconstruction* (1902) or Thomas Nelson Page, *Red Rock: A Chronicle of Reconstruction* (1898). To the many travelers' accounts long available should now be added John Richard Dennet, *The South as It Is: 1865–1866,* edited and with an introduction by Henry M. Christman (1965).

Franklin's volume contains an excellent bibliography of Reconstruction scholarship as of 1960, the year of the sit-ins and, in retrospect, a watershed date. Since 1960, Reconstruction scholarship has stressed two themes thrust forward by the modern civil rights movement—the treatment of the Negro in the South, and the motives for Reconstruction policy in the North.

Among recent books dealing with the Southern Negro during Reconstruction are Willie Lee Rose, *Rehearsal for Reconstruction: The Port Royal Experiment* (1964); Joel Williamson, *After Slavery: The Negro in South Carolina During Reconstruction, 1861–1877* (1965); Otto H. Olsen, *Carpetbagger's Crusade: The Life of Albion Winegar Tourgée* (1965); Charles E. Wynes, *Race Relations in Virginia, 1870–1902* (1961); and Frenise A. Logan, *The Negro in North Carolina, 1876–1894* (1964). The genesis and character of segregation are treated in Richard C. Wade, *Slavery in the Cities: The South, 1820–1860* (1964), and in C. Vann Woodward, *The Strange Career of Jim Crow* (1955, paperback), preferably the second revised edition (1966).

In addition to the works excerpted in this volume, recent studies of the formation of Reconstruction policy in the North include LaWanda C. and John H. Cox, *Politics, Principle and Prejudice; Dilemma of Reconstruction America, 1865–1866* (1963); Irwin Unger, *The Greenback Era: A Social and Political History of American Finance, 1865–1879* (1964); James M. McPherson, *The Struggle for Equality; Abolitionists and the Negro in the Civil War and Reconstruction* (1964); George M. Fredrickson, *The Inner Civil War: Northern Intellectuals and the Crisis of the Union* (1965); J. William Gillette, *Right to Vote: Politics and the Passage of the Fifteenth Amendment* (1965); and David Donald, *The Politics of Reconstruction, 1863–1867* (1965).

The persistent student will want to go on from these books to articles in *The American Historical Review, The Journal of Negro History,* and *The Journal of Southern History,* such as: Thomas B. Alexander, "Persistent Whiggery in the Confederate South, 1860–1877," *JSH* (1961); Vincent P. DeSantis, "The Republican Party and the Southern Negro," *JNH* (1960); Louis R. Harlan, "Desegregation in New Orleans Public Schools during Reconstruction," *AHR* (1962); Harold M. Hyman, "Johnson, Stanton, and Grant: A Reconsideration of the Army's Role in the Events leading to Impeachment," *AHR* (1960); James M. McPherson, "Grant or Greeley? The Abolitionist Dilemma in the Election of 1872," *AHR* (1965); Patrick W. Riddleberger, "The Radicals' Abandonment of the Negro During Reconstruction," *JNH* (1960); Louis Ruchames, "William Lloyd Garrison and the Negro Franchise," *JNH* (1965); Everette Swinney, "Enforcing the Fifteenth Amendment, 1870–1877," *JSH* (1962); Jack B. Scroggs, "Carpetbagger Constitutional Reform in the South Atlantic States, 1867-1868," *JSH* (1963); and Allen W. Trelease, "Who Were The Scalawags?" *JSH* (1963).

Finally, it will widen the student's sense of what might have happened if he reads about the aftermath of emanicipation elsewhere, as in John Bigelow, *Jamaica in 1850; or, The effects of sixteen years of freedom on a slave colony* (1851).